Coming Out Swiss

Coming Out Sw|ss

In Search of Heidi, Chocolate,

and My Other Life

Anne Herrmann

The University of Wisconsin Press

The University of Wisconsin Press
1930 Monroe Street, 3rd Floor
Madison, Wisconsin 53711-2059
uwpress.wisc.edu

3 Henrietta Street
London WC2E 8LU, England
eurospanbookstore.com

Printed in the United States of America

Library of Congress Cataloging-in-Publication Data

Herrmann, Anne, author.
Coming out Swiss: in search of Heidi, chocolate, and
my other life / Anne Herrmann.
pages   cm
Includes bibliographical references.
ISBN 978-0-299-29840-1 (cloth: alk. paper)
ISBN 978-0-299-29843-2 (e-book)
1. Herrmann, Anne.   2. Swiss American women—Biography.
3. Swiss Americans—Biography.   4. Swiss—United States.
5. Switzerland—Social life and customs.
6. Switzerland—History.   I. Title.
E184.S9H47   2014
305.893'5073—dc23
2013033113

In memory of

Elisabeth (Bethli) Herrmann-Rütschi
1921–1978

and

Juri/Georg/George/Georges [Ostroumoff] Herrmann
1921–2007

There are things so deeply personal that they can be revealed only to strangers.

Richard Rodriguez, *Hunger of Memory: The Education of Richard Rodriguez* (1982)

Given desire and purpose, I could make my home in any of them [French/English/Walloon]. I don't have a house, only this succession of rented rooms. That sometimes makes me feel as though I have no language at all, but it also gives me the advantage of mobility. I can leave, anytime, and not be found.

Luc Sante, *The Factory of Facts* (1998)

Having taken citizenship in April 1869, Nietzsche may be considered Switzerland's most famous philosopher. Even so, he on occasion succumbed to a sentiment with which few Swiss are unacquainted. "I am distressed to be Swiss!" he complained to his mother a year after taking citizenship.

Alain de Botton, *The Consolations of Philosophy* (2000)

When the history of the Revolution—or indeed of anything else—is written, Switzerland is unlikely to loom large.

Tom Stoppard, *Travesties* (1975)

In the course of her project, the Daughter must end up violating the values of her parents—themselves restless, westering—in favor of her own rootedness.

Richard Rodriguez, *Days of Obligation: An Argument with My Mexican Father* (1992)

Contents

Contents

Illustrations

Acknowledgments

I would like to thank those graduate students whose invaluable research assistance made parts of this book possible: Emily Lutenski, who began looking for things before I knew what the book was about; Monica Fagan, who learned things about the Swiss she wasn't sure she needed to know; and Alexandra Kruse, who expressed more clearly than I could what it is that the book had finally become. I am grateful to James Mitchell for bringing me the Swiss Family Robinson via Disneyland, to Tomomi Yamaguchi and Hiroe Sanya for acquainting me with Heidi in Japan, and to Navaneetha Mokkil-Maruthur for pursuing with me Switzerland in Bollywood.

I reminisce fondly about the hours I spent in the elegant building of the Stadtarchiv in the old part of Zürich, learning things about a family history that had remained untold, and in the Dokumentationsbibliothek Davos, where Timothy Nelson so kindly provided materials that made it possible for me to read all day, and even night, although I was in the Alps and expected to be out of doors.

I thank two writers: Eileen Pollack, who has written about a woman she imagined had to be Swiss and encouraged me even before there was anything legible to read, and Christine Rinderknecht, the Swiss author I most admire, whose ability to write fiction highlights the limitations of my own writing, even as she tries to convince me that the material is all there, I just need to narrate it.

Tricia Ortiz kindly drove with me around the Bay Area and joined the schoolchildren at Sutter's Fort, and Bert Ortiz generously accompanied me to a barely remembered New Glarus. To him I owe the freedom to write, the conversation that interrupts the solitude and a companionship that encompasses travel, even if it means hiking up one more Heidi path.

I am grateful to have had the opportunity to present "Heidiland: What's Heidi Got to Do With It?" at the "Homelands in Question: Re-locating 'Europe' in the Spaces of Cultural Negotiation" Conference at the Taubmann College of Architecture and Urban Planning in 2005 and "'Naïve Cartography': Aleksandra Mir's *Switzerland and Other Islands*" at "The Cultural History of Cartography: A Symposium" in 2012, both at the University of Michigan.

I remain indebted for institutional support from the College of Literature, Science and the Arts and Office of the Vice President for Research at the University of Michigan in the form of a Michigan Humanities Award. I thank the college for an additional term off, even if it meant signing an early retirement agreement, which has become its own kind of gift.

I would also like to recognize those colleagues whose friendship cannot be acknowledged simply by conveying gratitude: Michael Awkward, who has shared the pleasures and pains of being an author, kept me from losing courage and read various manifestations of this project; Abby Stewart, who has been with me in all things having to do with women and gender and has kindly read chapters of this book; Helmut Puff, who keeps me abreast of all things Swiss and reminds me of how American I am because I am not foreign born; and Susan Najita, who, although in a field far afield from my own, encourages me to experiment. Martha Umphrey remains an intellectual interlocutor par excellence.

I thank the *Southwest Review* for publishing "Coming Out Swiss/ Living in the Fifth Switzerland" and the *Yale Review* for making public "Heimweh, or Homesickness."

Finally, I would like to thank Raphael Kadushin for being such a strong believer.

Coming Out Swiss

SWISS GIRL PAPER DOLL

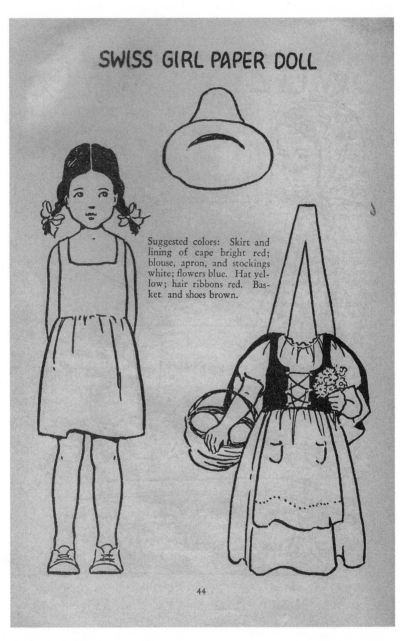

Suggested colors: Skirt and lining of cape bright red; blouse, apron, and stockings white; flowers blue. Hat yellow; hair ribbons red. Basket. and shoes brown.

44

Swiss girl paper doll, *Instructor Handbook Series: Handwork for all Grades* (F. A. Owens Publishing Co., Dansville, NY, 1937)

Prologue

Open Secrets

Coming Out Swiss

There are many kinds of secrets. Family secrets, bank secrets, skeletons in the closet. Sexual secrets are the ones we become most loquacious about, confessing them to priests, discussing them on cell phones. Sins cannot be forgiven, symptoms cannot be cured, until they've been exposed. Phone conversations, no longer confined to the privacy of the public phone booth, have made the public a space for private revelations.

What about linguistic secrets? Speaking a foreign language native to a European country half the size of Maine, in which it is not the only language people speak. Passing, for most of one's life, as monolingual.

Disclosing the fact that one speaks a foreign language, but not in that foreign language: an open secret. Confessing that one speaks a foreign language few others speak, even fewer want to learn, to someone who might not be interested: a form of coming out.

To come out Swiss is to come out speaking other languages— German, French, Italian, Romansch. I try to dismantle the myth that all Swiss speak all four languages. I point out that Romansch is like the Romance in Romance Languages. I explain that the Swiss understand German, but that Germans cannot understand Swiss-German. But will I be understood?

3

Growing up Swiss means knowing that not all nations are mono-lingual. In spite of attempts to legislate a single national language, many citizens speak one language at home, one at school, and one as a member of the "imagined community" of the nation-state. In Kerala, India, people speak Malayalam at home and English with friends, and begin to grow rusty in the Hindi they learned at school. In the German-speaking part of Switzerland, people speak Swiss-German at home, learn to read and write German at school, and conduct much of their work in English. Dialects make people feel like foreigners in a city half an hour away. They make people feel like they've gone abroad in their own countries.

Coming out a German speaker means coming out a member of the majority in Switzerland but a member of the minority in the German-speaking world of Germany, Austria, and Switzerland. Swiss-Bavarian is what a small town in north-central Washington calls itself. Bavaria is in southern Germany, Catholic, gregarious drinkers in Bier-garten. *The Sound of Music* takes place not in the Swiss, but in the Austrian Alps. The Austrians, formerly known as Hapsburgs, were the oppressor from whom William Tell liberated Switzerland with his crossbow. Now the crossbow is the official trademark for *Made in Switzerland*. William Tell was invented by a German who never set foot on Swiss soil.

The Swiss are not known for sharing their secrets.

Coming out Swiss rarely leads to meeting other Swiss, although occasionally it leads to "one of my best friends is Swiss" or "I grew up in New Berne, Indiana." It might lead to "what part of Switzerland?" The German-speaking part, which means learning a second language, German, in order to read and write. It means regressing to Swiss-German when one's emotional life is at stake. It means always already being bilingual.

Most Swiss anyone has ever heard of hail from Geneva: John Calvin; Jean-Jacques Rousseau; Madame de Staël; Henri Dunant, the founder of the Red Cross; Horace-Bénédict de Saussure, the botanist; Ferdinand de Saussure, the linguist; Tissot, the watchmaker. But is Geneva really Switzerland? It was the last canton to join the confederation and still calls itself a republic. It shares a hundred-mile border with France, but only six miles with Switzerland.

Zürich and Basel pride themselves on being the largest and most modern, the oldest and most cultured Swiss cities. Those from Zürich consider people from Basel snobs, that is, elitist; those from Basel consider people from Zürich arrogant, as in "pushy." My mother and father grew up in Zürich and Basel, respectively. Together they emigrated, first to Montreal, then to New York City, after what is still known as the War.

Swiss-German has no potential transnationally. It is not like Spanish, to which the manufacturer has devoted half the instruction booklet. It is not like Japanese, included in all the tourist information about Heidi, provided by the local visitor's bureau of Maienfeld. And yet the Swiss cross, whose colors the Red Cross inverted, has gone global. Swiss army blankets are cut up and resewn as backpacks. "Swiss Army" appears not just on pocketknives but on luggage.

Linguistic secrets are not written on the body, allowing for the entrance into a subculture. One who reveals them does not run the risk of being disowned or fired or excommunicated. Such revelation leads not to stigma but to scrutiny:

Does she have an accent?

Can she ski?

How many languages does she speak?

Are they all so reserved?

Americans assume I was born in Switzerland, because otherwise, how would I be Swiss? The United States tolerates dual citizenship, while Switzerland embraces it. The Swiss, who never disown one of their own, wonder when I will be returning home from the diaspora. Every summer I disappeared to a place where no one spoke English. Every fall I returned to the United States, where I continued to speak Swiss-German. No one knew where I went or what I did. We never used the telephone, in either direction. In Switzerland, the United States ceased to exist; in the United States, Switzerland was regularly invoked as superior.

The one secret my parents could not keep was their foreignness.

Their accents gave them away. When someone asked my mother where she was from, she said, "From here." She had lived in this country for twenty-five years.

No, where was she really from?

Why do they need to know?

"Switzerland."

"Sweden is such a beautiful country."

My mother taught me to read and write German. I began with children's books, including my namesake, *Anneli* (1919). I still read slowly and remember little. The language on the printed page is too unlike the language I speak. The language I speak has no written form, which makes it, when written, even more difficult to read. Every Swiss-German dialect has its own phonetic script, only one of which is recognizable, and only when read aloud.

I learned to write, initially by writing thank-you notes to relatives, dictated by my mother. Although German is highly phonetic—its orthography governed by completely reliable rules—I remained a poor speller. I didn't know what words looked like. Instead, I knew where to place their sounds by recognizing the location of the speaker. I knew what they meant when they were sounded out. I knew nouns had to be capitalized, but could I recognize a noun?

I had nothing to say.

I had no audience in German interested in America.

I had no audience in America who could locate Switzerland on a map.

Things seemed so simple in English. Sentences are short. Nouns are not inflected. Who cares if spelling remains a nightmare? And the number of lexical items exceeds those of all other languages? Conjugations are simple. Idiomatic expressions are everything.

My mother never felt confident writing in English, even though she was trained as a lawyer in Zürich (at the Uni), worked as a journalist for Swiss newspapers, and, by the time she was twenty, had mastered four languages, including Latin. My father, trained at the Federal Institute of Technology in Zürich (the Poly), relied on mathematical symbols to do what he did in applied mechanics, considered himself a citizen of the world, and, in his seventies, began to learn Spanish.

Prologue

What kind of secret is my Swissness?

It resides in a glass closet.

I display a CH on my car because only those in the know will know it means Switzerland. SW has already been taken, by Sweden, of course. CH means Confoederatio Helvetica, or Helvetic Confederation. Helvetia, the alpine provinces of the Roman Empire. I spied a car with a *CH* and stalked the driver, who told me his wife was Swiss, nothing more. A different driver pulls up next to me: "Does CH stand for Switzerland or Cape Hatteras?" "Where the heck is Cape Hatteras?" I ask an American friend.

English is cool, and often no longer translated into Swiss-German. Thirty percent of all magazine ads advertising Swiss products to Swiss use English. English recently appeared on the cover of the Swiss passport, along with the four national languages. Switzerland has four national but three official languages, meaning all government documents appear in all official languages. English has replaced the Latin of Confoederatio Helvetica as the lingua franca of a multilingual country. The canton of Zürich has gone so far as to defy a federal mandate that requires the first foreign language taught in schools to be another Swiss national language. English, not French, now comes first. What will happen to Italian? The Ticino—the Florida, the Riviera of Switzerland—has always sent its university students to Zürich or Geneva. And Romansch, spoken only in Graubünden, has fewer speakers than ever.

My name was Anneli. Any German speaker will know that *"li"* is the Swiss diminutive, as opposed to the Austrian *"erl"* (Annerl), or the German *"chen"* or *"lein."* Annachen was the nickname my brother bestowed on me. By pursuing a linguistic logic that produced a nonstandard form, he ridiculed his older sister and disavowed our subordinate relationship to High German. A friend of my parents pronounced it *Anna Lee,* thereby shifting my geographical allegiances within the United States toward Dixie. In late adolescence, I announced I was changing my name, unlike my mother, who remained *Bethli,* the Swiss form of *Elisabeth,* for the rest of her life. I wanted to grow up, to outgrow the diminutive. But what were my options? In German I could be only Anna, which in English sounded spinsterish. I could reclaim Anne in English, and locate myself outside of continental Europe. I could hope that others might resort to the French pronunciation, thus making it sound less foreign. In the end, my uncle would greet me, know my name was no longer Anneli, not remember what it was, and eventually say my name in a language he had learned in school, of which he remembered only "That's the way the cookie crumbles."

Swiss-German has borrowed recklessly from the French: *Trottoir* for "sidewalk," as opposed to *Gehsteig*; *Billet* for "ticket," as opposed to *Eintrittskarte*. The German, not the French, sounds pretentious. My aunt gave her French poodle a French name, "Le Vent." Every summer, she and my uncle, a dentist who was also a painter, drove to southern France. It all began when she, the daughter of a Swiss grocer, left to be the governess in a French château. After that, whenever my uncle fell asleep on the couch to the radio news in standard German, my aunt sat in her armchair reading literature in French. Her room, facing the back, was cool and impeccably groomed, her wardrobe, because of her size and aspirations, handmade from imported fabrics. She died, her glasses on her nose, a book still in her hand, the first corpse I ever saw, her armoire lined in *provençal* fabric.

I say my parents were both Swiss. But every Swiss person harbors a relationship to somewhere else, real or imagined. Everyone who leaves, for economic or humanitarian reasons, eventually returns. My mother, who wanted her ashes strewn, is buried in Davos. My father, who considered Davos his pied-à-terre, never lingered for more than a few days. My mother traced her ancestors to farmers along the Lake of Zürich. She never felt at home in English, she never felt at home in things English, including America. She never recovered from that Swiss malady known as *Heimweh*, or homesickness, the feeling one harbors for Switzerland when one would rather not be elsewhere.

My father lived in Moscow until he was twelve, with a Swiss mother and a Russian father. My grandmother, a prodigy pianist, trained my grandfather's voice for singing opera rather than litigating cases after the October Revolution. Following his affair with the leading lady on an American tour, my grandmother filed for divorce. She smuggled my father out of Mother Russia to Switzerland, where he changed his Russian name to his mother's maiden name. An engineer in the United States during the Cold War, he too harbored secrets. The Cold War insisted he not know Russian. His accent betrayed only his Swiss past, which, because it was not the only past, never led to being sick for that home he never had. He felt at home everywhere, and thus nowhere.

Do I ever panic?

I hear two young women speaking Swiss-German in Central Park. They have no idea I am listening, much less that I am able to understand every word they say. It sounds so strange, and yet so familiar. I've never liked the sound of Swiss-German, and yet Swiss-German was the private language I used with my mother to understand what seemed foreign to us about the United States, making the unfamiliar familiar by discussing it in a language no one else understood. I refrain from sharing my secret. I was born in New York City. I too find the scene, with its fresh dusting of snow, picture-perfect, but I won't be taking a picture to take back home. I could offer to take their picture, but that would require explaining that I'm not really Swiss, since I've lived here all my life; I'm not really an Auslandschweizer or Swiss abroad, since I never emigrated; and yes, it is amazing I still speak Schwyzerdütsch. And so I remain silent.

Switzerland took its name from the canton Schwyz, one of three original cantons to form the confederation by engaging in an oath on the meadow Rütli in 1291. It is there that in 1440 William Tell assassinated the Habsburg bailiff Gessler, that many of the mercenaries left from to fight in foreign wars, that citizens were taxed who married someone from another canton. The geographically central becomes politically marginal because it is Catholic and rural. It is typical, like any heartland. Like so many nineteenth-century narratives of nationhood, both the Rütli oath and the Tell legend have been deconstructed as historical fictions.

How would anyone know to ask, unless I had already told them? Once they know, what will they do with that knowledge? The other place remains a secret, an open secret, but isn't that the most dangerous kind? They will want to explain everything by saying it is because I am Swiss.

Prologue

They will want to visit Switzerland because it is so beautiful; they will want to avoid Switzerland because it is too expensive.

They wish they knew another language. They want their children to grow up bilingually.

No they don't.

How do they know?

A secret that is public knowledge, that one never stops explaining. Like people on their cell phones talking to a public that doesn't want to hear. A public that becomes increasingly privatized, where speaking to no one is no longer something others shouldn't know about.

Living in the Fifth Switzerland

Switzerland is a small place, a country slightly larger than the combined areas of Vermont, Connecticut, and Rhode Island.

It is the poorest country in Europe in natural resources. One-quarter of its sixteen thousand square miles is rock, ice, or water. Seventy percent of its area is covered in mountains.

One out of every ten Swiss passport holders lives abroad. One stays because it is impossible to leave—it is so beautiful—or one leaves because it is impossible to stay: 60 percent of Swiss living abroad are women.

The fifth Switzerland: all those who are Swiss citizens but don't live in Switzerland. Its current population, 715,710, makes it equivalent to the fourth largest canton. In 1992 Swiss abroad were given the right to vote. In 1996 the Swiss Abroad Place in Brunnen, Lucerne, received a granite plaque commemorating it as a site of potential pilgrimage.

All Swiss abroad begin in one of four Switzerlands.

German-speaking Switzerland. Zürich is its capital, the largest city in Switzerland, not Bern, the seat of the federal government, not Basel, fifteen minutes on the tramline to Germany or France. But German in what sense? German-speaking Swiss can understand all of the 120 Swiss-German dialects but refuse to speak any of them except their own. The German Swiss in part despise, in part shrink from, in part absorb what is German. Christopher Hughes has suggested, "There is a splendour in good High German, the German of the stage, the German that commands: in comparison, dialect sounds like a mixed farmyard, many hens and a few geese, unwomanly, unlearned, inurbane." Dialects exclude, including other Swiss; they also bind, the Swiss against the Germans. One would rather be speaking English: the language of neutrality, of capital, of the global.

When a German Swiss and a French Swiss meet, the language they have in common is foreign to both: German, the language of Germany. French Swiss pride themselves on their mastery of German, in particular the literary ambassadors who translate German Swiss literature into French; they wonder why their provincial compatriots insist on clinging to their dialects. By far the largest number of Swiss who live abroad in Europe live in France. In a recent poll, all French-speaking cantons voted to join the European Union; in a recent opinion poll, 29 percent of French speakers were not averse to the possibility of seceding from Switzerland.

My mother was able to choose between Italian and English as a second foreign language when she attended the gymnasium in the 1930s. In 1996 an amendment to the federal constitution mandated that German be taught as the second language in French-speaking cantons and French in German-speaking cantons. Zürich broke the contract by insisting that English be the first foreign language taught in its schools. Italian is spoken in the Ticino but also in Graubünden. In Graubünden they speak Swiss-German as well as Romansch.

What is Romansch? A language closer to Latin than either French or Italian. A language one learns, in one of three variants, only at home. Unlike Italian, it is spoken in a single canton. Romansch, the only national language I have never learned.

If one were to take linguistic communities the size of Romansch, Switzerland would now have ten languages, not four. But not all languages are equal. Italian resents its possible degradation to the status of an immigrant language: there is a difference between Albanian, Serbo-Croat, and Portuguese, on the one hand, and a Swiss national language, on the other.

Prologue

Of the Swiss abroad, 76,330 live in the United States. I am registered at the consulate in Chicago (to be disbanded and moved to New York City), which means I receive a complimentary copy of the *Swiss Review: The Magazine for the Swiss Abroad* six times a year. I am encouraged to vote, to send my children to Switzerland for summer camp, to return for the yearly reunion of the Swiss abroad. I have joined the 1 million Americans who claim Swiss descent, but I have failed to join a Swiss American club.

I am not that Swiss.

I am not that kind of Swiss.

I have lived in the fifth Switzerland all of my life. I have also resided in the other four. First grade in Davos (I and IV). Before I learned to read in any language, I was taken out of school. My mother, a nonnative speaker, taught me to read in English, in Switzerland. At the same time, I learned to ski. Skiing: the actual lingua franca of a mountainous, multilingual country. The year after high school, having studied French in the United States since sixth grade, I attended a language institute in Lausanne (II), where my two best friends were Japanese and German. I stayed on as a camp counselor in Montana-Crans (II), with a roommate from Paris. For a brief moment, I might have passed as trilingual. After college, I attended the University of Zürich (I), thinking I would stay to teach English as a second language. I stayed long enough to complete a *Licentiat* in English, as a native speaker, and watch my English deteriorate. I knew I wouldn't be staying. I knew I couldn't live in two languages, each of which diminished the other.

I remain a citizen of Basel, my father's community of citizenship, although I speak my mother's Zürich dialect, Züridütsch. We spent the summer months living with my grandmother in Zürich, in an apartment where three vacant rooms awaited our return. We spent one day each summer visiting my grandmother in Basel. After ten years in Agno, near Lugano (III), with a second husband whose name identified him, and thus her, as members of the Basel elite, she returned to the city a widow. My brother and I would stay with her in a house with

12

two grand pianos and a pergola, while my parents traveled and sent us postcards in English.

All Swiss citizens are entitled to provision in case of illness or poverty, but only citizens were allowed to use the common land. As resources, like communal fields and forests, diminished and populations increased, Swiss were encouraged to emigrate; foreigners are not encouraged to immigrate. In 1770 only 60 percent of the residents of Zürich were citizens. In 1789, no foreigner had become a citizen of Zürich for 150 years. With sufficient capital and skills, one can become a citizen, but only for a fee.

In 1734, thirty-five hundred emigrants left the canton of Zürich for America. The voyage took three to four months, with ten weeks at sea, where two hundred died. They were all agricultural laborers and tradesmen, most of them poor. There was no room to expand either resources or households. A third of the community would emigrate, although not all went to America. Half of those who emigrated already had been separated in some way from their community of origin due to death or divorce, abandonment, or illegitimacy. They received a small sum of money and renounced all future inheritance. The decision was absolute and irrevocable. Once they arrived, everything turned out to be different: the land was flat, there were no rocks, the wood was free, the soil was fine like in the garden. Inherited traditions were renounced, which made the pastors uneasy and encouraged them to denounce the undertaking. In many cases, there would be no letter; in most cases, no voyage home.

The fifth Switzerland exists because Switzerland, reluctant to extend citizenship, refuses to lose its emigrants. Until 1992, this did not include Swiss women, in particular those who married foreign men. If a Swiss woman abroad married a non-Swiss man and failed to alert the embassy or consulate where she was registered, she lost her Swiss citizenship. My mother, who received a law degree in 1948, never voted. As a woman, I live with 34,496 other Swiss women registered at embassies or consulates in the United States. As women, we received the right to vote in Switzerland in 1971.

Prologue

In 1874 Switzerland nationalized its army, requiring the entire able-bodied male population between eighteen and sixty to remain in its reserves. Eventually eighteen was raised to twenty, and sixty was lowered to forty-two. In 2003, the discharge age was lowered once more, to thirty, for an average of 262 days in service. For three weeks a year, young men of all classes and cantons who have not sought exemption for religious reasons enjoy a respite from the routine of daily life. On the one hand, there is the renewal of friendships in a homosocial setting; on the other hand, the lack of military involvement in any world wars.

Gertrude Stein thought that "writers have to have two countries, the one where they belong and the one in which they really live. The second one is romantic, it is separate from themselves, it is not real but it is really there." What, then, does it mean to have two countries, one in the rupture between spoken and written German, and another in the rupture between German and English? A high school teacher declared I would never write competently in English, given that I spoke another language at home. A college professor claimed to detect the Germanisms in my written English, frustrated they had not yet been eliminated. Where do I belong? Where do I really live? The United States is really there, a hyper-power, but is that what makes it real? What must it repeatedly disavow in order to maintain its positive illusions? Whenever I return, Switzerland seems real again, but is it really there, at the heart of Europe, increasingly not a part?

I have tried to live in Switzerland. To enjoy the stillness and avoid the sadness on Sunday afternoons in Zürich when only couples and families with perambulators are found on silent streets. To obey the unwritten rules in inheritance disputes that privilege married brothers with children over single sisters who are childless. To accept that the prodigal will never be welcomed home. But I have done so unsuccessfully.

I prefer a country where citizenship is determined by jus soli. No one judges me by my family name or asks what my father's profession is. Switzerland, without a monarchy or aristocracy, relies on the oligarchy of its elite families, whose names are common knowledge and who share a set of norms. These norms are largely urban, protestant or atheist, and middle-class. I too believe that good food should not be a class privilege; that drug addiction is a not a criminal or moral issue, but one of public health; that government is meant to protect minorities, not further empower elites.

How at home do I feel on this soil? Like many Americans, I too have lived like an itinerant. I have moved from the East to the Midwest to the West Coast to the East Coast to the Midwest, across the continent in the footsteps of my father's career, from one coast to the other pursuing an education. But I have settled. I have settled in the middle, where no one wants to be; in the heartland, where no one wants to stay. What do I say when people ask me where I'm from?

When did you move here?

I was born here.

I thought you said you were Swiss.

I am.

When are you coming back to Switzerland?

I'm not.

Where did you say Michigan was?

In the middle.

Since 9/11 I have felt increasingly like a foreigner; I feel more and more European. The norms I share with African Americans, Democrats, intellectuals, and Old Europeans have become more and more unfashionable.

Religious rather than linguistic differences make all the difference in Switzerland. Catholics claim their religion is that of the original nation; Protestants claim theirs is what made the nation modern, and therefore what it is. Very few Swiss attend church, and yet they are more likely to be theologians than philosophers, to build bridges than to write poems. They are more likely to climb mountains than to read, leading to such statements as "There is no such thing as Swiss writing" or "Swiss literature is a contradiction in terms."

In my reading, I have learned that Switzerland has always been a nation of newspaper readers. In the 1830s, it had one of the highest numbers of newspapers per capita in the world. The newspaper is the glue of the "imagined community," the community in anonymity. Benedict Anderson reminds us: "Reading a newspaper is like reading a novel whose author has abandoned any thought of a coherent plot." It is performed in silent privacy, repeated at daily intervals throughout the calendar, and replicated by myriads of other readers, whose existence one is confident of, but whose identity one will never know. A secular ritual. My Basel grandmother, who spent part of each summer in Montana-Crans, took all three of her newspaper subscriptions with her.

Outside of Switzerland, one easily forgets there is a Switzerland. There is little to remind one that it still exists. The Swiss are more likely to know the president of the United States than of their own nation. The Swiss executive consists of seven members, with each member also filling a cabinet post. Each year someone is designated spokesperson. At least one of the seven must be from the Italian-speaking part and one from the French-speaking part, even though each part represents less than one seventh of Switzerland.

The fifth Switzerland is a political fiction. It means living no place, nowhere.

It does not mean an imaginary island, impossibly ideal. Nor does it mean a perfect polity.

Writing from the fifth Switzerland means writing about an imagined country from a place that doesn't exist.

Swissness

Keynotes

Chocolate

The Facts

Switzerland leads the world in annual per capita consumption of chocolate, 22.7 pounds, although 20 percent of this figure includes tourists and cross-border commuters. Of this, 75 percent is milk chocolate, which in the EU means a minimum of 25 percent cocoa solids and in the United States a minimum of 10 percent cocoa solids.

Americans consume 11.6 pounds per capita per year, although the United States leads in cacao bean imports and chocolate production. The "confectionary coating" on a Baby Ruth candy bar, named after the youngest daughter of President Grover Cleveland, has replaced so much of the cocoa butter with vegetable oil that technically it cannot be called chocolate.

Chocolate is currently not about consumption but about tasting, which involves passion, connoisseurship, and rejecting the chocolate candies of your childhood. Tasting tips: Avoid coffee, tea, and mint before tasting, and taste in the morning or late afternoon, when you are just a little hungry. Taste each chocolate at least twice, and taste no more than seven to ten items. Between chocolates, drink room-temperature water and eat plain bread to de-fat the tongue.

The connoisseur has relegated Swiss chocolate to the status of a supermarket brand. In 1989 Lindt launched a 70 percent chocolate bar, making it the first supermarket brand to promote cocoa percentage. In 1992 it issued the first "country of origin" bar. Frey chocolate, the brand of Migros, the largest retailer in Switzerland, has appeared on the shelves at Target.

Cailler is the oldest Swiss brand of chocolate still in existence. François-Louis Cailler (1796–1852), like many Swiss chocolatiers, learned his craft in Turin. Unlike chocolatiers from the Ticino and the Grisons who leave Switzerland to open businesses in Amsterdam, Stockholm, Hamburg, Paris, London, or St. Petersburg, Cailler returns to Vevey in 1819 to open a mechanized chocolate factory. In 1875 his son-in-law Daniel Peter succeeds in creating the first milk-chocolate bar, called Gala Peter, by adding condensed milk. Made with much milk and little sugar, the chocolate bar not only provides a new use for Swiss milk and a way to distribute it worldwide but is marketed as nutritional for mountaineers and travelers. A friend of Henri Nestlé markets condensed milk as healthier for city dwellers and colonists than raw milk from tubercular cows potentially adulterated by contaminated water. Beginning in 1904, Nestlé markets Peter's chocolate worldwide, and by 1929 Cailler has become part of the Nestlé group.

In 1753 Linnaeus gives the scientific name *Theobroma cacao*, "food of the gods," to the cocoa tree. The tree grows only twenty degrees north and twenty degrees south of the equator in the damp, shaded understory of coconut palms and banana plants. Here midges, necessary to pollinate its flowers, thrive. The pod, which holds thirty to forty seeds, is attached directly to the trunk in a pattern known as "cauliflory." The pod never falls or opens of its own accord. Machetes are needed, or monkeys, who are seeking not the bean but the surrounding white mucilage, a sweet pulp. Fermentation, drying, roasting, and winnowing are necessary to transform beans into cocoa "nibs," which are milled to create cocoa liquor. Over half the nib is fat, extracted by means of a process called "Dutching." Cocoa butter is coveted for cosmetics and pharmaceuticals, while the remaining presscake can be pulverized into cocoa powder.

Chocolate

Alkaloids make up 1 to 2 percent of the cocoa bean in the form of caffeine and theobromine, known to stimulate the brain and central nervous system.

The Spanish learn of cacao not from the Aztecs but from the Maya, on the Pacific slopes of Chiapas and Guatemala, who, a thousand years before the Spaniards land, pour a dark liquid from one jar into another to produce foam, considered the most desirable part of the drink.

The pre-Conquest Aztecs in the Valley of Mexico count rather than weigh cocoa beans. Maize is added to chocolate drinks, as well as chili, vanilla, and black pepper. Drinking chocolate is enjoyed only by elites, served at the end of a meal in calabash cups.

Columbus never tasted chocolate, but on his fourth voyage he discovered the gold he had been looking for on the island of Guanaja in a canoe full of "almonds" used as money.

The Spanish in Mesoamerica insist on drinking chocolate hot, introducing cane sugar, adding familiar spices such as cinnamon and anise, and beating the hot chocolate with a large wooden stick or *molinillo* to produce foam. Cocoa liquor is stored and shipped or issued to soldiers in the form of a wafer or tablet to which one can add sugar and water.

Cocoa arrives in Europe as a medicine "appreciated for its taste, its filling nature, and its stimulation." It is reputed to be mood enhancing and to aid digestion.

It arrives at the Spanish court as a hot beverage, although the cup now has a saucer with a ring, to prevent it from slipping, and a spoon, to stir the chocolate when it settles.

Is chocolate a drink or a food? Does it or does it not break the ecclesiastical fast?

The Italians add flavors like musk, lemon peel, and ambergris; the French invent the *chocolatière* or silver chocolate pot, with a straight wooden handle at a right angle to the spout and a hole in a hinged lid for the *moussoir,* or froth-maker.

Tea, coffee, and chocolate arrive in England simultaneously. Tea is the most expensive; coffee provides the most stimulation.

By the time the European market doubles the need for chocolate, the indigenous population in Mesoamerica has plummeted. In 1537 Pope Paul III vows to excommunicate any Christian who enslaves an Indian. Planters on the Guayaquil coast of Ecuador and in Venezuela step in to supply Guatemalan and Mexican markets. African slaves replace Indians in the cacao groves. The fast-growing and disease resistant forastero bean replaces the more aromatic but lower-yielding criollo bean. In Trinidad the two beans are hybridized to produce trinitario.

Today, the Ivory Coast is the leading producer of cocoa beans, a legacy of nineteenth-century French forastero cocoa plantations. Most cocoa is grown by peasant farmers who have never tasted chocolate: it is too expensive and it liquefies too quickly. "Blood cocoa" funds an enduring civil war that allows both governmental officials and rebels to buy weapons with revenue from cocoa production. Children from Mali are smuggled in as slave laborers, increasing the gap "between the hand that picks the bean and the hand that unwraps the candy" (Off, *Bitter Chocolate*).

Chocolate has been a favorite disguise for poison.

In eighteenth-century Europe, chocolate is seen as southern, Catholic, and aristocratic while coffee is northern, Protestant, and middle class. Chocolate is identified with papal and/or royal absolutism while tea symbolizes civilization and liberty.

In 1847 J. S. Fry & Sons produces the first chocolate for a mass market, the chocolate bar, by blending cocoa beans and sugar with melted cocoa butter to make a paste that can be cast into a mold. English Quakers promote chocolate drinking as an alternative to drinking gin. Fry supplies the Royal Navy, while Cadbury becomes the purveyor of chocolate to Queen Victoria. In 1868 Cadbury offers the first decorated chocolate box, which remains long after the chocolates are gone; in 1875 Cadbury introduces the first chocolate Easter egg, making chocolate an integral part of the most important celebration on the Christian calendar.

In 2007 Cadbury is fined £1 million for putting unsafe chocolate on sale. Chocolate and salmonella go well together. The abundant fat, low moisture levels, and high sugar content help preserve the bacteria. In Europe there are two or three chocolate-based salmonella outbreaks every decade.

Godiva, founded in Brussels after World War II, claims to be "The World's Best Chocolate," and many people think it is. In 1974 it is bought by Campbell's, which then promptly tries to sell the brand, which has never fit its product line. In 2006 Hershey buys Scharffen Berger Chocolate Maker and Dagoba Organic Chocolate and in 2007 *Consumer Reports*–trained panelists taste fourteen dark chocolate bars and choose Hershey's Cocoa Reserve Extra Dark with Cocoa Nibs as the winner. Milton Hershey's great-grandfather flees persecution as a Mennonite in Switzerland and settles in Pennsylvania.

The Kekchi Maya of Guatemala introduce chocolate to Prince Philip of Spain in 1544. In the 1990s, the Maya of Belize are persuaded to abandon the hybrid cocoa trees introduced by Hershey and return to their semi-wild trees to produce Maya Gold for Green & Black's, the first chocolate brand declared a "free-trade" product.

Chocolate has a high concentration of antioxidants, diffusing free radicals that cause premature aging. Dark chocolate has twice as many antioxidants as milk chocolate and the same number of flavonoids as red wine and green tea, said to reduce risks of heart attack and cancer.

Knowledge about production has become a requirement for the consumption of prestige cultural goods. Today chocolate labels indicate cocoa percentage (weight from cocoa beans), country of origin (anywhere in the country), plantation (never more than five acres), bean variety (criollo is always a hybrid of criollo and trinitario), and vintage (year of the cocoa crop).

In 1997 Domori, a chocolatier from Genoa, buys a plantation in Venezuela, where he replants criollo trees by grafting them onto trinitario, using seeds from a gene bank in Trinidad. The first "pure criollo" bar appears in 2003.

"White chocolate" is not chocolate but rather cocoa butter, and therefore confectionary.

The most significant improvement to chocolate making is conching, invented—both the process and the machine—by Rodolphe Lindt, in 1879. Conching kneads the chocolate for up to three days, causing it to be aerated, thereby helping aromas to develop, acids to evaporate, and the texture to become smoother. Since then the greatest technological progress has been in packing: "Where in the past women stood at long tables, and later conveyor belts, carefully placing chocolates in boxes, today robots do the same job in a fraction of the time. Attentive staff check and correct the work of robots" (Chocosuisse, *Chocology*). In 1899 Lindt sells his factory in Bern, his brand name, and his secret production process to Sprüngli of Zürich.

In 1845 Rodolf Sprüngli-Ammann opens the first chocolate factory in the German-speaking part of Switzerland. In 1859 Confiserie Sprüngli, which in 1892 separates from the factory Lindt und Sprüngli, opens on the Paradeplatz in Zürich. In 1970 it opens the first outlet in a shopping mall. All outlets must be within an hour of its manufacturing plant in Dietikon to ensure the quality of its chocolates, made with fresh cream. Its best known and most popular product is not chocolate but tiny meringue macaroons in dozens of flavors called Luxemburgerli, named after the place of origin of the young confectioner who begins making them in Zürich in 1958. Luxemburgerli, like *truffes du jour*, must be sold within twenty-four hours of production.

Quevedo Bittersweet: "Quevedo's extremely dark color foreshadows its powerful but flowery chocolate taste. The intensity of this rarified Forastero varietal produces rich, green forest, tea and slight nut flavors with a lingering banana and pound cake finish" (according to a Guittard chocolate wrapper). These are taste notes. Make sure you taste the chocolate before you read the notes. To find your own words, look for associations with the world around you. What natural products, such as fruit, flowers, woodlands, or spice, does the taste remind you of?

Toblerone, invented in 1908, is the most famous of all Swiss chocolates. Forrest Mars learns what he needs to make the Mars Bar by working on the Toblerone factory floor.

Chocosuisse, the Union of Swiss Chocolate Manufacturers, defends itself against the misuse of the "Swiss chocolate" label. "Swiss chocolate" must refer to chocolate products manufactured only at production sites in Switzerland. Good chocolate, according to Chocosuisse, "melts like butter, does not stick to the roof of the mouth or feel gritty, and leaves hardly any aftertaste" (*Chocology*).

The heyday of the Swiss chocolate industry, between 1890 and 1920, coincides with the golden age of Swiss tourism. Visitors from around the world spread the word. Lindt aimed his advertising at exclusive girls' schools in the French-speaking part of Switzerland. By 1912 Switzerland had cornered 55 percent of the world's chocolate-export market.

Of worldwide cocoa bean harvests, 1 percent ends up in Switzerland, and 57 percent of its chocolate is exported.

The EU allows chocolate to contain up to 5 percent other vegetable fat, which until now no Swiss producer has taken advantage of.

Swissness: Keynotes

Venezuela and Ecuador are the first bean-producing countries that manufacture high-quality chocolates and successfully export them, the El Rey and the Vintage Plantations brands, respectively; this is otherwise known as "bean to bar."

In 1860 Etienne Guittard boards a ship for San Francisco, bringing with him his uncle's chocolates from Lyons, which he hopes to exchange for gold-mining supplies. Wealthy miners are willing to pay premium prices for them, and after three years of failing to find gold, he opens a shop on Samsone Street. Guittard is the oldest family-owned chocolate company in America. Ghirardelli, who also arrives in California during the Gold Rush, gives his name to a company now owned by Lindt.

> We reach for chocolate when we feel a little hungry; when doing housework, out for a walk, during the rigors of military service. Chocolate has even ventured into space with astronauts and cosmonauts. You can always rely on chocolate. It does not make you "high," is not addictive, and contains no hallucinogenic substances. No allergies to cocoa have yet been recorded. (Chocosuisse, *Chocology*)

Cailler is a small Swiss brand, whose exports make up only 5 percent of its sales, owned by Nestlé, the largest food and beverage company in the world. In 2006 a French architect, Jean Nouvel, is commissioned to revitalize Cailler's look, which he does by creating translucent PET wrappers for bars wrapped in colored foil. A French-Swiss consumer group discovers that a 100-gram Frigor bar wrapped in 50 grams of packaging produces five times more nonrecyclable waste than the old packaging did. This in addition to an 8 percent price increase. Denner, a discount retailer, refuses to stock the chocolates, and the Swiss refuse to buy them, and sales plummet by 20 percent. What the Swiss reject as a higher-priced and over-packaged bar, international consumers might embrace as the latest luxury from Switzerland.

The language of chocolate has borrowed its terminology from the language of wine, in particular from the internationally accepted reference standard of French wines. Because of its complex chemical composition and its ritualized consumption, chocolate remains distinguished by the need for "an apprenticeship in taste" (Terrio, *Crafting the Culture and History of French Chocolate*).

To be invited "to go to the king's morning chocolate" (*aller au chocolat*) was to enjoy royal favor and social status; to be like chocolate (*être chocolat*) was to be deceived or to play the fool. To act like chocolate (*faire le chocolat*) meant to be naive or gullible and to court numerous social risks, from deception to death. The noun *chocolat* has long signaled not only a tropical foodstuff, but men of African descent. (Terrio, *Crafting the Culture and History of French Chocolate*)

In the 1980s the French become leaders in chocolate connoisseurship by setting a new standard of taste. Although not known historically for luxury chocolates, to increase consumption, its chocolatiers begin to celebrate an artisanal craftsmanship and aesthetic. *Grand cru* marks a reeducation of the palate by privileging dark chocolate over mass-produced milk chocolate. Dark chocolate is marketed as distinctly French, whereas the origins of milk chocolate are placed outside of France, in the United States and Switzerland. By marketing dark chocolate as better, both in terms of taste and healthfulness, because it has less sugar, France continues a tradition of principles established by nouvelle cuisine.

Chocolate-covered pretzels are an Amish Christmas tradition.

The Fictions

The most popular fictions about chocolate, apart from Roald Dahl's *Charlie and the Chocolate Factory* (1964), have been written by, for, and about women: Laura Esquivel's *Like Water for Chocolate: A Novel in Monthly Installments with Recipes, Romances, and Home Remedies* (1989) and Joanne Harris's *Chocolat: A Novel* (1999). These books, made into highly successful films, offer female-centered histories that assume the primacy of the mother-daughter relationship. In *Chocolat*, the mother-daughter dyad is positioned as the most reliable, even when threatened by church doctrine that seeks to run the mother out of town, and in Esquivel as the most restricting, cemented by a family tradition upheld by the mother that prohibits marriage for the youngest daughter. In both cases, in the absence of the father, the daughter is too much on the move or too confined to the kitchen, while the mother continues to pay for a sexual transgression and provide for her progeny.

The chronologies of these novels are seasonal, the chapters marked by dates that succeed each other with predictability yet are punctuated by ceremonial occasions. Food is prepared either for daily consumption or for commemorative gift exchange. In Mexico, chocolate enters recipes with chilies, onions, and almonds; in France, it takes confectionary form. In either case, it mediates the relations that provide for alternative communities, primarily female homosocial ones, while exposing the male-headed household as perpetually elusive, if not inherently bankrupt.

In Mexico, chocolate is made into squares, dissolved in hot water and beaten until covered with foam. To be "like water for chocolate" is to be "on the verge of boiling over," to be enraged. Tita is enraged at having to forego marriage, at having to live with her lover as his sister-in-law. She rejects a family tradition that keeps the youngest daughter obedient to her mother for life. By learning to cook, by nursing her nephew, she joins the servant class.

In France, chocolate is grated, melted, tempered, from blocks of *couverture*, and made into squares whose names are reminiscent of the aristocratic culture of the ancien régime. Chocolates are sold over the counter in boutiques with elaborate window displays, where candies are treated like jewels. Easter is the privileged moment for expensive confectionary purchases; chocolate competes with the church for the souls of its parishioners. In *Chocolat*, Vianne, for whom Catholic doctrine is synonymous with patriarchal law, lives by the credo that "chocolate, I am told, is not a moral issue."

In *Like Water for Chocolate*, as surrogate father, the mother demands filial obedience. She runs a ranch on the U.S.-Mexican border, with three daughters and two female servants. "Never needing a man for anything," she embodies paternal law. Jovita González in *Life along the Border* explains: "In his large, strongly built stone or adobe house, the *ranchero* led a patriarchal existence. As head of the family his word was authority, no other law was needed and there was no necessity for civil interference. An offense, where criminal or moral, met with severe punishment." To care for her mother, Tita, the youngest daughter, is forbidden to marry; the second daughter, Rosaura, is presented in marriage to Pedro, originally the lover of Tita; Gertrudis, the oldest daughter, runs off with one of Pancho Villa's men, works in a brothel, becomes a general, marries a general, smokes cigarettes, and learns to drive a car. Knowledge that Tita has been conceived out of wedlock causes her mother's husband's death and leaves the daughter fatherless. She is raised by surrogate mothers, women who neither marry nor have children, servants who can neither read nor write. Undernourished by a mother whose sexual transgression has left her a widow and in a man's role, Tita is raised in the kitchen and learns to cook.

In *Chocolat*, Vianne is raised by a single mother who struggles to feed her only daughter because she has no patience for cooking, for food that demands time. Always on the move, she is a traveler, a fugitive, changing places, changing names, on the run from the law for infringing minor laws to ensure her survival. She has taught her daughter to read tarot cards, not recipes. Vianne is also illegitimate, with the law of the father re-embodied as "the Black Man," the priest, the figure of death, threatening to steal the daughter from the mother who refuses to remain in place. The daughter eventually nurses her mother, who wants to see America before succumbing to a terminal illness. When the mother is hit by a cab in New York City, the daughter moves to France and gives birth to a daughter.

Men are symbolically powerful but socially marginal. Male lovers appear as mulattos and gypsies; they mirror the social ostracism of rebellious daughters but fail to make them respectable. One man refuses to marry the daughter he loves in order to obey her mother; another, unable to commit to the mother, will never know his daughter. Fire is their fate—forms of arson that turn them into patients or deprive them of property. Like Rochester, who loses his sight in the fire at Thornton Hall before he is entitled to marry Jane.

As unmarried women, Tita and Vianne prepare the food for ceremonial occasions that mark rites of passage for others. Vianne is self-taught, poring over menus from restaurants where she and her mother could not afford to eat. She learns the names of dishes she has never tasted, and she collects recipes, torn from magazines abandoned in train stations, into a scrapbook. Compared to cooking, chocolate-making is not considered time-consuming. Tita is taught by Nacha, the cook, and she collects recipes handed down to her in a cookbook that will be the only object left once the ranch has burned down and will in turn become the novel the reader is reading. Recipes require enormous labor: fattening up and castrating roosters to make capons or breaking 170 eggs for a wedding cake. Tita prepares the wedding feasts for her lover when he marries her sister and for her niece who marries the son of the American doctor, perpetuating the tradition for which she herself remains ineligible.

Vianne opens an artisanal *chocolaterie* in a small village in the southwest of France, an area that claims to be the oldest site of continuous chocolate manufacture, authentically local and distinctly French. On Shrove Tuesday, while others think about fasting, La Céleste Praline opens the doors of what used to be a bakery. Easter Sunday, the privileged moment for expensive confectionary purchases, is greeted by a chocolate festival across the square from the church. While self-employment in the provisioning crafts is premised on the work of a married couple and the creation of a new business tends to coincide with marriage, Vianne pays for the building with cash. Unlike her mother, she has a bank account and a trade.

A chocolatier is known as a "*maison*" or "house," "a corporate family unit that held commercial property (ideally) in perpetuity," "a unit of production encompassing the dual roles of enterprise and household," identified by a patronym. The husband produces chocolates in the private space of the workshop, and the wife sells the chocolates in the public space of the boutique, as explained by Susan Terrio. Vianne greets her customers with "I know everyone's favorite" and proceeds to offer them their favorites "on the house," bypassing commercialized relations with village locals. Selling requires sustained emotional labor that is less demanding than that required of a daughter, in hotel rooms too small, caring for a mother who believes "we don't need anyone but each other."

Tita, after the death of her surrogate mother, takes on the role of ranch cook. If she is denied marriage, is she allowed love? Afraid of becoming "the last chile in walnut sauce left on the platter after a fancy dinner," Tita prepares meals like "quail in rose petal sauce," "a dish for the gods" according to Pedro, and assists in the birthing and feeding of his children. The daughter accuses the mother of killing her nephew by banishing the family to San Antonio, while the mother accuses the daughter of producing an illegitimate child with her brother-in-law. Rosaura, who wants her daughter to grow up in "the sacred institution of the family," agrees to a pact whereby Tita agrees not to have a child if Rosaura agrees that her sister and her husband may continue to meet in secret.

In September, while Tita is making chocolate, roasting the cocoa beans and reserving part of the cocoa butter for lip ointment, Gertrudis arrives for a cup of freshly whipped hot chocolate. Tita, having wished for her sister's appearance so that she might discuss her unwanted pregnancy, serves her: "In this house they made hot chocolate like nobody else's, since they took so much care with every step in making it, from its preparation to the whipping of the chocolate, yet another critical procedure. Inexpert beating can turn an excellent-quality chocolate into a disgusting drink, either by under- or overcooking, making it too thick or even burnt." Chocolate reminds Gertrudis of the maternal home she is nostalgic for, while for Tita the home is where the mother repeatedly returns from beyond the grave to chastise her youngest daughter. When Gertrudis gives birth to a mulatto baby, Tita reveals their mother's secret, an illegitimate pregnancy with a Negro escaping the Civil War, legitimized by the unwanted marriage to Tita's father.

Vianne serves a hot chocolate that is stronger than espresso, transforming her shop into a café, creating an ambience that combines the intimacy of home with the pleasure of celebration, regardless of the day. Blurring the line between the personal and the professional, she drinks chocolate while serving it to others. She becomes an empathic confidante to those whose losses are graver than her own: the owner of a dog who is dying, the wife of an abusive husband, a grandmother prevented from seeing her grandchild. Rather than demystifying the family as sacred institution by exposing its secrets, Vianne provides for those outside its traditional structures within a public space.

French chocolatiers trace their craft to the Aztecs. The cocoa bean was revered before Christ and thereby transcends the moral imperatives and hypocrisies of a church that seeks to control women's sexuality through marriage. In *Chocolat*, the melting of *couverture* takes place in a petit bourgeois enterprise across from the cathedral by producing the "raw and earthy tang of the Americas." On Easter, a giant chocolate statue of Eostre, with corn sheaf in one hand and a basket of eggs in another, dominates the window display. Swiss chocolate appears in the novel in the form of supermarket chocolate the priest remembers having as a boy, too expensive then and not sufficiently sophisticated now.

Chocolate enables a mode of production in which reproductive and productive labor are no longer at odds. Mothering takes place within an economy that clouds the distinction between profit and gift exchange and diminishes the difference between public and private. The unpaid labor of the cook on a ranch and confectionary offered "on the house" are forms of social reproduction that maintain gender roles even as they offer a critique of familial and ecumenical traditions.

While the French try to increase the consumption of chocolate that relies on a repressed colonial past, the Swiss try to preserve within a global economy the name "Swiss chocolate" for confections to be consumed the very same day.

Crossing the U.S.-Mexican border or American expatriation in France considers local consumption part of transnational flows, enabling fictions that legitimate relations seeking to survive in spite of interdictions.

Gold

History

Secrets are shared. Numbers are whispered into unwilling ears. Every day in the orphanage they are recited, like a catechism. They are marked underneath tabletops, inside wooden chests. The name of the bank. The number of the account. Eventually, the name and number are forgotten. The furniture is removed. Sums have been deposited under someone else's name. A stranger has been told "in a bank." Revealing additional specifics might encourage theft by an imposter.

Article 47(b) of Switzerland's 1934 Banking Act: "Anyone who in his capacity as an officer or employee of a bank . . . violates his duty to observe silence or his professional rule of secrecy . . . shall be liable to a fine of up to 20,000 francs or imprisonment of up to six months, or both." Tax evasion, as opposed to tax fraud, is a civil matter, not a criminal one. William Tell was a tax evader. Article 47(b) was not invented for Jews but, some say, was first used to protect Jews: Swiss bankers refused to repatriate funds to Germany or provide information about the accounts of German nationals.

French Huguenots secure their capital against Catholic kings, and following the French Revolution royalists protect their property by seeking out private banks in Geneva, hidden behind small brass plates. The portfolios of the rich are managed with discretion, to secure rather than increase wealth not tied up in land. Protestantism liberates finance from both ecclesiastical rule and individual guilt. Private banks are not allowed to advertise, can't solicit deposits, don't publish balance sheets, are not governed by the Banking Act. They are not entitled to buy gold.

> Swiss banks rely on a steady stream of clients with liquid assets who are fearful of the future and deposit money they then pretend they don't possess. (Faith, *Safety in Numbers*)

Bank secrecy belongs to the *Privatsphäre*, not the private but the secret sphere, not the private understood as the bedroom or the body, but an individual's entitlement to secrecy about health, family life, and financial affairs. The right of refusal to provide information to anyone outside the *Gemeinde*. Secrecy is what makes Swiss banking unique. The abolition of bank secrecy could lead to a withdrawal of funds by foreigners and the collapse of the Swiss economy. In 1996 bank secrecy is lifted for all dormant and heirless accounts belonging to victims of the Holocaust. In 2009 bank secrecy is lifted for 250 UBS clients suspected of U.S. tax evasion.

Until 1990 there existed in Switzerland a Form B that entitled an attorney to open an anonymous account for a client. The account was opened in a fiduciary capacity, with the principle's name withheld. These are numbered accounts, where the rightful accountholder never appears and is known only to the bank's director. When a client withdraws money, he or she remains seated upstairs in a boardroom while the director goes to the cashier to withdraw the requisite sum. Dormant accounts fall into two categories: for the first, for which creditors exist for material assets conveyed to Switzerland before or during the early stages of the war, heirs present themselves without death certificates or documentation proving they are the deceased's sole heir. These are dormant accounts, where no transactions have taken place for years. The second, or heirless accounts, have no identifiable heirs. Whole families have been gassed or shot. If a creditor cancels a custodial agreement, the bank is at liberty to destroy relevant documents after ten years. If the creditor is unknown, that is, has not closed the account, the bank may not destroy any records. If an account is orphaned, the bank is legally bound to seek out the person's heirs. In the early post-war years, dormant accounts were transferred to so-called collective accounts. Eventually they disappeared into the bank's undisclosed reserves.

When the Berlin Wall falls, and the Iron Curtain comes down, the fiftieth anniversary of the end of World War II is celebrated, national archives are declassified for the first time in fifty years, and the final chapter is once again not closed.

Laundered money is money "washed in the Alpine snows" (Faith, *Safety in Numbers*). Swiss bankers are the chief launderers of looted Nazi gold; they organize sophisticated laundry routes. The Germans deliver gold to Switzerland and are reimbursed in Swiss francs. They take these francs to Turkey, Portugal, Sweden, and Spain (the other so-called neutrals) to buy raw materials. The central banks of these countries buy back the Nazi gold from the Swiss National Bank by using Swiss francs. Looted gold is gold that has been taken from the gold reserves of the national banks of eleven occupied countries (monetary gold) and from wedding rings, gold dental crowns, bracelets, watches, earrings, artificial limbs, and spectacle frames of concentration camp victims (*Totengold*) delivered by the SS to the Reichsbank under the code name "Melmer." This gold-laundering machine remains in operation until three weeks before Hitler's suicide. In the subterranean galleries of the Kaiserode potassium mine near Merkers, U.S. infantrymen discover the gold reserves moved out of Berlin after the Reichsbank was hit by an Allied air raid. In a huge, unventilated room they find bags of paper money and gold currency, neatly arranged in rows, as well as gold bricks, Passover goblets, and paintings from the German National Art Museum. It takes four days to unload twenty-two railcars into a mine with five hundred kilometers of tunnels. In 1946 Britain, France, and the United States establish the Tripartite Commission for the Restitution of Monetary Gold to redistribute 303 tons of gold to claimants "in proportion to their losses." Claims from central and eastern European nations, already behind the Iron Curtain, take years to resolve.

Swiss francs are as good as gold. (Smith, *Hitler's Gold*)

Manganese, a resistant metal, used in the manufacture of gun barrels, is imported from Spain; tungsten, also called wolfram, the metal with the highest melting point, used in making dies for shells, comes from Portugal; stainless steel, used to manufacture ball bearings, is imported from Turkey. All of this is paid for in gold.

Gold does not oxidize in air or water and is the most malleable and ductile of pure metals. Too soft for monetary use, it is alloyed with copper or silver. Much of the gold mined in history is still in circulation. Gold is a chance discovery. Europe has produced little gold while South Africa has produced 50 percent of all gold ever mined. In 1971 the dollar was no longer convertible to gold, and in 1975 the price of gold was left to the free market. Hoarding gold bars, some think, provides a hedge against inflation.

"In general, real gold and non-existent gold were equally important in the Discovery, Conquest and the Colonization of the Americas" (Vilar, *A History of Gold and Money, 1450–1920*). Gold was born in the Indies, died in Spain, and was buried in Genoa. If Spain was poor, it was because it was rich. The strangeness of the New World enhanced gold's worth. Columbus, who failed to find gold, provided substitutes for wealth in the form of wonders. Indians used gold for ornamentation, the visibility of adornment promising the possibility of hidden treasure. Indians were wiped out by the hard labor of "river gold" (Vilar, *A History of Gold and Money*) with no opportunity to plant crops, engage in childbirth, resist organisms. "The economy of gold . . . was actually an economy of flesh, because selling and renting captured Indians as slaves became more profitable than mining" (Vilches, *New World Gold*). Queen Isabella banned imported brocade embroidered with thread made of precious metals, worried that her subjects were "squandering their fortunes, enriching foreign merchants and dissipating the national treasury" (Vilches, *New World Gold*).

"Money, which itself changes in value, is therefore a strange measure of value" (Vilar, *A History of Gold and Money*). It should circulate like blood in the body. The central bank is like the heart, and should not let money lie stagnant. Money is not wealth, but gold is. Gold is a symbol of value, not a measure of wealth. "Gold-money embodies the functions of archetype, token, and treasure in one single object" (Vilches, *New World Gold*). Money is a medium of exchange that can take the form of metal or ink. The generation of money by money breeds illegitimate offspring. All the gold that arrived in Seville generated an ocean of paper.

Gold is a monetary metal used for international transactions and the wages of mercenaries. Metallic money becomes a commodity when its monetary value is in conflict with the market value of its metal. England is the home of the gold standard, gold as the incarnation of transcendental value. Switzerland is the last country to tie its currency to gold.

Gold is melted down by the Prussian mint and given pre-1939 German serial numbers. Convoys of trucks cross the Swiss border at Basel for the subterranean vaults of the Swiss National Bank in Bern. Bars are counted, classified, and registered below ground, then stacked on shelves. Every bar possesses its own identity card.

Belgian gold is sent to France prior to occupation and by France to Dakar before the French collapse, then moved inland to Kayes in September 1940. The Vichy government agrees to return the gold, some 4,944 sealed boxes weighing over 240 tons, to the Reichsbank. At Kayes it is loaded on a train to Bamako on the Niger River, then light trucks and riverboats transport it to Timbuktu, and finally to Goa. From there, it is moved by truck and camel north through the Sahara to Colomb-Béchar and by train to Algiers. It is moved the ten thousand kilometers by air to Marseilles with French and German aircraft (two tons per trip). The gold reaches Berlin in May 1942.

> We are in the presence of a crime without a name. (Ziegler, *The Swiss, the Gold, and the Dead*)

"How can our border guards tell the difference between politically motivated German emigrants and German Jewish asylum seekers?" (Ziegler, *The Swiss, the Gold, and the Dead*). The Swiss offer two suggestions: underline the names of Jews in red ink or stamp the front page of their passports in the top left corner, with a circle approximately two centimeters in diameter around the letter "J." Berlin opts for the latter. Switzerland admits three hundred thousand refugees, including twenty-five thousand Jews. Beginning in 1942, thirty thousand Jews are refused sanctuary when the border is sealed off. "Refugees are subjected to a rigorous interrogation before being allowed to benefit from the right to refuge on the soil of the Confederation. Capital benefits from the right to asylum without any enquiry" (Faith, *Safety in Numbers*).

Wilhelm Gustloff, the Swiss Nazi leader and former tuberculosis patient, maintains his headquarters in Davos until his assassination by the Jewish student David Frankfurter in 1936. Wounded Nazi soldiers and airmen as well as Allies are sent there to recover. Front companies purchase hotels to convert them into sanatoriums to channel money to and from Berlin through their bank accounts. Pro-Nazi organizations are provided cover by, for instance, the Savoy Hotel, which is made into a sanatorium renamed the Konsul Burchard Haus, owned by the Tuberculosis Association in Berlin, which provides meeting space for Nazis. Nazi youth disguised as tuberculosis patients are brought to the Fridericianum, a gymnasium. The Swiss become nervous about an economic enclave on Swiss soil and declare that hotels and land can no longer be purchased by foreigners.

> Most Swiss were anti-Nazi during the war, but that doesn't mean they were pro-Jewish. (Bardach, "Edgar's List")

Gold

Switzerland's neutrality is first recognized under the Peace of West-phalia in 1648 and renewed by the Congress of Vienna in 1815. To be neutral means to be neither one nor the other. Does that mean queer? Is it a morally indifferent neutrality, simply an abstract opportunity for two enemies to meet on neutral ground, or a self-interested neu-trality, whereby gold cannot be refused from either side?

Hitler has a bank account at the Bern branch of Union Bank of Swit-zerland for the foreign royalties of *Mein Kampf*, whose sales, once it becomes a school textbook, run into the millions, managed by the owner of the Max Amman publishing company.

In 1943 the United States implements Project Safehaven to prevent neutral countries from becoming safe havens for Nazi spoils. In 1944 the Allies declare gold transactions with the Third Reich illegal. In 1945, under the Currie Agreement, Switzerland promises to freeze German assets and not purchase anymore gold. In 1946 Switzerland signs the Washington Agreement, which results in a voluntary contri-bution of CHF250 million (in compensation for looted gold considered worth CHF1.7 billion), the return of nongovernment German assets (supposedly forbidden by its status as a neutral and eventually com-pleted in 1952, when Germany repays its debts to Switzerland), and CHF20 million to compensate for dormant assets (a voluntary advance to establish the United Nations).

Israel has not yet been founded; there are no Jewish organizations at the table. There is an unwillingness to impose one's will on allies; there is the task of rebuilding Europe; there is the growing threat of communism. Switzerland is not a defeated state, even if it believes it is being treated like one.

As the Swiss Inscription says: *Sprechen is silbern, Schweigen ist golden* (Speech is silvern [*sic*]; Silence is golden) (Carlyle, *Sartor Resartus*).

Swiss law firms approach wealthy Jews and offer to buy the freedom of their relatives in occupied countries; the assets of deceased or heirless

Poles are returned to the Communist government of Poland to settle claims against the nationalization of Swiss property.

Switzerland has been outed. "The image of Switzerland as a small, independent nation bravely defending democracy, law and justice, refusing to get involved in the conflicts between its neighbors while maintaining generosity, solidarity and an openness to the world, especially through its humanitarian commitments" (Braillard, *Switzerland and the Crisis of Dormant Assets and Nazi Gold*) is put into question.

"I ask myself if Auschwitz is in Switzerland," says the outgoing Swiss president Jean-Paul Delamurz; Rolf Bloch, president of the Swiss Federation of Jewish Communities, says "Switzerland was not Auschwitz"; *Wenn Auschwitz in der Schweiz liegt* (If Auschwitz were in Switzerland) (1997) is the title of a series of essays by the Swiss writer Adolf Muschg. Switzerland is finally on the map; it is no longer confused with Sweden. How un-Swiss, to have banks audited, to be publicly probed in front of foreigners, to be subject to global scrutiny.

The World Jewish Congress (WJC) is founded in Geneva in 1936 to fight Hitler and defend the Jewish community in eastern Europe. The WJC is part of the World Jewish Restitution Organization, a group of international Jewish agencies seeking restitution of former Jewish property and assets from former East European communist countries. In 1997 the president of the WJC is Edgar Bronfman, CEO of the Seagram Company, one of the world's wealthiest men—with a personal fortune of $3 billion—who develops an interest in his Jewish faith when his father dies. He has brought Kurt Waldheim to trial, Russian Jews to Israel, and now international media attention to Switzerland. Survivors are dying. Their assets lie dormant in Swiss banks. The WJC takes on the cause of the rejected heirs.

The response to being outed is shame or denial. The Swiss response is defensive, legalistic, obstructionist, and self-righteous. France has fallen, and Switzerland is completely surrounded by Axis powers.

Germany is Switzerland's principal European trading partner. Maintaining good economic relations remains vital to preventing an invasion. In case of a German victory, it remains prudent to continue business as usual.

On December 19, 1996, the Swiss Federal Council names the members of the Independent Commission of Experts Switzerland—Second World War (ICE), chaired by Jean-François Bergier and composed of eight historians, to conduct a legal and historical probe into the gold trading and foreign currency transactions within the context of World War II.

On February 6, 1997, the Swiss banks create a $70 million humanitarian fund for "needy victims of the Holocaust" in the United States, Europe, and Israel.

On August 12, 1998, Credit Suisse and UBS agree to a global settlement of $1.2 billion, in response to the class action suit filed by 18,000 plaintiffs for $20 billion in unreturned Holocaust assets.

The largest public pension funds in the United States threaten to divest their shares in Swiss corporations. The United States threatens to block the merger of SBC and UBS that will create the largest bank in Europe. Is this a conspiracy to destroy Switzerland as a world financial center because it threatens markets like London and New York, or is this the last chapter of the Holocaust coming to a close?

Swiss get up early but wake up late. (Swiss saying)

Swissair stops serving Swiss chocolates wrapped like gold bars on both domestic and international flights. In 1997 the Swiss business community reprimands Swatch for its ad campaign during the World Ski Championship in Sestriere, Italy, saluting the two Swiss athletes who have won gold medals: "As always whenever there is gold, a good part of it ends up in Switzerland."

Is secrecy a sign of insecurity? What motivated my father to open numerous accounts and leave them unaccounted for? Was it a desire to secure wealth by circumventing the state? Was it lack of loyalty to any nation state? Was it a need for anonymity once the American wife he sought to divorce filed a deposition that threatened to reveal the names of the buildings with tiny brass plates? "The nature of the secrecy laws made it such that a depositor was often closer to his Swiss trustee with regard to financial matters than he was to his own family" (Vincent, *Hitler's Silent Partners*). Customers for secrecy services are always located elsewhere and in that sense do not exist.

Art

Christian Boltanski was born in Paris in 1944 to a secular Jewish physician father who converted to Catholicism and a gentile novelist mother who wrote under the pseudonym Annie Lauran and briefly opened a gallery that showed only Yiddish art. His mother came down with polio, which made her unable to walk, so she used her sons as canes. When the war broke out, Boltanski's parents divorced, and his father lived for a year and a half under the floorboards of their apartment. After the war, his parents remarried, and his mother became a Communist. His parents and four children lived in a large apartment on the rue de Grenelle, where they all slept in the same room. "Eighty percent of my parents' friends were Jewish survivors of concentration camps, and almost all of them were Communists" (Gumpert, *Christian Boltanski*).

In the early 1990s, Boltanski creates a series of installations with titles like *The Dead Swiss, Reserve of Dead Swiss, Archive Dead Swiss,* and *Dead Swiss on Shelves with White Cotton. Dead Swiss* consists of 174 black-and-white photographs clipped from the obituary pages of Swiss newspapers sent to him at the rate of sixty to seventy a week. Boltanski reshoots the already grainy images and enlarges them to slightly larger than life-size. In *Reserve of Dead Swiss*, hundreds of rusted biscuit tins with snapshots pinned to them form a tall, narrow corridor. The stacks are unstable; during one installation they fall to the floor and are left there. The exhibit includes the photograph of one Swiss who is not dead, with a document inside the tin that says the image is untrue. "Of course someday it will be true." In *Archive Dead Swiss*, the photographs rest on wooden shelves with the light bulbs of small gooseneck desk lamps just inches away. Boltanski remembers when the Tate Gallery bought one of his pieces, *Dead Swiss on Shelves with White Cotton*: "When I sold it, the curator mentioned that the cotton would go yellow in a few years time, so I told him that he could change it. He also said that the photos would fade, so I told him that's okay, there are always more dead Swiss—I don't care which ones you use. Moreover, even the shelves were not going to fit, as they had been made for a different room! And the curator asked, what did we buy? And I said well, you've bought photos of dead Swiss and shelves with white cotton. But it's not an object, it's an idea" (Semin, Garb, and Kuspit, *Christian Boltanski*).

Boltanski has no particular interest in the Swiss or Switzerland.

"Before, I did pieces with dead Jews but 'dead' and 'Jew' go too well together. There is nothing more normal than the Swiss. There is no reason for them to die, so they are more terrifying in a way. They are us" (Alphen, "Deadly Historians").

"I chose the Swiss because they have no history. It would be awful and disgusting to make a piece using dead Jews—or dead Germans for that matter. But the Swiss have no reason to die, so they can be anyone and everyone, which is why they are universal" (Semin, Garb, and Kuspit, *Christian Boltanski*).

"The Swiss . . . are 'naturally healthy,' and yet they are dying all the time . . . just like everybody" (Wilson, "Christian Boltanski").

The word "reserve" suggests that when the Swiss die, as one critic surmises, "they quite naturally end up in a bank vault" (Wilson, "Christian Boltanski").

Swissness

Keywords

Heimweh, or Homesickness

A cat is as subject as a mountaineer to homesickness.

(Oxford English Dictionary, 1805)

Heimweh, or homesickness, was first recorded by Swiss physician Johannes Hofer in his 1688 medical treatise, *Dissertatio de Nostalgia oder Heimweh*. He describes the illness suffered by a young man who, to complete his studies, travels from Bern to Basel. The patient begins to feel sad. He develops a fever, fails to eat, loses sleep, becomes distracted. He scorns all things foreign: the air, customs, conversation. He thinks only of his fatherland. He is reminded of it in his wanderings; he creates images of it when he is alone. He weakens to the point that it looks like he is dying. There is no remedy other than returning home. Simply hearing of this possibility, he begins to breathe more easily. By the time he arrives just a few miles outside of his *Heimatstadt*, he has fully recovered.

Hofer names this illness "nostalgia," *nostos* meaning "return to one's native land" and *algos* meaning "suffering" or "sorrow." Greek is the language that in the late seventeenth century turns a set of symptoms barely distinguishable from sadness or melancholia into a diagnosable disease. Two centuries later, the symptoms will have disappeared. They acquire other names: shell shock, post-traumatic stress syndrome, depression.

Nostalgia medicalizes as well as Europeanizes a condition whose national idiosyncrasies get lost in translation: *maladie du pays* is the name given to the suffering of Swiss mercenaries in France; *el mal de corazón* is the illness diagnosed among Spanish soldiers in Flanders toward the end of the Thirty Years' War (1616–48).

Among soldiers and seamen, nostalgia is diagnosed primarily as an excess of memory. Soldiers are conscripted, often displaced for the first time from the villages they have never left. Sailors are impressed, kidnapped onto the next ship as soon as they arrive in port. They are prevented from engaging in farewells. Their stays are indefinite, with no hope of leave or return. Their activities are limited, frequently characterized by tedium. If in the eighteenth century interest in nostalgia takes place primarily in German-speaking regions, in the nineteenth century it shifts to France, to those physicians seeking to reduce desertions from national armies like Napoleon's. Leave is granted only to those suffering from nostalgia. Knowing this, soldiers feign its symptoms. It becomes known as "hypochondria of the heart." The symptoms, among them idleness, daydreaming, even erotomania, infer a lack of manliness.

Is nostalgia an attempt to medicalize an afflicted imagination, or the symptom of a medical imaginary?

A long-haired cat appears out of nowhere. The afternoon feels like Indian summer, and he finds me hanging linens on the line. Once the temperature drops, he insists on coming in. Sick of not having a home, he already knows where the food bowl he has never had might be.

One estimate puts the number of Swiss who served as mercenaries in foreign armies between 1400 and 1800 at 1 million, another at 2 million. Treaties were made between cantons and foreign princes granting a monopoly of recruitment for a stated number of soldiers for a term of years. During the Reformation, under Huldrych Zwingli's influence, the practice began to come under attack. A national foreign policy required the control of individual military service; mercenaries could not compete with professional armies. In Protestant cantons like Zürich, industry came to replace military service abroad as a way to enlist an excess of workers. The Swiss constitution, ratified in 1848, made it illegal.

Theodor Zwinger, who in 1710 published *De Pothopatridalgia*, claimed that Swiss soldiers became nostalgic when they heard the "rustic cantilena," *Kühe-Reyen* or *ranz-des-vaches*, the sound of bells as cows are being driven to pasture on the alp. Others, like Johann Georg Zimmerman, writing in 1764 of his experiences as a doctor in Switzerland, claimed that the condition was not limited to or preeminent among Swiss. It was not cowardliness but constraint, the prohibition against an accustomed "native freedom" that produced longing for one's native soil.

Is it cowbells or church bells that make one feel at home, when place is governed by two seasons—on and off the alp—and time is marked by fifteen-minute intervals chiming from a clock?

In the nineteenth century, unmarried girls enter domestic work as an alternative to factory employment. In Johanna Spyri's story, Heidi's aunt Dete leaves the village of Maienfeld for Frankfurt, exchanging work as a maid in a hotel in Bad Ragaz for life as a domestic worker in a German family. She insists that Heidi accompany her. As the companion to Clara, the only child of a wealthy widower—twice her age and confined to a wheelchair—Heidi develops symptoms of homesickness, diagnosed by a friend of Clara's father, a doctor.

Marie, the Swiss maid in Virginia Woolf's *To the Lighthouse*, is heard crying in the attic room, the only one with an open window, because she "would rather go without a bath than without fresh air." Is she crying because her father, dying of throat cancer in a valley in the Grisons, will leave her fatherless, no longer at home in the world, or because, "at home, she had said, 'the mountains are so beautiful'"? Mrs. Ramsay, having taught her "how to make a bed, how to open a window, with hands that shut and spread like a Frenchwoman's," is irritated by the lack of hope. She would like to say something, but fails to find the words.

Jamaica Kincaid's Lucy arrives on the Upper West Side ashamed to be from a place where the only thing to be said about it is that one had fun there. In the twentieth century, unmarried girls become au pairs in domestic spaces meant to simulate home. Lucy has read about homesickness, "from time to time, when the plot called for it": "A person would leave a not very nice situation and go somewhere else, somewhere a lot better, and then long to go back where it was not very nice." She is surprised that this has happened to her, that having longed to leave, she now longs to go back. When Antigua comes to her, in the form of an emissary from her mother, "apart from everything else, she left behind her the smell of clove, lime, and rose oil, and this scent almost made me die of homesickness."

Homesickness may be susceptible to semantic vagueness, but the condition can feel lethal.

My mother had a lifelong longing for Zürich, her *Heimatstadt*. This is where she was born; where she grew up not far from the lake; where she attended the *Höhere Töchterschule*, or girls' gymnasium; where she waited out the war years, studying law and discussing politics, with mostly male friends. She will marry one of these men, and together they will leave for America. Before the war, she spends a year in Geneva becoming a simultaneous interpreter. After the war, she is offered a job as an attorney in a juvenile court outside of Zürich. She is eager to leave; she never anticipates staying. They settle first in Montreal and then in New York City. Montreal is a French-speaking city, and French is a Swiss national language. In New York, German speakers with limited English seeking work are in enormous surplus. The law she has studied is Roman law, and thus superfluous. She was never meant to be an emigrant. She will suffer her entire life from homesickness.

Psychoanalytic critics such as Jane Gallop imagine the daughter as the nostalgic. The mother as mother is lost forever because the mother as homeland is irretrievably past. The female subject is hence in a foreign land. If the masculine fears losing something it never had, the feminine regrets never having had anything in the first place: "Man's desire will henceforth be linked by law to a menace; woman's desire will legally cohabit with nostalgia: she will not be able to give up her desire for what she can never have (again)" (Gallop, *Reading Lacan*).

Heimweh, or Homesickness

We returned every summer to live with my maternal grandmother in Zürich. This is the place that remains constant, as we settle and resettle from east to west across the North American continent. Now my mother lies buried in her homeland, and I, in a foreign land, return as the emigrant's daughter. Expected to feel at home, I instead feel intensely homesick. Is it for her, or for this place? What is it about this place? Is homesickness the fate of the second-generation emigrant daughter, or a secondhand emotion passed down to the next generation? In America, they say you can't go home again; in Switzerland, they know that even if you leave, sooner or later you'll be back.

Following the death of my mother, I transport a cardboard box from the West Coast to the East Coast to the Midwest. It is marked *"Artikeln E.R."* I open it and discover copies of articles my mother wrote for Swiss newspapers between 1951 and 1964, when she was no longer able to practice law and had not yet entered the college classroom. She signed them *Elisabeth Rütschi*. The woman she might have been, "E.R.," before emigration, before her entrance into English.

Home seems to mean more than a reliable food source. Otherwise, why would he roll on his back on the wide plank floor and close his eyes to the sound of human voices? Or curl up in the sea-grass basket and listen to Monteverdi?

On August 23, 1957, my mother publishes a piece in the *Zürcher Woche*, titled "Zürcherinnen, denen es schwer fällt, Newyorkerinnnen zu werden" (Women from Zürich who find it difficult to become New Yorkers). She claims that women from Zürich are among the most adventurous and curious, thus it is not surprising to find a number of them among the Swiss in New York City. Some of them have careers. These are the active ones, the most ready to adapt, free to return to their native city, where they easily reestablish old ties.

Other women arrive with families. They follow husbands lured to America by intriguing career possibilities enabled by their degrees from the Eidgenössische Technische Hochschule (Federal Institute of

Technology, ETH). Their hands are tied. They will need to awaken their pioneer spirit, to cultivate patience and adaptability. Under new conditions and in possibly estranging circumstances, they have the opportunity to combine the best of the old with the best of the new, to create "*ein Idealzustand.*" Whereas men often solve conundrums through emigration, women continuously encounter new ones as emigrants.

My mother was destined to be the first kind of Zürcherin, which is why becoming the second kind felt like such a betrayal.

The scene is afternoon tea in a New York suburb: an immaculate lawn slopes down to a pond mirroring a stand of mature trees next to a recently acquired single-story home. The only signs of Swissness are the hazelnut cake, a ceramic dish brought back from Switzerland filled with chocolate, and the sound of Swiss-German. The topic under discussion in Zürich dialect is everyone's *Heimatstadt*. All are suffering from a certain *Heimweh*, ranging from "*verzehrender, geradezu lähmender Sehnsucht*" to "*einer leisen Wehmut, wie wir sie allgemein dem Vergangenen und den Jugenderinnerungen entgegenbringen,*" "an all-consuming, downright paralyzing pining away to a slight sadness induced by childhood memories or other reminiscences." They begin by praising their *Heimatstadt*: so small, and yet so varied, so livable, and so versatile. Women and store windows are dressed up with equal elegance. On a single day one can take a dip in the lake, shop for groceries on the way home, and arrive in time for the theater. A paradise for women with small children. And the parks, with those beautiful green lawns that one doesn't have to mow, with canvas chairs anyone can relax in, unlike the hard metal ones they have in Paris or those dreary cement blocks they call benches in New York City. Not to speak of those parks surrounded by cyclone fences where any mother feels like she's been caged in. It's impossible to shop on the spur of the moment with children on Fifth Avenue. If one had to take a break, there would be no appropriate tea room.

My mother admits that Zürich is beginning to resemble a forgery: the white boats on the blue lake; Saturday-night church bells; concerts in the nave of the Grossmünster; festivities with dancing in every public square. Were their husbands wrong in bringing them to America? Someone chimes in: "Don't you remember the tram conductors who close the door on you if the children don't hurry? Or the landlord who, when he sees the kids, won't rent to you? How can you forget how often it rains, making it impossible to go to the park, much less recline in a canvas chair?" My mother gently reminds them that even people in Zürich dream of the south, of overseas, imagining life will be easier there. Although "*wenn sie der Schuh der Wirklichkeit etwas drückt,*" "when the shoe that is reality begins to pinch a bit," Swiss emigrants will put a golden glow on their *Heimatstadt*.

In the same box, I come across a poem, written on a manual typewriter on a loose sheet of onionskin. It is dated Davos, March 1958. I am still in first grade, but my father is on sabbatical and we are spending part of the year in Davos. This is where he began his sojourn in Switzerland in the 1930s in the children's sanatorium, having arrived from Russia with tuberculosis and a Swiss mother and no knowledge of German. This is where my brother completed the Alpine Mittelschule, after leaving a midwestern high school with a low lottery number, fluent in Swiss-German but with little command of written or High German. And where my mother lies buried in the *Waldfriedhof*, because the cancer had already metastasized, after the divorce proceedings had already begun. And where my father has now joined her.

The poem, untitled, is written in English:

> Heimweh is a sound that never dies.
> It sometimes quiets down.
> It can be a man that means what you have lost,
> It may be a lake with an island or
> a mountain covered with glittering snow.
>
> It sometimes almost goes away
> and comes again and holds you in its grip
> when you, with tears, read "Heidi"
> to a little girl.

Swissness: Keywords

My mother writes in a foreign tongue even though she has returned, at least temporarily, to her *Heimat*. The daughter, who has been taken out of school, has not yet learned to read. The mother, a nonnative speaker, will have to teach her, but she has little patience. She reads *Heidi* to her instead, but in what language? The daughter will mimic her mother's tears, induced by Heidi, a girl with whom she never quite identifies. She inherits her mother's homesickness and, having learned to read, will find her home in English.

Resisting selves thrust into alien languages.

Heidi is a girl who has been told by a boy, Peter, the goatherd on her grandfather's alp, that reading is difficult, too difficult, and thus something to avoid. When Heidi arrives in Frankfurt, it is not her companion Clara's tutor, but Clara's grandmother who motivates Heidi to read, by generating interest in a book she plans to give her as a gift. The story, told not just in words but in pictures, is that of the prodigal son. This has been understood as the grandfather's story; he squanders the family fortune, serves as a mercenary in Naples, returns with a son whom the village refuses to recognize, and, when his son dies, ends up a recluse on the alp. Heidi's desire for literacy is fueled by a longing to see herself as the protagonist. But to become the prodigal daughter, she must suffer from homesickness. In Frankfurt, Heidi sleepwalks, is mistaken for a ghost, and leaves the front door wide open, ostensibly an invitation to thieves, but obviously a way to stage her departure. Returning home means not just returning to the alp but to God. To him, one can say all, even as Heidi learns he will not necessarily answer her prayers at the time they have been received. When she teaches Peter to read, it is so that he, in her absence, can read to his grandmother who is blind.

My mother's desire, as an urban Protestant, is neither for the alp nor for God. It is for her *Heimatstadt*. Unlike my mother, I have no *Heimatstadt*. I become nostalgic for the very home that might have made me homesick.

The cat continues to wander over to the Catholic church, in search of those who will lean down and pet him on their way to mass. Even he has feelings of homesickness, for those who originally thought that he belonged to them.

Nostalgia is the desire for what cannot be defined, *le désir d'on ne sait quoi*. French has no word for home: "*pays*" can mean the part of the country one is from, or the country itself; German confuses "*Heim*" with "*Heimat*": "home" is meant to coincide with "nation," and the nation inflicts itself on those along its nonnatural borders. In my mother's case: "*Dieses Heimweh ist der verborgene Maler, der das Bild, das die Betroffenen von Amerika haben, oft ungerechterweise trübt und grau erscheinen lässt und das ferne Zürich in einenen goldenen Schimmer zu tauchen vermag, in dem alles Menschlich-Allzumenschliche einfach wegtouchiert ist.*" "Homesickness is like the painter behind the scenes, who allows the picture of America to become too grim and grey, and immerses the image of a distant Zürich in a golden haze, thereby erasing all that is human—all too human" (Rütschi, "Zürcherinnen, denen es schwer fällt, Neuyorkerinnen zu werden").

In *The Book of Laughter and Forgetting* Milan Kundera writes: "*Litost* is a Czech word with no exact translation into any other language. It designates a feeling as infinite as an open accordion, a feeling that is the synthesis of many others: grief, sympathy, remorse, and an indefinable longing. The first syllable, which is long and stressed, sounds like the wail of an abandoned dog."

Eva Hoffman in *Lost in Translation* describes nostalgia as "pregnancy without the possibility of birth": "As I walk the streets of Vancouver, I am pregnant with the images of Poland, pregnant and sick. *Tesknota* throws a film over everything around me, and directs my vision inward. The largest presence within me is the welling up of absence, of what I have lost. This pregnancy is also a phantom pain."

Europe moves east; the writer replaces the doctor. Homesickness, difficult to translate, finds its home in metaphor: it is like an accordion that ceases to close, like a pregnancy that fails to terminate.

Nostalgia returns once again in the form of a German neologism. *Ostalgie*, nostalgia for the very thing no one thought one could feel the loss of: the material things made in the GDR everyone thought no one wanted. These are the products for which consumers constructed product biographies, ways of using non-user-friendly products impervious to product innovation, enmeshed in the biographical narratives of their users. These products enjoy a symbolic afterlife, defying the very capitalism that put them out of business, fueling the very capitalism that seeks to exploit them as ossified commodities. They symbolize the desire for a desire that has vanished—for a socialist state, for a western materialism—leaving its products to be consumed as a form of camp. They appear in glossaries and dictionaries that keep the old brand names alive among citizens whose country has disappeared. They reappear in a shared language where memory (*Gedächtnis*) and memories (*Erinnerung*) require two different words.

Ostalgie: an excess of memory in a time of amnesia.

Fernweh, or "Farsickness"

Fernweh. The antithesis of *Heimweh*, or homesickness.

The longing of those from small places for open spaces, those from the north for the south, those who know where they belong for somewhere they have never been.

It doesn't go both ways.

The Swiss have *Fernweh* for Italy, for burnt sienna and empty piazzas as opposed to the myriad shades of green resulting from endless rain.

Italians appreciate the cleanliness of Swiss streets and the punctuality of Swiss trains, but they don't long for either. They respect them.

Swiss can have *Fernweh* for America, because it is big and empty and ugly, which makes it exotic. The landscape makes up for whatever is lacking in the buildings, whether loveliness or longevity.

Americans don't have *Fernweh.* Many have never been out of the country; some have never left the ranch. They are in search of something else. When they can't find it, they forget what they've been looking for. When they do find it, they become surprisingly sentimental.

The Swiss no longer have *Fernweh* for America. On every city block, last-minute vacations beckon to the Seychelles to Mexico to Shanghai to Dubai to the Maldives. Why travel to the same place twice? Why decide today when tomorrow's bargain might be even better?

The far away has become the new near.

The near is so close it is no longer worth noticing.

Where is the traveler who has unexpectedly gone missing?

The Mountains

The Alp(s)

A is for alp(s).

The Alp

The Alps separate Switzerland from Italy, providing twenty-three passes for the journey to Rome, with one hospice at St. Bernard. Early travelers are terrified: some ask to be blindfolded, and others hold a vinegar-soaked sponge to their noses to mitigate altitude sickness.

The Alps cover two-thirds of Switzerland and are the site of 60 percent of its tourism.

The alp is the communal summer pasture that supports the village cow herd from June to September, in order to allow the grass in the valley meadows to be harvested as hay. Meadows are fertilized with composted manure so desirable grasses predominate and hay can be harvested each year without letting fields lie fallow. No one is permitted to send more cows to the alp than he can winter, to bring animals for temporary pasturage, or to sell a cow within a stipulated period of time after the end of the alp season. Trees anchor the mountainside soil, protect the watershed, reduce avalanche danger. They shelter livestock during storms. The alp limits the growth of forests and the spread of settlement and thus makes possible the Alps, a vacationland.

The communal localism that resists (male) in-migration and favors out-migration, regulates existing renewable resources by preventing overgrazing. Men emigrate as mercenaries or to build tunnels. They become Swiss Guards at the Vatican or royal bodyguards to the French king. Men and women inherit equally through partible inheritance, but residence, even if it includes ownership but does not include descent through the male line from a prior member of the community, does not include citizenship. Descendants who have never lived in the village are citizens; those who are not citizens, in spite of wealth and influence, are denied membership in the community. Thrift is encouraged, and risk is to be avoided. No one ends up landless; no one ends up rich. Many remain celibate.

Those who go to school might become priests or postal bus drivers or ski instructors. Those who leave are likely to return to spend their vacations harvesting hay.

The Alps are the most environmentally threatened mountain system in the world.

Of all tourists, 75 percent arrive by private car.

The Mountaineer

The first mountaineers are people who live in the mountains, chamois hunters, and crystal gatherers. Those who come to the mountains are known as travelers or "strangers." In 1827 "Switzerland" is still used to describe any area of France, Savoy, Piedmont or Italy that contained mountains.

The initial strangers are scientists who come with thermometers and barometers to study glaciers, avalanches, thunderstorms, the boiling point, and red snow.

In 1723 Johann Jacob Scheuchzer, a Swiss professor of physics and mathematics at the University of Zürich, fellow of the Royal Society of London, and correspondent of Isaac Newton and Gottfried Leibniz, draws up a compendium, canton by canton, of all species of dragons known to exist in the Swiss Alps. He is the first to study the *Föhn*.

In 1729 Albrecht von Haller, a Bernese physician and mathematician, compiler of the first book on Swiss flora and director of the salt-works at Roche, publishes a poem titled *Die Alpen*, a didactic poem subtitled "An Attempt at Swiss Poetry," reprinted thirty times in his own lifetime. The first edition is printed anonymously, the second with Haller's name, and subsequent editions with his name followed by numerous honorary titles. He is the first Swiss to be read outside of Switzerland, although German is for him a foreign tongue. He speaks Swiss-German and French, but he writes in German to prove that it is as suitable as English for didactic poetry. For some, "Swiss writer" is no longer an oxymoron. From 1976 to 2000, Haller appears on the Swiss 500-franc banknote.

Then come those inspired by the view. Wordsworth describes his walking tour of the Alps, journeying three thousand miles, including two thousand on foot. Rousseau reads Haller; Shelley and Byron read Rousseau, in a boat on Lake Geneva. Queen Victoria is carried to the top of the Rigi by sedan chair while she mourns the death of Prince Albert, who sent her a pressed flower from its summit. Mary Shelley likens the Alps to the Arctic. Emily Dickinson, in a poem that begins "Our lives are Swiss—/ So still—so Cool—" likens the Alps to a curtain that stands guard between Switzerland and Italy that might be drawn to enlarge her view from Amherst. Dickinson's Alps are as imaginary as those of Friedrich Schiller, who also never set foot in Switzerland, although his play *William Tell* has been performed every evening during the summer months since 1912 in an open-air theater on the shores of Lake Lucerne.

Then come the true mountaineers, in search of exercise, excitement, and self-enlightenment. They come with ice axe, ropes, and nails in their boots. Their holidays are short, and instead of enjoying long walking tours, they ascend virgin peaks and cross crevasses with the aid of ladders carried by guides. Most of the early climbers in the High Alps specialize in one summit, and once they climb it they give up. By the middle of the nineteenth century, some continue after a first ascent to dedicate their entire summer holidays to alpine scrambles. In the 1850s Mont Blanc could be reached from London in twenty-four hours and the Swiss Alps in fifty-six. The Continent was now accessible to those with a long vacation, one that lasts at least six weeks.

The golden age of mountaineering begins in 1854, with the first climb of the Wetterhorn near Grindelwald by Alfred Wills, High Court judge who presides over Oscar Wilde's trial, who claims the pursuit is worthwhile in itself and does so in writing. It ends in 1865 with Edward Whymper's ascent of the Matterhorn whose descent ends in four deaths, including that of Lord Francis Douglas, whose brother Alfred takes Oscar Wilde to court. Of the thirty-nine major peaks ascended during that time, thirty-one are ascended by British amateurs, most of them accompanied by Swiss guides. By the time mountaineering enters its silver age, 1900–1910, the piton and carabiner have been invented; the most familiar mountains are attempted by the most dangerous routes; and the competition between nations, primarily Austria and Germany, takes place between climbing buddies rather than the Englishman and his guide.

> What on earth can you find to do in Switzerland. For goodness sake, don't take to climbing mountains. Every newspaper almost, has a Matterhorn tragedy in it. Are you anywhere near the Matterhorn? I have the vaguest idea of your or anybodies [*sic*] geography. (Letter from Virginia Woolf to Emma Vaughan, August 8, 1901)

> How could I think mountains and climbing romantic? Wasn't I brought up with Alpenstocks in my nursery, and a raised mp [*sic*] of the Alps, showing every peak my father had climbed? Of course, London and the marshes are places I like best. (Letter from Virginia Woolf to Vita Sackville-West, August 19, 1924)

Leslie Stephen makes first ascents of the Schreckhorn and the Blümlisalp in the Bernese Oberland, the Zinal Rothhorn near Zermatt, the Monte della Disgrazia in the Grisons, the Mont Mallet in Chamonix, among others, crosses most of the high Oberland passes and finds new routes up many peaks, including the Allalin and the Weissmies. He is dismissive of scientists, but on the Blümlisalp he agrees to take a barometer, which, unbeknownst to him, slips out of the guide's rucksack and falls into the Lake of Oeschinen. When he climbs the Mont Blanc, he times it so that he will be at the summit at sunset, thus his companion, the French painter Gabriel Loppé, can capture the landscape against the sinking sun. The Col des Hirondelles owes its name to him because during his first ascent he finds a pile of dead swallows on the snow at the foot of the pass. He never climbs the Matterhorn, thinking the guides will be too nervous after the Whymper disaster, but he ventures into the much-less-traveled Dolomites and Carpathians. He criticizes guideless climbing and invites his favorite Swiss guide, Melchior Anderegg, who has never been in a city larger than Berne, to London. An early member of the Alpine Club, also its chairman, vice president, and president, as well as editor of the *Alpine Journal*, Stephen walks from Cambridge to London in twelve hours to attend a club meeting. He wears the same tweed coat in the mountains and in London, its waistline stained yellow from the ropes that have been fastened round it.

In 1871 Stephen publishes a collection of essays titled *The Playground of Europe*, about which he writes: "I have published a small book about the Alps, a collection of articles called the Playground of Europe, the best part of wh. is the name." The essays are intended for the Alpine Club, describing routes that might be followed by fellow members while decrying the crowds that are increasingly encroaching on what they consider their private playground. In spite of the impossibility of solitude given climbing with guides, Stephen is at his most philosophical when he writes: "The mountain solitude is so intense because the mountains are, in one sense, so far from secret. . . . You know that you might fall, for example, from the summit of a cliff, upon which a hundred sightseers are gazing at the time, and yet they would be unaware that a tragedy was being performed before their eyes." The view, which for the Romantics begins at the foot of the mountain and for the Victorians involves looking down from a peak, has become a show for sightseers whose sight is enhanced by the eyeglass. "Solitude in a crowd is supposed to be the worst kind of solitude; but perhaps the most impressive is the solitude on a point visible and familiar to half a nation." For the mountaineer, solitude has become a spectacle whose spectators remain unsuspecting.

The Mountains

It is this solitude that Stephen exchanges for his first marriage.

The Honeymoon

On June 19, 1867, Leslie Stephen and Minny Thackeray marry and spend their honeymoon in the Alps. In Grindelwald, Minny is left to read in the hotel, elegantly dressed in her "grey & blue French costume," having packed only a pair of "dancing-boots." She sends Leslie for a walk while she watches him through an eyeglass. She is startled by the size of the mountains, one of which, the Schreckhorn, Leslie was the first to climb. "We are so close to these enormous brutes," she writes to her sister Anny, "that even I could see anyone running up & down their sides." In Zermatt she writes to Blanche Warre-Cornish: "I am trying not to look out of the window, for if I do I shall see the Matterhorn with the moon shining on it and you can't think how horrid it looks, like a great hooky sort of gleaming ghost. I always think it will come and poke its great hook nose into the window." The journey to an unfamiliar landscape in the form of the upper-middle-class honeymoon is meant to realign the gaze of the single subject with that of the married couple; so observes Helena Mitchie in her study of fifty-three honeymooning couples whose wedding dates range from 1829 to 1886. If for Minny the honeymoon means a reorientation in terms of learning not to fear a landscape and therefore a body identified as masculine, for Leslie it means returning to the mountains as a final turning away from his exploits as a mountaineer. The "ideal honeymoon as a learning experience in which the husband figures as a guide" is an impossible one for a mountaineer who can only abandon, rather than share, the "sight" from the summit of an alpine peak. His solitude is now complete.

The fundamental change that marriage brings to the groom, rather than the bride, finds its expression in the more recent and most frequent use of the honeymoon in the Swiss Alps, the Bollywood film. In Raj Kapoor's now classic *Sangam* (Meeting of souls) from 1964, Sundar, a member of the Indian Air Force who returns after two years missing in action, has his first posting in London, which allows for a honeymoon in Europe with his bride, Radha. In the first Indian film to be shot in foreign locations, the couple journeys from London to Rome to Venice, and then to Paris, which Mitchie identifies as "a privileged site of contestations between sexual innocence and experience." This contestation takes a more oblique form in the contest between two consumer goods, the expensive handbag that Radha desires and the new set of bagpipes Sundar purchases. It becomes more explicit when Sundar suggests that the show he will attend at Place Pigalle is only for men and Radha puts on a show just for him, wearing black tights, playing the new bagpipes, with a lampshade for a hat and window curtains for a gown. Switzerland provides the obligatory scenes on the train and rolling around in the snow, but more unusual is the invitation Sundar extends to Gopal, his best friend and the man Radha is still in love with and would have chosen to marry. It is Radha's birthday, and Gopal, who "will bring warmth to these icy mountains" from Bombay, is Sundar's gift. The day begins with Radha listening to the church bells from her hotel balcony, but it is in a mountainous gorge, rather than in a meadow or on a peak, that Sundar shouts, "Gopal," and he appears. Radha makes clear to Gopal that he is never to return, and by the time Sundar has set a table for three in the hotel room, he has once again disappeared. Sundar pages him in vain at the Geneva airport, still unaware of a groom's need to realign his gaze from a homosocial friendship to his marriage.

In Yash Chopra's 1995 *Dilwale Dulhania Le Jayenge* (The brave heart will take the bride), the longest-running film in Indian cinema, the story begins in London, where a son and daughter of Indian immigrants decide to travel to Europe after college. Simran is given permission to travel by her patriarchal father before she marries the stranger she has been promised to in India, and Raj's millionaire father encourages him to take a trip, even though he has failed to graduate. The pair meets on the Eurostar shortly after leaving St. Pancras Station, Simran using her eyeglasses in an attempt to read a book in solitude while Raj uses his sunglasses to avoid solitude, playing the role of seducer. The first foreign scene is in Paris, where light opera becomes an occasion for Simran to embarrass Raj and Raj to declare his attraction to

The Mountains

Simran's "magic." When they both miss the train from the mountains back to Zürich, the Alps become the scene not for a honeymoon but for an extended courtship that mimics scenes from a marriage. Raj pretends to be Simran's husband when the Swiss police ask for her passport; Simran wakes up wearing Raj's shirt in the chalet where they have been marooned for the night. He tries to convince her that in spite of his joking, he is still a Hindustani who would not only not take advantage of her but refuses to elope with her when it becomes clear that she would rather marry him than the stranger waiting for her in Punjab. While he claims "I hate girls" and she dismisses boys by saying "they are all the same," this journey to the Continent becomes one not only away from England toward compulsory heterosexuality but away from the India of their parents and its arranged marriages. Raj removes the Swiss cowbell from Simran's front door in London before he follows her to India. There, the scenes from Switzerland are replayed as a way of motivating an apparently endless courtship that finally ceases when the bride's father allows his daughter to marry for love.

Over two hundred Bollywood films have scenes filmed in Switzerland. This is due in part to political difficulties making it impossible to film mountain scenes in the Himalayas and in part to the filmmaker Yash Chopra, who spent his honeymoon in Gstaad in the 1970s, where he promised his wife that every movie he made would include a romantic scene or song filmed in Switzerland. In April 2010 Chopra, in conjunction with his production company Yash Raj Films and the Kuoni Travel Group, with its origins in Switzerland, organized a fifteen-day tour, "The Enchanted Journey." Groups of middle-class Indians are taken to the sites of their favorite Bollywood films, have their picture taken in the same poses as their favorite actors, watch films while they are traveling, and receive a package of five Bollywood films to take home. Chopra has been presented with a prize from the Swiss government for "helping rediscover Switzerland," while the town of Thun had its first Bollywood film festival in May 2010. The attraction of Switzerland? "No noise, no pollution, no crowds." "A place for romance and natural beauty." Like Byron and Shelley on Lake Geneva, these tourists hope to make the fictional real by revisiting the scenes that produced the original intensity of their reading or viewing experience. Swiss hotel managers complain that guests cook curry dishes on camping stoves in their rooms, just as they complained when the first English expected afternoon tea, water closets, and Anglican church services. It will nevertheless not be Swiss ambivalence toward foreigners that encourages filmmakers to look elsewhere. It has become both less expensive and more novel to shoot scenes in countries such as Hungary, Poland, and Czechoslovakia.

The Alps

Napoleon crossed the [St. Bernard] pass [in 1800] on the back of a mule but apparently said nothing about the beauty of the scenery; his wife, Joséphine, on the other hand, was so taken with the place that she later invited a Swiss farmer and his wife, along with seven cows and a bull, to live with her in a mock-Alpine chalet on the outskirts of Paris.

Andrea Beattie, *The Alps: A Cultural History* (2006)

Of the numberless attractions offered by the Exposition, the most extensive, picturesque and animated, as well as the most interesting for novelty, is the Swiss village; and this chalet is one of the collections of houses that compose it. Here we have Switzerland in the heart of Paris, a living synthesis of the incomparable little country whose beauty and grandeur of scenery excite the wonder and admiration of thousands of intelligent tourists who are attracted thither annually from all parts of the world.

Paris Exhibition reproduced from the official photographs (1900)

I change planes in Amsterdam, between the midwestern university town where I live and my initial destination, a minor European city.

I choose a hotel in Zürich on the street where my mother grew up, in a building that reminds me of my grandmother's house: the curved staircase, the polished banisters, the creaks in the wooden floorboards.

The Mountains

My uncle dies, he has disinherited me, and my brother inherits the house that has been in the family for over a hundred years. I am forced to abandon the one room I have returned to all of my life. Here, closer to the lake, I am reminded of the grandmother with whom I fed bread to the ducks and a mother with whom I went swimming while she kept her head above water in order to enjoy the view.

I recover from jetlag, return to the main train station, and continue my journey into the Alps. The trip to Davos Platz requires changing trains in Landquart, something I have done numerous times. From here the tracks narrow, the train ascends inside spiral tunnels, and I remain seated until the final stop, one stop farther than that of Hans Castorp in *The Magic Mountain* when he arrives in Davos Dorf in the early 1900s. I breathe in the thin alpine air, the cure of many ills, although not his, and most likely not my own.

After escaping from Russia to Switzerland, emigrating from Switzerland to America, migrating from the East Coast to the West, my father chooses this "city in the mountains" as his permanent residence. He pauses briefly between Palo Alto and St. Petersburg, St. Petersburg and Rhodos, Rhodos and Majorca, his bags arriving before he does, waiting at the train station ready to be repacked. Although I have entered a vacationland, why am I not enjoying myself?

My father pulls out an old photo album and reminisces about the early years of his first marriage, the one to my mother. How after the war there were so few people traveling and resources were so scarce that one accepted without hesitation the invitation of a stranger. The itinerary in the album, recorded in my mother's handwriting, documents a series of international conferences attended by my father, accompanied by a wife eager to resume traveling, even if adverse to playing the role of an accessory. I am his oldest child, although I am neither a son nor a daddy's girl. Two subsequent marriages bring two additional daughters. The first my father refuses to adopt, even though her mother is dying of cancer; the second he insists on adopting, in spite of her mother needing someone else's kidney, filling the daughter's closet with countless pairs of shoes.

My journey continues to an even more remote valley in Graubünden, a place no one in my family has ever visited. In the 1850s,

The Alp(s)

The author (*right*), with mother and brother, Graubünden, 1950s (photo taken by author's father)

children between six and sixteen left for Swabia to earn money for food and clothing, setting out on foot across the Alps in March and returning in November. They suffered, excessively homesick and deprived of shoes, but if fortunate enough to land a benevolent employer, they would have been places, they would have seen things, beyond those confined to a barely accessible valley.

This time my father decides to accompany me.

He invites himself to Vals.

I insist on taking the train. I try to explain that I live in a part of the country that invented the automobile, on which I, like others, am utterly dependent. Vacation allows independence from a private means of transportation. He will make me feel like a prisoner in a vehicle that will take me to friends I have never met, who possess wealth I fail to admire and embody success I refuse to esteem—"trophy friends," one of my friends calls them. The meal will be opulent, the wine abundant, the view impressive, but my feeling will be one of redundancy.

I change trains in Bad Reichenau and then disembark in Ilanz, where I board the postal bus that travels up the valley with place names I can barely pronounce, in the one national language I have never learned to speak. It will blow its horn around tight curves to announce itself to oncoming traffic. It will navigate the steep, narrow road with trucks carrying bottles of mineral water, Valserwasser, now owned by the Coca-Cola Company. It will deposit me at a hotel where as soon as I arrive I am invited to enter the mineral baths, owned by the local community, designed by a Swiss architect. Peter Zumthor is known as an architect's architect, with a small oeuvre; his stark granite pools and views framed by striated granite openings bring architecture students and professors from as far away as Oregon. I recognize the "severe, minimalist perfection" that Matt Tyrnauer has identified as an aesthetic I call my own, providing an oasis in austerity from the sadness that comes with irreconcilability.

He calls to say he will arrive a day late.

He arrives early and wonders why I am not waiting for him. He treats himself to a leisurely lunch that includes a bottle of wine. He reprimands me for not being there when he shows up. He is raising his voice. I imagine he is raising his hand, like Lily Biscoe facing Mr. Banks at her canvas in *To the Lighthouse*. His lunch, which cannot yet be put on his tab, ends up on my bill. He, who checks in as the professor, will be confused with his daughter, also a professor, although she rarely identifies herself as such.

I take his hand and guide his frail body across the granite floor. I accompany him from pool to pool. The one that amplifies sound and the one with scented petals. The not so small and very hot one in red, the very small and very cold one in blue. The one that moves from indoors to outdoors and frames the hay huts dotting the hillside across the valley. The water that turns the grey granite to saffron, that tastes like sulfur from cups dangling on metal chains.

The entrance, he says, reminds him of a pissoir in Paris.

We agree on a time for dinner, when wine will supplant most of the interest in food, and interest in the wait staff will surpass much of the interest in his daughter. He will try to persuade me of things that make me think he is dining with someone else. This time it seems to be how to reconcile science and religion. They have proven that religion is biological by telling children a story about a crocodile and a mouse. The crocodile eats the mouse. Does the mouse still miss its mommy? Yes. This proves the mouse has an afterlife. This proves children have religious feeling, and because it is expressed by children, it must be innate.

I have spent my life in literature, interpreting fictions and insisting that their meanings remain undecidable. Religion has been of interest as another kind of fiction. Science, like religion, imagines that what it knows can be elevated to the status of truth. I begin to speak; I fail to articulate my views; I end up in tears.

I will excuse myself, and when I return we pretend nothing has happened.

Is it true that he has sold the apartment in Basel that was once my grandmother's for one in St. Petersburg, where she once lived? Will he own it with the second in command of the Russian Orthodox Church, and his so-called sister, who might never have been related and most likely was more than a companion? The metropolite has made a vow of celibacy, although apparently not one of poverty. He is retrieving my father from the diaspora and returning him to Mother Russia. Does it matter that her son, his adopted "brother," does not believe in God? It turns out he had an apartment not in St. Petersburg but in Spain, an apartment registered not in his own name but in that of a fictitious corporation. I am told that he was in love with the "sister" and that she was in love with Spain.

No, I have no interest in visiting St. Petersburg.

I already uncomfortably inhabit the position of the American whose relatives live in Switzerland, or is it that of the Swiss who lives in America?

He reminds me that I am one-quarter Russian, but the city once known as Leningrad is not one I need to know.

Visiting a place that will leave me illiterate will not cure the homesickness of the daughter for whom the Alps, rather than their lack, instills a sense of homelessness.

The Mountains

A woman is playing piano in the hotel bar. As the evening progresses, she leaves her classical repertoire and turns to jazz. She begins to sing, in a sultry voice. She is attractive in an unconventional way. Her back is very straight as she leafs through her notebook, looking for the next song. She tells me, in a voice that sounds American, that they want her not just to play but to sing more. I am the only one listening.

Epilogue

In 1912 Paramount Pictures makes its official logo the Finsteraarhorn, at 4,272 meters the highest peak in the Bernese Oberland. Like the Matterhorn, it stands alone with a shape like a pyramid. At the turn of the century, it is more famous than the Matterhorn, after Mark Twain writes about it in *A Tramp Abroad* (1880) and Gertrude Bell, the first woman to attempt the northeast wall in 1902, nearly loses her life. Since the early 1990s the mountain has been protected as a trademark.

After ten referenda, the voters of Graubünden finally allow automobiles on their streets. Until then, drivers must turn off their motors and hitch their cars to a horse. In 1925 they are permitted to drive only on the main roads. One young driver, so impressed by the purity of the air at the top of the Julierpass, flattens his tires and refills them with alpine air to take back with him to Berlin.

Glaciers cover 3 percent of Switzerland's land mass. In the past two decades, they have lost 15 percent of their surface. By the end of the century, small and middle-sized glaciers will have completely disappeared.

Davos, or "How the English Invented the Alps"

∞∞

Davos is likewise a rare "find" for young men looking out for a spot in which to read during the "Long" [a vacation that lasts at least six weeks]. It is not "slow" enough to be voted tiresome, nor so "fast" as to induce the conscientious student to leave the inevitable books in the unopened portmanteau. The English colony which, summer and winter seems to have pitched its headquarters in the Hôtel Belvedere, always finds something to do. Excursions are constantly planned. Gay parties of picnickers may often be descried having themselves "carted" up the lateral valleys. Some again test their walking powers on the various peaks and summits; while yet others go in for a favourite hobby with select and sympathising friends.

[Mrs. Elizabeth MacMorland], *Davos-Platz: A New Alpine Resort*
for Sick and Sound in Summer and Winter
by One Who Knows It Well (1878)

The theory of a cure for phthisis by means of dry, pure, rarified mountain air is so essentially consistent with common sense that we wonder it was not put into practice long ago. But consumption has always been too timorously, too leniently, too indulgently dealt with. Parents and doctors unite to humour and soothe the patient at home, and, when the last stage was drawing nigh, sent him to end his sadly useless life, fittingly enough, in some romantic southern region. Davos demands

The Mountains

qualities the very opposite of the resigned sentimentalism in which too frequently the phthisical youth or maiden was encouraged. Here is no place for weak and despairing resignation; here you are not pusillanimously helped to die, but are required to enter into a hard struggle for life.

Davos, with 20 illustrations by J. Webber, and a Map (ca. 1880)

January in London, with few exceptions, had been a month of raw and foggy days—days that were bitter cold, with the coldness of a damp cloth, and stuffy with the airlessness of that which a damp cloth covers. Far otherwise was it at Davos, where morning after morning, after nights of still, intense cold, the sun rose over the snow-covered hills, and flamed like a golden giant, rejoicing in his strength, through the arc of crystalline blue.

E. F. Benson, *The Relentless City* (1903)

What a contrast! Here at Platz, a bit of a city in its way, with enormous hotels, elegant villas, large shops, all flooded at eventide in a brilliant sea of illumination, the streets and pavements alive with a gay crowd, representing every language, every range of education, every faith, gathered here from off the face of the whole earth, the strangest town in all Europe, at an elevation of more than 5000 feet,—and there, close by, the old folk, simple and content, the world forgetting, by the world forgot, living in their lonely farm-houses, away there in the folds of the Sertig, in the Spina, on the Hitzenboden, where never a stranger is known to stray.

Davos as Health-Resort: A Handbook (1906)

Right: Villa auf'm Egg, Rütistrasse 17 (today Rosenhügelweg 6), ca. 1890, also known as "Boulevard des Anglais" (Dokumentationsbibliothek Davos)

Davos.

The Mountains

Scene I

Characters

JAS: John Addington Symonds (1840–93) author of the seven-volume *The Renaissance in Italy* (1875–86) and coauthor, with his daughter Margaret, of *Our Life in the Swiss Highlands* (1892). He fails to write *The History of Graubünden*. He first arrives in Davos in 1877 and lives in Am Hof from 1881 to 1893.

RLS: Robert Louis Stevenson (1850–94), author of *Treasure Island* (1883), which he completes in Davos, and four essays on the Alps collected in *Essays of Travel* (1905). He fails to write *History of the [Scottish] Highlands*. He resides in Davos for two winters, 1880–81 and 1881–82.

LS: Leslie Stephen (1832–1904), author of *The Playground of Europe* (1871) and editor of the *Alpine Journal* (1868–72). He visits Symonds in Davos in 1893.

Place

Am Hof, the house John Addington Symonds built in Davos in 1882, the first house in a meadow of the same name, a queer composite of Swiss architectural style and English amenities. The water supply comes from a spring above the house, pouring through pipes that produce a "continuous and sonorous sound of rushing waters" (M. Symonds, *Out of the Past*), at times disturbing the sleep of unaccustomed guests. A *Wandelbahn*, or "ambulatory," a covered veranda built at right angles to the house, provides a place to walk under cover on wet or snowy days, as well as a place to sit for breakfast or tea. The attic is filled with the scent of apples, a Union Jack, and pith helmets left over from the aborted trip to Egypt. The basement has a kitchen supervised by M. Bérard, a superb cook who prefers cooking for men; the two wine cellars are filled with casks of wine from the Valtelline valley.

Davos, or "How the English Invented the Alps"

JAS occupies a bedroom and two studies paneled in cembra or Arven wood. The largest knots have been reserved for these rooms, which are permeated with the sweet smell of wood not varnished, or oiled, or waxed. The inner of the two studies is known as the carpenter's shop, furnished with a green serpentine stove, old peasant furniture, a Persian rug, and a large table with a slate top. There are photographs of people, places, and pictures. Books line the walls, except for an old medicine chest with two skeletons of fine inlaid wood on its door, and a shelf with a collection of pipes. Piles of miscellaneous papers, known as precipices, are stacked on the table, which also contains "fancy articles" such as Venetian beads, stuffed owls, Japanese match-boxes, and select stationary. It is a tidy room, excessively tidy.

JAS changes his clothes, because he has so many, several times during the scene.

Ciò, the Venetian boat dog, enters and exits at will.

Sequestered in his study, JAS lives up to ten hours of each day in Italy and Greece.

Time

The early 1880s.

JAS: The life can be exceedingly monotonous. I think we can agree on that.

RLS: Smoking eases it, as can talk. "Cigarettes without intermission except when coughing or kissing" is how I describe my nicotine habit (Harman, *Robert Louis Stevenson*). I've been limited to three pipes a day, one after each meal.

JAS: I've just come in from smoking a pipe with the grooms. It's not too late for a glass of Valtelline.

LS: When Stevenson came for dinner with Edmund Gosse in London, Anny, my sister-in-law, did all the talking. The summer before I married Minny, the two sisters visited the Alps for the first

79

time and I failed to propose, in spite of a romantic picnic by the Riffelhorn.

JAS: In my household, I encourage vigorous discussion rather than sitting in silence. When invited to the house of a lady or gentleman, my daughters are told: "You are not invited merely to enjoy yourself and to think about yourself and to stare and take notes about your fellow-guests in silence. You are there to contribute to the general pleasantness" (M. Symonds, *Out of the Past*).

RLS: "In short, the first duty of a man is to speak; that is his chief business in this world; and talk, which is the harmonious speech of two or more, is by far that most accessible of pleasures. It costs nothing in money; it is all profit; it completes our education, founds and fosters our friendships, and can be enjoyed at any age and in almost any state of health" (Stevenson, *Memories and Portraits*).

LS: I was horrified when RLS, a twenty-nine-year-old groom, married a forty-year-old widow. JAS and I have quite different relations to alpine natives: I argued against guideless climbing; I consider married homosexuals to be blackguards.

JAS: I gesticulate and leap up in mid-sentence to take down a volume.

RLS: Talk is impromptu, collaborative, *to be continued*, like the many books I have never finished. I read aloud the stories I am writing and ask my stepson, Lloyd, to take notes and discuss them with me. Later they will perceive our collaboration as a form of pederastic seduction.

JAS: We both had moderate talents, but what genius we had for work! By producing no discernible masterpiece, we made it difficult for posterity.

RLS: I include you in my "Talk and Talkers." I name you "Opelstein." "He does not always, perhaps not often, frankly surrender himself in conversation. He brings into the talk other thoughts than those which he expresses; you are conscious that he keeps an eye on something else, that he does not shake off the world, nor quite forget himself" (Stevenson, *Memories and Portraits*).

JAS: I encourage reserve, but no taboos.

Davos, or "How the English Invented the Alps"

RLS: Our second winter in Davos. Fanny, Lloyd, and I were living in the Chalet am Stein, just above the Hotel Buol, where you occupied a suite of rooms. You and Catherine came to visit almost daily. I was too ill to write; "dry rot," Fanny called it. Fanny became ill: the doctors thought she was too stout. Even Woggs the dog fell ill.

JAS: Your first winter. I sought you out at the Hotel Belvedere the day after you arrived. You appeared with a letter of introduction from Edmund Gosse, an early admirer of Whitman. I wasn't sure how to spell your name. All I knew was that you were a friend of Leslie Stephen, who as the editor of the *Cornhill* nursed both of us to fame. I consented to writing a letter of reference for the Professorship in History and Constitutional Law at Edinburgh University. Needless to say, it was unsuccessful, since you held none of the necessary qualifications.

RLS: My favorite chalet, the happiest of all our homes, was La Solitude, in Hyères-les-Palmiers, a miniature Swiss chalet constructed for the Paris Exposition of 1878, relocated to southern France. There I developed ophthalmia and sat in the dark wearing bandages or goggles. Fanny was afraid I was going blind.

JAS: I put in my name and then withdrew it for the professorship in poetry at Oxford, not because of my "Arcadian tastes" but because of my agnosticism. Once I became consumptive, I could hardly use my eyes, inflamed under blue spectacles and green eyeshades. I was forced to hire readers.

RLS: Bertie Sitwell dies of consumption in the Hotel Belvedere, leaving his toy theater to Lloyd, my stepson. His mother, Mrs. Francis Sitwell, is the initial "bereaved matron with an absentee husband" I fall in love with, seven years earlier. "Madonna" I call her, the endlessly eager and sympathetic listener with a reputation for "nurturing a string of needy young men" (Harman, *Robert Louis Stevenson*). I write a poem in memory of Bertie, the only means I have for assuaging his mother's grief: "I begin to hope I may, if not outlive this wolverine upon my shoulders, at least carry him bravely like Symonds and Alexander Pope" (Lockett, *Robert Louis Stevenson at Davos*).

The Mountains

JAS: Our health was our greatest trial; our weakness, needing the attendance of women.

RLS: I paint scenery for the theater and help Lloyd give performances, sliding the actors in and out on their tin stands, making sounds for galloping horses and screams for damsels in distress. I remember buying dozens of printed cutouts for Skelt's Juvenile Drama on Antigua Street in Edinburgh, the playbooks imprinting a lifelong sense of adventure and romance. My father, the last in a line of engineers who built lighthouses on the Scottish coast, thought that leisure was the proper place for letters.

JAS: Madge, our second youngest, joins Lloyd in your attic, where you and he play elaborate war games with six hundred miniature lead soldiers on the floor made into a map, "with mountains, towns, rivers, 'good' and 'bad' roads, bridges, morasses, etc." (Osbourne, *An Intimate Portrait of R.L.S.*). You need playmates and prefer them not to be girls. After you leave, the cardboard theater remains in our attic for years. Margaret, or Madge, as we renamed her, after my favorite mare, is forced to imagine the Switzerland she has never seen every time Catherine and I return from one of our interminable journeys abroad. What she sees is "a sort of *décor de theatre* place in my imagination, made up of high mountains cut out of cardboard which rose at regular intervals like teeth, and with a perpetual and most vivid 'afterglow' upon their snows; and edelweiss and gentians here and there upon the foreground" (M. Symonds, *Out of the Past*).

RLS: I kept my costume on as long as possible after any performance, as one young woman observed, as if "he were acting to himself being an actor" (Harman, *Robert Louis Stevenson*).

JAS: I remember playing with tin soldiers the day my sister died of consumption.

RLS: I changed my name from Lewis to Louis and adopted the black velvet smoking jacket of French bohemianism. They called me "Velvet Coat." I met Fanny in France, in Grez-sur-Loing. She was still Mrs. Samuel Osborne, originally Fanny Vandegrift from the backwoods of Indiana. She was one of fifty-seven women in a silver-mining camp in Nevada. She owned a pocket derringer pistol and smoked roll-ups. When I followed her to Monterey, I stayed in the French Hotel and befriended its owner, Simoneau. She finally divorced Sam and we spent our honeymoon in Silverado.

JAS: My affection for Rosa Engel taught me to love the Alps. I met her in Mürren when she was fifteen, when she reminded me of Goethe's Margaret. We spoke French, and I presented her with a love poem and a ring. She rejected my proposal, never married, and after her hair turned white appeared in Davos for one last visit. That same year, I met Catherine North, also in Mürren, who together with her sister was among the first women to discard the crinoline for traveling. I followed her to Pontresina, where she accepted my proposal. She reminded me of Dante's Beatrice. We exchanged rings on Piz Languard. We picked a blue *Eritrychium* and placed it inside a golden locket I wore on my watch chain until the day I was robbed in the Public Gardens in Naples. We honeymooned not in the Alps, not even in Italy, but in Brighton.

RLS: I didn't want to become a permanent invalid, a "Symonds person." I was a "workhorse supporting a household of idling adults" (Harman, *Robert Louis Stevenson*).

JAS: I called it "the wolf," "that undefined craving coloured with a vague and poignant hankering after males" (*The Memoirs of John Addington Symonds*), which I thought would be cured by marriage.

RLS: My only friend at the Hotel Belvedere was the head waiter, Christian, who, as described by Lloyd, "like many Swiss of mediocre position, was an extremely intellectual man" (Osbourne, *An Intimate Portrait of R.L.S.*). Together we would pace the empty dining room in interminable discussion while the tables were being spread for the next meal.

JAS: My first winter. I spent three weeks sitting all day on the gravel terrace in front of the Hotel Belvedere. Then I was allowed to go into the wood. "My manservant took me up in a little carriage, hung a hammock between two pine trees, and placed me in the hammock, and when the sun came near to setting fetched me again in the carriage" (*The Memoirs of John Addington Symonds*).

The Mountains

Catherine read to me for two hours every afternoon. Dr. Jenner advised interrupting the journey to Egypt with a sojourn in the High Alps. My sister Charlotte and her husband, T. H. Green, suggested joining them in Davos. It is not a beautiful valley, like Mürren, which has no invalids, but the air is still and dry and cold. I delivered a lecture on Michelangelo for the Literary Society in the dining room of the Hotel Angleterre.

RLS: The south-sea climate was considered bad for the tubercular, but once I arrived there, I throve. I became the "South Sea Don Quixote," the "Polynesian Walter Scott," even Tusi Tala, the "teller of tales." I wanted to be buried on Mount Vaea. It took forty Samoans, including several chiefs, to cut a path through the jungle up the mountainside.

JAS: "*L'amour de l'impossible est la maladie de l'âme*. It cannot be doubted that the congenital aberration of the passions which I have described has been the poison of my life" (*The Memoirs of John Addington Symonds*).

RLS: There was concern that your erotic preoccupations were destroying your intellectual gifts. Henry Sidgwick persuaded you to lock all of your poetry in a black tin box on the bank of the Avon, where he dramatically threw the key into the water.

JAS: I was not a poet, but I had an irresistible urge to write poetry. Writing poetry was like a holiday from the profession of literature, the *via dolorosa*. "Had I wanted to live a poem, I should have chosen Venice" (*The Memoirs of John Addington Symonds*).

RLS: What they call my English style is really my alertness to an unknown native tongue, namely Scots. I admit my native tongue is dying in a foreign tongue that is my first language. Some things I can only express in Scots. Most of my Scottish books I wrote under tropical trees.

JAS: "The quest of ideal beauty, incarnated in breathing male beings, or eternalized in enduring works of art, was leading me to a precipice, from which no exit seemed possible except in suicide or what I then considered sin" (*The Memoirs of John Addington Symonds*).

Davos, or "How the English Invented the Alps"

LS: "I confess . . . that I am a fanatic. I believe that the ascent of mountains forms an essential chapter in the complete duty of man, and that it is wrong to leave any district without setting foot on its highest peak" (Stephen, *The Playground of Europe*).

RLS: I was attracted to the underworld, where I had relations with many fallen women. I remained oblivious to how men fell in love with me. "Hauf a laddie, hauf a lassie, hauf a yellow yite!" (Harman, *Robert Louis Stevenson*) is what the boys called after me on the streets of Edinburgh. Either that or I was seen as the reincarnation of Shelley. When I did come out, to the deep chagrin of my parents, it was as an atheist.

JAS: You had one incurable malady, although it was difficult to name, while I had two: disease of the lungs and perversion of the sexual instincts. The son of an eighth-generation physician in Bristol, one of Shelley's earliest admirers. Was work an opiate for *l'amour de l'impossible?*

RLS: "I have a more subtle opium in my mind than any apothecary's drug" (Harman, *Robert Louis Stevenson*), namely my overworked imagination.

JAS: "Nevertheless, the mountains take a lasting hold upon their foster-children, and foreigners who have lived among them long acquire something of the Nostalgia, or *Heimweh*, which the natives feel for Switzerland" (Symonds and Symonds, *Our Life in the Swiss Highlands*). Of course I never would have agreed to have Johannes, a handsome peasant, marry Madge, which is why we sent her to England, to live with the Leslie Stephens, ostensibly to study painting. We also believed it was wrong to marry an invalid, because tuberculosis was thought to be inherited, but Katherine, our youngest, known in town as the Symonds *Büebli*, did so anyway.

LS: Virginia worshipped Madge, to whom she first opened up about her literary ambitions. Then she thought Madge wasted her talents by marrying the future master of Rugby, and she became Sally Seton in *Mrs. Dalloway*.

JAS: One needs a mental occupation.

The Mountains

RLS: My occupation: "I sling ink" (Harman, *Robert Louis Stevenson*).

JAS: Christian Buol. Financial gifts cemented our friendship. When he drove the sledge, he seemed like a Greek charioteer. When we traveled to Italy, where he had never been, we shared the same bed, so I could view the "naked splendor of his perfect body." When I visited the cembra-paneled house of the Buol family, it was like a scene out of a Whitman poem, the Swiss peasantry as democratic ideal, "their noble, because absolutely natural, breeding" (*The Memoirs of John Addington Symonds*). You and I never agreed about Whitman, I the hot lover and you the cool admirer, whether his poetry was art, whether comradeship included sex.

RLS: The intoxication of tobogganing alone and at night. The speed, the "spinning round a corner, and the whole glittering valley and all the lights in all the great hotels lie for a moment at your feet" (Stevenson, *Essays of Travel*).

JAS: The intoxication of the day-long sledge drive with my favorite postillion, "the only noise—this short, sharp shriek of the frozen snow; that and the driver's whip, and the jingling bells of the harness." We called these "Little Changes," something that broke the monotony of life in an alpine valley (Symonds and Symonds, *Our Life in the Swiss Highlands*).

RLS: I courted adventure and escaped with my life.

LS: I admired your boyishness and mistook it as a sign of genius. I fault myself for the fact that our friendship never ripened.

JAS: I overtaxed my strength but knew when to lie still.

LS: When I came to visit shortly before your death, that is what made me think we could never be friends. "Poor man—he seems always to have to patch himself up" (*Selected Letters of Leslie Stephen*, vol. 2).

JAS: I am buried near Shelley in Rome. The day after my death, Sophie Girard, my beloved Swiss governess, who, like Rosa Engel, lived near Thun, also dies. The last letter I write to you I never send: "A curious sense of being drawn to you is on me to-night" (Lockett, *Robert Louis Stevenson at Davos*). I become wistful of your life in the South Seas. My little "Study of Walt Whitman," which I send to you, appears on the day of his death.

RLS: "He is a far better and more interesting thing than any of his books" (Lockett, *Robert Louis Stevenson at Davos*).

JAS: "I asked a friend of mine—a staglike youth from Graubünden, tall and sinewy, like young Achilles on a fresco at Pompeii—how all the gymnasts in this country came to be so brotherly. 'Oh,' he replied, 'that is because we come into physical contact with one another. You only learn to love men whose bodies you have touched and handled'" (Symonds and Symonds, *Our Life in the Swiss Highlands*).

It is getting late. I will invite some of the peasants to come in and sing for us. Then we will offer them supper.

Scene II

Characters

JCS: Janet Catherine Symonds, wife of JAS.

MS: Margaret Symonds (Mrs. W. W. Vaughan), third daughter of JAS and JCS; author of *Out of the Past* (1925), a memoir.

KS: Katherine Symonds (Dame Katherine Furst), fourth daughter of JAS and JCS; author of *Hearts and Pomegranates: The Story of Forty-five Years, 1875–1920* (1940), a memoir.

FS: Fanny Stevenson, wife of RLS.

MM: Mrs. Elizabeth McDonald MacMorland, author of *Davos-Platz; A New Alpine Resort for Sick and Sound in Summer and Winter By One Who Knows It Well* (1878).

BH: Beatrice Harraden, author of *Ships that Pass in the Night* (1893), a novel.

The Mountains

Place

The sitting room of Janet Catherine Symonds at Am Hof. The walls are paneled in cembra wood up to six feet, at which point a shelf runs around the room under three feet of Morris-blue fruit paper. There is an old carved Swiss cupboard, smelling of hay, a dark-green stove with figures in relief and on the walls photographs of people such as Lady Mount Temple and Julia Stephen, as well as a signed photograph of Queen Victoria, JCS having been born the year she ascended to the throne. There are paintings of apple blossoms and anemones by her sister, Marianne North, nicknamed "Pop." In addition there are several of her own landscapes, including a water color of hyacinths, narcissus, and crocuses in full flower with the window open, a view of the Davos Valley deep in snow with the Tinzenhorn in the distance. There is a Persian carpet on the floor, and a big, soft divan runs around two sides of the room. The room is tidy, and JCS hopes to keep it that way.

Masses of plants are hibernating on every windowsill. Ivy in pots are trained around the window frames and across the ceiling. Harts-tongue ferns from England are growing in earthenware bowls. An old orchid in a grey Delft jam pot has been brought from Clifton Hill House in Bristol. The porter at the Kurhaus has given JAS two wooden boxes of carnations, over which she reigns like a queen. She has hauled them in because of a sudden snowstorm, places them on two inverted blue stone jars in front of the window, and feeds them with liquid manure procured from a peasant friend.

A Kentucky cardinal flies free in the room, brought across Europe after the death of Pop. When evening falls, it perches on the frame of Queen Victoria's portrait and roosts there.

JCS sits at her table painting a giant saxifrages (*Saxifrago pyramidalis*), which she has placed in a jug of water with its stalk supported by a strong paper collar. She has been sitting here nearly a week, painting, occasionally interrupted by guests.

Time

The late 1890s.

Davos, or "How the English Invented the Alps"

JCS: Fanny. You're back. I hear you have the only row of peas in the Pacific.

FS: I asked my devoted servant to plant some vanilla seedlings, which he put in upside down. My daughter Belle and I replanted them root-downward, only to find that Lafaele redid his work to surprise me.

JCS: I've been carrying rocks again, which makes my fingers so rough that working with embroidery silks becomes unmanageable. In the middle of a hayfield, where the scent of flowers mingles with that of Alpine herbs, sheltered by the wooden *Wandelbahn* and watered by a tiny stream, the garden is a never-failing source of happiness and interest to a quiet person like myself.

MS: "People sought my mother out just because she hid herself away from them" (M. Symonds, *Out of the Past*).

KS: She called herself the "Missing Link," sandwiched between a distinguished husband and an accomplished sister. Pop, a well-known painter of flowers, whose paintings are on exhibit at Kew Gardens, was one of the first women to travel around the world alone.

JCS: JAS becomes annoyed when I all I do is talk about flowers. My passion is not for old art but for open air.

FS: I was both feminine and "one of the boys." I began to write fiction and became increasingly confident in my writing. I contributed first ideas, then entire chapters. Some say my literary skills were on par with his.

JCS: Once we abandoned Clifton House by burning the letters of five generations of Nonconformists and burying the busts of emperors gathered on grand tours, I was against building a house at Davos. I thought tent life would be the most prudent. When our Janet, my eldest and most perfect child, died of consumption, I embroidered a *Horsefieldii* daffodil on a white satin pillow for her coffin.

FS: When Hervey was born, Sam was living openly with a mistress in San Francisco. When he arrived in Paris, Hervey was almost dead. Hervey's death marked the end of our marriage. From then on, every illness of Lloyd's, and then Louis's, became a crisis.

The Mountains

JCS: I envied Pop her freedom from responsibilities on the eve of her setting sail for Japan.

FS: I suffered from what I called "brain fevers" or brain congestion, what Louis later called the "sulks." Much later he described me as "a violent friend, a brimstone enemy," with "insane black eyes, boy's hands, tiny bare feet, a cigarette, wild blue dress usually spotted with garden mold" (Harman, *Robert Louis Stevenson*). By the end, he was convinced I was deranged.

JCS: I suffered from postpartum depressions, which became more severe with every birth. We agreed not to have more children, to lie in separate beds, to live in separate rooms.

FS: I was never well in Davos: sore throat, stomach disorder, heart trouble. When I went to Bern, they thought I might have a gall bladder infection; I thought it might be malaria. Without Mrs. MacMorland, it would have been intolerable.

JCS: She tells the story of the first two patients in Davos, a German medical man with a bad lung and his young consumptive friend, with so effeminate an exterior that he was thought to be a Polish princess in disguise. It turned out he was a publisher and bookseller. The pair, whose accommodations consisted of an unheated room and barely enough food, improvised by laying on haysleighs in the open air.

MM: I arrived in Davos with my husband, the Reverend John Peter MacMorland, in 1871, for the benefit of my health. We were the first English, or rather Scotch, family to spend a winter here. We stayed at the original Kurhaus, which burned down in 1872, then at the Flüela Post Hotel, then at the Hotel Schweizerhof. There we met a German visitor named J. C. Coester, who wanted to build a hotel for English visitors. Mrs. Bradshaw-Smith, my mother, laid the foundation stone for the Hotel Belvedere. We were its first guests when it opened in 1875, and we returned for thirteen years. In 1877 I published a pamphlet, anonymously, based on my exploration of the geology, flora, fauna, people, and history of Davos. It didn't seem sufficiently comprehensive, so I wrote a complete guide book for the English public. I felt obligated to make the healing influences of the valley more widely known.

Davos, or "How the English Invented the Alps"

JCS: Your paintings show the dreariness, untidiness, and emptiness of the old Davos, without a single tree.

FS: When we arrived at the Belvedere, the Reverend, Elizabeth MacDonald MacMorland, their little daughter Bessie, and Mrs. Bradshaw were also staying there. Like Louis, Mrs. MacMorland was born in Edinburgh. Louis used to spend hours in Mrs. Bradshaw's sitting room, listening to her stories of Scottish life. She nicknamed him "the Sprite."

MM: After you left the second time, you wrote a letter saying you had a dream about me.

FS: "I dreamed that you said that you had grown to dislike me so intensely that you could not stay in the same hotel with me" (Lockett, *Robert Louis Stevenson at Davos*). I said I would be the one to move, which you agreed would be the best.

MM: I regularly ran up and down the steep path that led from the Hotel to the Chalet am Stein, seeking out your company.

FS: I asked you to send several photographic views of Davos, which you did, but I never acknowledged them or repaid you. I asked Louis to write for me, but he never did. We met some Dutch people who had just come from Davos, but they couldn't tell me anything about you. Finally I wrote and hoped that we were still friends.

JCS: Beatrice Harraden! What a surprise!

BH: I arrived in October 1890 and left the following spring. I was twenty-six at the time I came with my sister Gertrude. We stayed at the Villa Germania, a *dépendence* of the Kurhaus.

KS: I remember you living in the Kurhaus with your red-haired sister and the shy, silent man who became the hero of your book.

JCS: Your first novel became a bestseller translated into nine languages and has been chosen as an English reading book in foreign schools and colleges. It sold five hundred thousand copies in America, and in 1921, with your adaptation, it was made into a film.

BH: I published *Ships that Pass in the Night* in 1893. I renamed Davos "Petershof." I made the heroine, Bernadine, a working woman and suffragette, like myself. She works in her uncle's secondhand bookshop in London, teaches, writes for newspapers, attends socialist meetings. At twenty-six, she falls ill with "an overstrained nervous system," and travels alone to Petershof. There she meets another loner, a tuberculosis patient known as the "Disagreeable Man," with whom she shares her ambition to write a book. He has been there seven years, is staying alive only for the sake of his mother, and lends Bernadine his camera. His response to her ambitions to become an author: "There are too many books as it is; and not enough people to dust them" (Harraden, *Ships that Pass in the Night*).

MS: I remember him saying: "My dear young woman, we are not living in a poetry book bound with gild edges. We are living in a paper-backed volume of prose" (Harraden, *Ships that Pass in the Night*).

BH: She recovers, returns to London to dust books, and he writes a letter he never sends, revealing the depth of his feeling. His mother dies, which leaves him free either to die or to return to the mountains. He finds Bernadine in the bookshop where she has begun to write her own book. Although she has revealed the depth of her feelings to her uncle, she convinces her suitor to choose life by returning to the mountains. By evening she has been run over by a wagon.

MS: She never had to make a decision for or against marriage. In the film it is Robert Allitson, the architect who has been given first the design for city hall and then a death sentence, and not Bernadine, who suffers from collapse from overworking for the "advancement of Women's Position," who serves as protagonist. "No two less lover-like" (Harraden, *Ships that Pass in the Night*) people fall in love only to have their ambitions thwarted again when Robert returns to the mountains without Bernadine and she appears to him in a vision.

JCS: Every afternoon from four to six I read aloud to JAS in his study, where he lay on his sofa, his head supported by a brick-colored cushion with an immense plant of *Saxifraga pyramidalis* embroidered all over it. I used to say I was the only married woman who had read aloud to her husband not only the whole of Boswell's *Life of Dr. Johnson* but the entire *Decline and Fall* of Gibbon two separate times.

FS: RLS claimed I had the soul of a peasant rather than an artist. When Belle, my daughter, and I arrived in Europe to study at the Antwerp Academy of Art, we discovered they did not admit women.

JCS: Dear Mary Clifford: "We are all as loyal as ever to that stern, wholesome Alpine valley, which has gained so much of true home-feeling for us in these two winters. I love it better than the South really, one feels a better human being, physically and morally, among the snows" (M. Symonds, *Out of the Past*). Yours, JCS.

FS: I never liked England, the animosity of Louis's friends.

JCS: For RLS you were "his fantastically gifted wife—that woman of the quick live heart and the keen incisive genius" (M. Symonds, *Out of the Past*), although he never thought much of your house-keeping, given how often you misplaced things.

FS: You are an artist. You sketch, paint, and embroider flowers. You make the house beautiful while leaving the housework to others.

JCS: Your garden has become part of the National Botanical Gardens of Samoa. Editing the autobiography of my sister, who died in 1890, is too much for me. It is eventually published by Macmillan as *Recollections of a Happy Life*. I prefer listening to the singing of her cardinal. By 1892 JAS encourages me to leave Davos. KS eventually decides that my deep melancholy is too much for her boys to handle.

KS: J. G. Jung, whom I consult in Zürich, advises me against settling in Klosters. In his view, it is the duty of a healthy woman to live among her own people down in the valleys.

FS: My house on Hyde Street survived the fire that devastated San Francisco after the 1906 earthquake only because those who knew it contained the papers of RLS left other firefighting duties to protect it.

JCS: Since his death, all I want is to sit still, to live without responsibility and to recover in spirit from the turmoil of my earlier life.

◇◇

The Library

The first English library at Davos was established at the Hotel Buol when John Symonds lived there, with thirty books in addition to volumes he contributed. In 1886 a public library was started, with a hundred books in a room rented in the Villa Sereinig, that after a year, in need of more space, moved to the Villa Florenza Magdalena. In 1887 a small chalet was built for the library next to the Villa Flora, later Villa Richmond, belonging to Dr. Ruedi, the favorite doctor of the English colony, opposite the Hotel Victoria. It became the only piece of property owned by the English community. In 1897 it was transferred to a stone building across from the Hotel Belvedere, next to the tennis courts, in time to commemorate the queen's Diamond Jubilee. By now it contained more than five thousand volumes, half of which circulated, mostly in the categories of fiction and natural history. It was considered one of the most significant English libraries on the Continent. Open four days a week for an hour and a half, it was supported by subscriptions, donations, entrance fees to lectures of the Literary Society, and books left behind by visitors. Tauchnitz and other continental editions of English Authors were the most coveted. Symonds supported the library with both a donation and a subscription, although he didn't expect to use it: "I have always found it best to buy the books I want; and I am of the opinion that people in general spend far too small a percentage of their income on the purchase of books" (J. A. Symonds, "Davos English Library"). In 1980 the building was torn down to make way first for the clubhouse of the tennis club and then for the Kirchner Museum, which was built in 1992. No one knows what happened to the books.

This is the history I have been able to construct with materials found in the Dokumentationsbibliothek Davos, although the building

I remember across from the Hotel Belvedere, even then no longer in use, was wooden clapboard with a pointed roof. Why an English library in Davos? It belonged to an English colony I never knew existed because no one I knew was interested. The library has become what Pierre Nora calls a "realm of memory," the repository of a life in English, a life in books, of no interest to those, like my parents, seeking to repatriate themselves not by reading but by rambling through landscapes that said they had come home.

The Cemetery

The *Waldfriedhof*, or woodland cemetery, is an invention of the early twentieth century. The terrain is sculpted by a stand of trees rather than landscaped like an English garden, and plain, uniform gravesites are loosely distributed, rather than arranged in geometrical uniformity. It is meant to provide a place of intimacy for the dead and their visitors in a natural setting. The *Waldfriedhof* in Davos, the second such cemetery in Switzerland, was designed by Rudolf Gaberel and completed in 1920, two and a half kilometers outside of town in a grove of larch trees, known as *Wildboden*.

The request for a separate burial place for Jews began in 1903 and was finally successful in 1931. The Jewish cemetery stands adjacent, owned by the Swiss Federation of Jewish Communities and separated by a stone wall. The idea of a cemetery, at first unknown to Jews, becomes a site of refuge for those in the diaspora: Antwerp, Berlin, Prague, Vilna, Kiev, and Odessa are some of the places of origin marked on the graves. Although room was made for 900, there are currently 185. The number of Jewish tuberculosis patients declined, and Davos has no Jewish community, apart from seasonal visitors who know it as a preferred summer resort due to the availability of kosher restaurants and shops. Unadorned stones face Jerusalem, and graves include the remains of unknown Jews from Buchenwald and three Jewish mountaineers from Vienna who lost their lives in 1923 in the region of the Jungfrau. Their graves were transferred from a decommissioned cemetery in Bern.

The Mountains

Simple crosses made from larch wood with pointed roofs, increasingly weathered grey, stand in compact rows on the uneven topography of the forest floor. Although graves in Switzerland are dug up after twenty-five years, my mother's has been there for more than thirty. After a lifetime in America, she settles in Davos to rehabilitate the library of the Hochgebirgsklinik or German sanatorium in Wolfgang that had treated primarily tuberculosis patients and had been closed for years. When she fell ill, a physician friend who directed the Thurgauisch-Schaffhausische Höhenklinik, a short walk from her apartment, diagnosed tuberculosis. Initially the Queen Alexandra Sanatorium, this was the only English sanatorium in Davos, opened in 1909 and closed in 1914, when the number of English dwindled from one thousand to thirty. When my mother failed to respond to antibiotics, her pain was construed as psychosomatic, given my parents' pending divorce. She traveled to Zürich to seek additional medical advice; there she was diagnosed with cancer, lung cancer, although the primary tumor was never found. She died within a month. My brother and I transported her ashes in a cardboard box to the "city in the mountains." Although my mother asked to have her ashes scattered, my brother decided on a grave. My father, having been nursed by my mother following a recent heart attack, never crossed the Atlantic to attend her funeral.

My father lived another thirty years and once he retired from a university in northern California claimed Davos as his primary residence. He first arrived in Davos in the 1930s, when his mother, to escape the ravages of Stalin's famine, smuggled him out of the Soviet Union. She placed him in the *Kindersanatorium*, where he didn't speak a word of German, while she, a pianist divorced from her Russian husband, looked for work in Basel, her *Heimatstadt*. Six years ago, on his way to Lucerne to celebrate Russian Christmas, he waited for the train at the Zürich Hauptbahnhof. Sitting on a bench on the platform, his head dropped against the shoulder of his oldest friend and his heart ceased.

My parents lie in separate graves, which is my decision. My mother is buried in a cemetery with the man she might have married, a native of Davos, who during the war studied law with her in Zürich; and the man she did marry, an engineer who after the war took her to America. My father married two more times, a woman in his field who moved to California from Poland and soon died of ovarian cancer and an American of Russian descent who lived in San Francisco and awaited a kidney transplant at the time he sought a divorce in order to return to Switzerland.

The most illustrious grave belongs to Ludwig Kirchner, a German expressionist who arrived in Davos during World War I, lived in close proximity to the *Waldfriedhof*, and took his own life.

The City

Public Histories

"Athens on the Limmat"

"A True History
That Never Happened"

In the 1870s Zürich sheltered the largest and most politically active émigré community in western Europe. When two exiled populists, Petr Lavrov and Mikhail Bakunin, came to recruit followers from among its university students, the city became the center for Russian revolutionary activity abroad. Lavrov posited the acquisition of knowledge as a moral imperative; Bakunin likened it to the accumulation of capital. Switzerland was open to asylum seekers and had no extradition law for political crimes, and the authorities intervened only if Swiss citizens were involved or foreigners interfered in Swiss politics. Because of a lack of cooperation on the part of the Swiss police, the city on the Limmat became home to a well-organized system of Russian spies.

By May 1873 the Russian colony had reached a total of 300 inhabitants, 104 of whom were women, of whom 73 were studying medicine at the university. In May 1873 the tsar issued a decree, or *ukaz*, stating that any woman student who remained in Zürich past January 1874 would be denied entrance into institutions of higher learning and access to government jobs. The women were accused of advocating free love and learning obstetrics to perform abortions. Higher Courses of Education for Women had been opened in St. Petersburg, and the

Medical Surgical Academy, under the auspices of the Ministry of War, had inaugurated a special training program for midwives. At the Trial of the Fifty in 1877, considered the first judicial platform used to propagate revolutionary views, between eight and eleven of the sixteen female defendants had studied in Zürich. Most belonged to the Fritchis, an all-female group of revolutionaries, named after their Zürich landlady.

Nadezhda Suslova arrived from St. Petersburg in Zürich in 1865 to complete her medical studies, after women were expelled from the Medical Surgical Academy following the Polish revolt in 1863. The University of Paris, which opened its doors to women in 1863, the first university in Europe to do so, did not accept her, and the women's medical colleges in America did not meet her expectations. Two years later, she asked to sit for her doctoral exams, without ever having registered as a student. By law women were neither allowed nor disallowed from registering, so Suslova became the first woman to acquire her degree from the University of Zürich. She responded: "I may be the first, but not the last. Thousands will follow me." Following the assassination of Alexander II in 1881, quotas for Jews were established at universities, and the Women's Medical Courses in St. Petersburg were closed once again.

Zürich provided the site for what came to be known as "the experiment." Its university was young and small, its professors recruited in part from the ranks of those who had participated in the revolutions of 1848, primarily in Germany. The goodwill of a group of enlightened patriarchs sanctioned by law what had already become custom, namely women auditing lectures, including anatomy classes, in a coeducational setting. The professors referred to students as *Studierende*, rather than *Studenten* or *Studentinnen*. They hoped other universities, especially German-speaking ones, would follow, but Prussia, the last to open its doors to women, did so only in 1908.

Once women completed their degrees, they failed to find employment in public institutions. Instead, they created their own. Marie Heim-Vögtlin, the first Swiss woman to obtain her medical degree, opened her own practice in 1874 and later cofounded the first women's hospital—funded by women and run by female doctors for female patients—and nurses' training school in Zürich, the Pflegerinnenschule. Susan Dimock, her best friend at the university, returned to Boston to establish a nurse's training program at the New England Hospital for Women and Children. Dimock died in 1875, at twenty-eight, when the steamship *Schiller* went down crossing the Atlantic to Europe.

Scene I

Characters

sk: Sofia Kovalevskaia (1850–91), the first woman to receive a doctorate in mathematics and hold a chair in mathematics at a European university.

eks: Emily Kempin-Spyri (1853–1901), Europe's first female doctor of law and founder of Emily Kempin's School of Law for Women at New York University.

mct: M. Carey Thomas (1857–1935), the second president and primary architect of Bryn Mawr College.

fk: Florence Kelley (1859–1932), general secretary of the National Consumers' League, chief factory inspector for the state of Illinois, and resident of Hull House.

Setting

The Jules Verne Bar, a panorama bar on the eleventh floor, with a view of downtown Zürich.

Time

The 1880s.

The City: Public Histories

FK: I arrived in Zürich in 1883, having lost my degree from Cornell University. My trunk had been taken off the train on the way to Oxford. I asked to have it put back on, but it was left there. When I reached the university, I was told I didn't need a degree, that the degree I had from an American university had no value. I wanted to study social science, but instead I became a student of government, or *Staatswissenschaft*. I was the only woman to study with Julius Platter, a Tyrolean, who transformed political economy from the study of laws into that of significant social questions, until a Swiss woman joined me the following year.

EKS: I wanted to study law, but as a woman I had to register under *Staatswissenschaft*, which remained the case until 1902. By the time women were allowed to practice law in Zürich, in 1898, I will have been certified mentally incompetent. Initially I thought the new tramway, built by an English firm and powered by horses, too expensive, so I walked for over an hour from the Enge, where I lived with my husband and three children, to the university.

MCT: In Leipzig women were allowed to attend lectures but not to stand for degrees. In Göttingen women were barred from lectures, but the university granted degrees to foreigners in absentia. When the entire male faculty voted on my petition in Göttingen and turned it down, Mamie and I decided to leave Leipzig, the center of comparative philology, for Zürich. It was provincial, of course, but generous. Unlike Leipzig, where we were violating centuries of student culture, five hundred male heads no longer turned "like fields of wheat in the wind" (Horowitz, *The Power and Passion of M. Carey Thomas*) when we walked across the town square.

SK: I arrive in Zürich in 1873, for the birth of my sister's first child. Aniuta has married Victor Jaclard, a Communard, who manages to escape to Switzerland on my husband's passport. She wants me to stay, to study with a student of Karl Theodore Weierstrass, with whom I have been studying mathematics in Berlin. After four years of private lessons, where I visit him every Sunday and he visits me one other day a week, Göttingen agrees to grant me a degree. My sister imagines Weierstrass and I are getting too close, but in the end she discourages me from leaving him. My parents begin to suspect my marriage is not a real marriage. I am beginning to think this "fictitious marriage" should not have lasted this long.

EKS: We all knew who you were, Sofia. I from reading a book titled *Das Buch der Frauen* (1896) by Laura Marholm, which devotes one of its six psychological portraits to you.

MCT: In a speech I deliver in 1907, where I argue for the importance of graduate schools for women's colleges, I mention your name as an example of female genius.

FK: I marry one of your compatriots, a medical student. We keep our marriage secret. We speak only German together. He provides me with books from a secret library, the Russian library. "Coming to Zürich, the content of my mind was tinder awaiting a match" (*The Autobiography of Florence Kelley*). I discover socialism. I discover scientific solutions to social problems. Once the University of Pennsylvania rejects me for further study in advanced Greek, my father agrees to allow me to enroll at the university in Zürich.

MCT: In Zürich I write a thesis, "Swinburne's Place in the History of English Poetry," in three days, but Mamie and I have been reading his *Poems and Ballads* since we were students at Cornell University. I replace the religious renewal my mother experienced as a Quaker with the religion of culture, with reading literature as a source of spiritual renewal. Mamie will help me write the thesis. I will never reconcile my longing to be an artist, to transform the beauty and pleasures of Europe into poetry, with my interest in comparative philology as a form of evolutionary science. I will try to make Bryn Mawr College an outpost of Leipzig in America.

FK: I want to ensure that German economic writings are known throughout America, where, in 1886, after the first May Day parade in Chicago, I say to Engels that this is where the revolution will take place. May Day is followed by the Haymarket riots and the hanging of anarchists. I will translate *The Conditions of the Working Class in England* into English. As an English speaker, I will remain suspect within the Socialist Labor Party. I never succeed in learning Russian, the language one hears most often in sections of Zürich like Oberstrass and Fluntern. "It was a joke among the polyglot students that the Russians were so busy with the future that they never knew whether the snowcaps were clear and lovely or shrouded in fog, any beauty that survived despite our modern capitalist civilization being unworthy their notice" (*The Autobiography of Florence Kelley*).

SK: I will do some translating for my husband, Vladimir Kovalevskii, a publisher of scientific and political writings, without pay, of course. He kindly agrees to enter a fictitious marriage with me. Otherwise, how would my sister Aniuta, my cousin Zhanna, and Zhanna's cousin, Iulia, and I have been able to travel abroad? A Russian woman in the 1860s, although she was entitled to own property, and as a property owner to vote via male proxy and was protected by law from wife-beating, remained on her father's or husband's internal passport. The three of us all meet again in Heidelberg, where, in spite of Vladimir, we establish a women's commune.

EKS: You will fall in love with a younger man, a distant cousin of your husband's, after Vladimir inhales a bottle of chloroform. He is in debt to oil entrepreneurs and no longer appears for his classes. He will be remembered as one of the founders of evolutionary paleontology. As a widow, you will finally be respectable. Mathematicians begin to invite you to meet their wives. I too fall in love with another man, but he will fall in love with my daughter. She will bear his child, while I imagine the tumor I am growing is a man inside my stomach.

FK: When I return to America in 1886, I am greeted by the newly erected Statue of Liberty.

EKS: Lady Liberty is a French concept. The French will bestow you, Sofia, with their most prestigious prize, the Prix Bordin, but the

Swedes will make you the first female professor at a European university. In Stockholm you will quickly learn Swedish, but you will always long to speak Russian. You will hope for a position at a Russian university.

MCT: I pursue my degree with the same determination I pursue Mary Garret, who, like Mamie, I meet at Cornell. Why should the fact that I am only twenty-five years old and have never been employed prevent me from becoming the president of Bryn Mawr? After fourteen years, Mary finally returns my love. If they make me president, she says, she will pay 10 percent of the college's annual budget. Mamie begins as my graduate student and eventually becomes a professor of English. She wants to be recognized for the lectures she wrote and I delivered for eleven years in a two-year survey course of Western literature required of all entering students.

FK: Your name and that of Jane Addams will be linked, as those belonging to the two women with the greatest influence on American girls. Jane takes me in when I leave Lazare, who accuses me of speaking English with the children and has become physically abusive. I arrive at Hull House, win custody in a court battle, and leave the children with friends in Winnetka. In Jane, I finally find a peer. I become her closest friend. The settlement feels like home, the relations between women reserved, rather than intimate.

MCT: Unlike Hull House, a settlement of unmarried women, Bryn Mawr feels like "a fairey palace," "a house of cards that 13 men could destroy in an instance" (Horowitz, *The Power and Passion of M. Carey Thomas*), that is, the college's thirteen male trustees.

EKS: I set sail for America because my father casts his long shadow across my fatherland. There is no public swimming place for women along the lake because he has voted against it. I learn to swim in the French-speaking part of Switzerland, where I am sent to be polished up for the marriage market. But I keep my swimming a secret. "Zürich, the barb in the center of my heart" (Hasler, *Flying with Wings of Wax*). When I begin studying at the university, my father refuses to speak to me. When I come back from America a professor, he fails to recognize me on the street.

MCT: I live at 43 Plattenstrasse. Ten years later, Rosa Luxemburg, who remains on the periphery of Russian-emigrant bohemia, will take up residence a few doors down. Once I become the first woman ever to graduate summa cum laude from the University of Zürich, people treat me like a celebrity. For the first time, I enjoy being stared at on the street.

SK: I arrive during the final months of the Russian colony and visit the Russian library on the first floor of the Pension Frauenfeld in Fluntern. Apparently I am following in my husband's footsteps. He was here already in 1864, cofounding a pension for Russian students and emigrants. In the reading room, I find Russian exile publications, the most recent writings about the French revolution, tracts by German and French socialists. There are dozens of newspapers in numerous languages, including Georgian, Armenian, and Yiddish. The only thing I can't find is literature. "It is impossible to be a mathematician without the soul of a poet" (Koblitz, *A Convergence of Lives*). There is a lot of coming and going, tobacco smoke and loud voices. It is difficult to read, but it is well heated. The samovar is on. There is always tea for those with "pale faces, thin jackets, doubtful shoes" (Schirmacher, *Zürcher Studentinnen*). The Russian women are not all nervous, loud, unkempt, with short hair, blue glasses, and a cigarette. They are not all "nihilist girls."

FK: When I arrive at Cornell, I fall in love with Margaret Hicks, who is in love with M. Carey Thomas. When Margaret dies, I come down with a fever that alarms even my Zürich physician. The doctor puts me on a diet and for a fortnight forbids me to read heavy books or to write. Before I fully recover, I agree to receive the attentions of Lazare. As a Jew, he is barred from teaching, so he studies medicine; a medical degree will allow him to reside outside the Pale of Settlement. I refuse to allow the publisher to omit my unpronounceable name, his name, Wischnewetzky, from the cover of my book.

MCT: I considered marriage, for just a moment, as a way to get abroad.

EKS: I went abroad, that is, sailed for America. "She arrived in the New World bringing with her the Old: twenty-two crates, an out-of-work husband, three small children, and a homesick house servant" (Hasler, *Flying with Wings of Wax*). That is how my daughter remembers it. She has no idea what it is like to have a law degree and not be able to practice because without the vote women do not enjoy active citizenship; not to be able to continue teaching at the university because as *Privatdozent* I have no staff affiliation or salary, only the private fees of a diminishing number of students; not to be able to teach the law to women earning their own living because I am unable to find a space large enough. In New York, Walter can't take root, but I fly, even if only with "wings of wax."

SK: I have become friends with both Suslova and Bokova through Aniuta's radical circle in St. Petersburg. Suslova has just returned from Zürich with her degree. Bokova introduces us to Vladimir as a potential fictitious husband. Although Aniuta is older, he prefers me. Maria Bokova, whom I adore, is the model for the heroine at the center of the ménage à trois in Chernychevsky's *What Is to Be Done?* (1863). Maria Bokova has entered a fictitious marriage with Petr but is in love with I. M. Sechenev, a physiology professor she meets at the Medical Surgical Academy. Petr is my daughter Fufa's godfather, and Vladimir, in his suicide note, asks Maria, an ophthalmologist now married to Sechenev, to raise her. I should never have consummated my marriage. We should have continued to live in separate rooms.

Scene II

A lull enters the conversation as the women divert their attention to the view. The fog has lifted. The Fraumünster comes into focus. The snowcapped mountains appear at the end of the lake.

FK: This is how I remember it: "Zürich in those days was a small and simple city, with many steep and narrow streets, some of them beautifully curved, and lined with impressive remnants of old walls. There was abundant music, and a little repertory theater subsidized by the city. The forest, owned by the canton and maintained according to the highest standards of forestry then known, extended down from the top of the Zürichberg almost to the Polytechnicum [where the university inhabited the south wing until it moved into its own building in 1914]. It was an enchanting forest with broad allées cut as fire safeguards, and between the endless rows of pines, wild flowers such as I had never seen" (*The Autobiography of Florence Kelley*).

EKS: In Zürich, only my father-in-law's bookshop, on Stadelhoferplatz 5, where the Russian students met to protest the *ukaz*, offers an oasis. I want to study law, like my cousin Bernhard, the son of my aunt, Johanna Spyri. She has carved out a life for herself, but she has done so writing books like *Heidi*, which I read to my children. I want to write books on modern trusts and the influence of Roman law on England and America.

SK: Some, like the revolutionary Vera Figner, were eager to leave but disappointed when they arrived: "It was a clear April day in 1872, a remarkable, invigorating day, abounding with sunlight and the scent of spring, when my sister and I set out from our native village of Nikiforovo [Kazan], traveling briskly on a troika with bells ringing. From the administrative center of our district we had taken a steamship, then a train, to Switzerland. Now I was in Zürich, with its ancient, narrow streets, its miserable lake, unappealing in the rain, and that ugly view of the tiled roofs from my window" (Engel and Rosenthal, *Five Sisters*).

FK: I am not invited to eat in the dining hall on Clausiusstrasse, a three-room apartment with kitchen, where up to fifty students, all of them Russian, have lunch. This is often their only meal of the day. I learn from the memoirs of the anarcho-communist Peter Kropotkin that "tea and bread, some milk and a little slice of meat cooked over a spirit lamp, amidst animated discussion of the latest news from the socialist world or the last book read . . . was their regular fare. Those who had more money than was

needed for such a mode of living gave it for the common cause"
(Meijer, *Knowledge and Revolution*). During summer vacations
they travel on false passports to smuggle revolutionary literature
back into Russia, or they escape into the Swiss mountains.

MCT: I call on Dr. Heim-Vögtlin when I become ill after my three-day
written exam. She is the most prominent female doctor in Zürich.
But it is Dr. Emma Culbertson, who lives in a Boston marriage
with a Dr. Smith, who makes me drink two cups of strong tea
with milk before my oral exam: three hours in front of the entire
philosophical faculty. I have to speak German and be examined
by professors under whom I have never studied. I am hoping my
summa will secure me a professorship in any women's college in
the country, even though my uncle has practically promised me a
position at Bryn Mawr. I too began by thinking I wanted to study
medicine, but I am instantly chastised: "What we want in the
cause of women are not doctors and lawyers (there are plenty of
those), we want scholars" (Horowitz, *The Power and Passion of
M. Carey Thomas*).

FK: I have been ordered to the Riviera with my brother who is going
blind; I am the only person who can accompany him on such
short notice. Jane will call this the "family claim," a lifetime of
dependency on and service to relatives as an unmarried woman,
the answer to "after college, what?" After being detained for
months in Avignon, M. Carey and Mamie spend the night at our
hotel. M. Carey has just received her summa cum laude distinction, and they are on their way to Italy. She says I should skip
Oxford and head straight for Zürich.

MCT: Is it true that Dr. Heim decides to become a doctor when the man
she is engaged to marries someone named Nadezhda Suslova?
That she climbs the Glärnisch, which requires ropes, seven times,
including with her future husband, a geologist, commissioned to
draw its panorama? That she too studies in Leipzig, where, when
the male students become too disruptive, the professors agree to
wait with her in an antechamber so that they can enter the lecture
hall together? She writes letters that are sometimes sixteen,

sometimes twenty-four pages long, to her son who has immigrated to, among other places, America.

EKS: I am too much the lawyer to be a feminist. I insist on my own exclusivity. There is a haste to my initiatives. In the end, I have no support system, only fantasies about fleeing to England with my doctor.

MCT: They want me to publish my dissertation, but I never return to the British Museum to do the needed work. I never become a scholar. I dedicate myself to the cause of women, but I never fully choose a life of action. I often feel rushed, overworked, irritated, and angry. I am delighted that Mary, one of the richest women in America, will renovate the Deanery, an eight-room cottage on the Bryn Mawr campus the trustees have allowed us to live in for life. We add a guest wing and housekeeper's apartment; leaded windows and a copper-beamed ceiling; Tiffany glass, Persian rugs, Indian chests. John C. Olmsted agrees to design the garden.

EKS: Standing on the university terrace, I float high above the roofs of the old part of the city. The city can be taken in at a glance, who is sitting with whom on the benches by the lake. I observe how Swiss men marry Russian female students to become better socialists. Some of them travel to Russia, like Fritz Erismann, an ophthalmologist, who leaves for St. Petersburg with Nadezhda Suslova, who will have one of the most sought-after gynecological practices in the city. He marries a second Russian student, Sofia Gasse, a friend of his first wife's, who, after the *ukaz*, continues her medical studies in Bern. He becomes a professor of public health in Moscow, and eventually they return to Zürich, where he acquires a seat on the city council. Women who study law are restless, not like doctors who have a clear, delimited career goal. Medical knowledge is scientific knowledge easily translated into social service. Women are naturally suited to medicine because of their traditional roles as healers and comforters of the sick.

MCT: I insist that as women enter the professions, their education must be the same as men's: "Given two bridge-builders, a man and a woman, given a certain bridge to be built, and given as always the unchangeable laws of mechanics . . . it is simply inconceivable that the preliminary instruction given to the two bridge-builders should differ in quantity, quality, or method of presentation because while the bridge is building one will wear knicker-bockers and the other a rainy-day skirt" (Horowitz, *The Power and Passion of M. Carey Thomas*). And yet I remain a lifelong advocate of single-sex education. A single female scholar does more for human advancement than thousands of ordinary college graduates.

EKS: I insist on the separation of goods in marriage, against the future author of the Swiss civil code, who favors a law that will merge the property of married partners. In marriage, a woman is always at a disadvantage.

SK: There were Russian students who were openly contemptuous of Swiss values. They found Swiss bourgeois expectations of behavior more restrictive than those of tsarist Russia. Maria Subbotina says: "There is no such depressing atmosphere of routine and habit as in free Switzerland" (Meijer, *Knowledge and Revolution*). The Swiss condemn the tsarist regime, but Swiss students have a reputation for wanting to marry rich women and make money. The Russians are uninterested in Switzerland, except as a place where for the first time they meet those who are like-minded in an atmosphere that is politically tolerant. As Vera Figner writes: "I must tell you that Switzerland is the most bourgeois place in the world, in the sense of reverence for convention, propriety and external appearances" (Engel, *Mothers and Daughters*). Russian women have men in their rooms, but they have renounced sexual relations.

EKS: When Franziska Tiburtius, the first German woman at the university, becomes a student, she is no longer received at the homes of two friends she has known in Zürich.

FK: Two women in the waiting room of Dr. Heim-Vögtlin's practice on Hottingerstrasse: "She's from Russia, isn't she?" "No, she's from Brugg." "Only from Brugg?" (Siebel, *Das Leben von Frau D. Marie Heim-Vögtlin*).

The City: Public Histories

EKS: If prison is the final schoolroom for Russian revolutionaries, my counterpart to the university is the Burghölzli, the insane asylum of my *Heimatstadt*, where I have been asked to be transferred.

MCT: Like Chernychevsky, I delighted in triads.

Scene III

The sun begins to set. A multitude of tiny lights glimmers along the shore on the other side of the lake. The Limmat flows past the Schipfe and under the Lindenhof, where in 1292 women saved the city from its enemies by dressing as men. The bar gets dimmer as couples replace those who have been conversing in single-sex groups.

In the 1890s the brain of Sofia Kovalevskaia is among those of eminent scientists investigated for the correlation between achievement and brain size.

In 1895, after reading Krafft-Ebing's *Psychopathia Sexualis*, M. Carey Thomas comes to realize that the passionate feelings of sentimental friendship are the expression of female homosexuality.

In the 1890s Florence Kelley mentions to Engels that she continues to find "the Russian Hebrew immigrants" in Chicago to be "the most-open-minded workers" among union organizers in the women's garment industry (Sklar, *Florence Kelley and the Nation's Work*).

It will be 1983 before the University of Zürich makes the second woman after Emily Kempin-Spyri a *Privatdozent* in law.

<><><><><><><><><><><><><><><><><><><><><><><><><><><><><><><><><><><><><><><><><><><><><><><><><><>

Coda

The degree my mother receives as parliamentary interpreter and translator in French, German, and Italian, after attending the University of Geneva, leaves her unprepared for a world at war and the closing of national borders. She returns to Zürich and decides to study law; she is one of a handful of women. Her dissertation, published in 1949 as

"Athens on the Limmat"

Die Staatsangehörigkeit der Kinder aus national-gemischten Ehen (The citizenship of children of mixed-nationality marriages), asks, "How is it possible for Swiss women to lose their Swiss citizenship by marrying a non-Swiss? How is it possible for those women who continue to live in Switzerland to become foreigners in their own country and raise children who do not share their nationality?" A wife should not be required to forfeit her citizenship for that of her husband, given the increasing mobility of populations since World War I and the growing participation of women in social life.

Mixed marriages raise the question of affective or virtual citizenship, one based on socialization, environment, and daily influence, something not just given, but acquired. Swiss law should grant *ius sanguinis* not just through the father, but also the mother, at least for those mothers who continue to reside in Switzerland. Dual citizenship, my mother claims, is not an ideal solution: *"Besitzt er aber ständig beide Nationalitäten, wird er viel eher hin- und hergezerrt, und es fällt ihm am Ende schwer, sich zu entscheiden."* (Should he be in constant possession of both nationalities, he will be torn two ways, and in the end will find it difficult to choose.)

My mother will marry a man born to a Swiss mother and a non-Swiss father who remains stateless for eight years because his mother refuses to acquire her husband's Russian citizenship and is unable to confer Swiss citizenship on her son. Together my parents will immigrate to America and become naturalized citizens. With their two children, they will inhabit the very dual citizenship my mother initially argued against. Their son will eventually renounce his U.S. citizenship, but not before he provides each of his children, who have a Norwegian mother and reside in Switzerland, with an American passport.

After college, I attend the University of Zürich to find out how Swiss I am. For my *Licentiat*, I am required to pass a Latin exam by translating passages into German, not the Swiss-German I speak at home or on the street, but the written German I have never mastered because all of my schooling has been in English. The first time, I fail the exam; the second time, the examiner takes pity on me. I become credentialed in English to teach it as a foreign language, even as my so-called native proficiency is deteriorating daily.

By the time I sit for my final exam in comparative literature, I no longer remember the ending to *Madame Bovary*. In answer to the question "What do you think it means?" I remain silent. My mother is dying of cancer in a hospital on the other side of the Limmat, and I have not reread the novel since I was in high school. By the time I complete my exam, she will have passed away, and I will be dressed in a black skirt, black tights, and black clogs with white socks. After a brief graduation ceremony, I walk alone in the nighttime fog down the Freiestrasse from the university to my grandmother's apartment, which I have been sharing with my brother. "You're absolutely right," the examiner says. "The meaning of the ending is undecidable." I will come to understand the meaning of undecidability only once I return to America to complete a PhD.

My mother, who was never able to practice law, is afraid that, like her, I will return to America with a degree that will end up useless. She hoped to use her languages for work in international organizations, only to land a job in New York translating for Hanover Bank and Trust Company, into English, the one language she never studied; she hoped to practice law, only to teach German and French at a two-year college in a midwestern university town because of nepotism rules; she hoped to continue teaching in a German department, only to be replaced by the German mistress of the department chair.

I return to America in order to find a home in the one language no one in my family has comfortably inhabited.

Dada in Zürich, Continued

I always have loved this city for its beautiful location on the lake in the shadow of the mountains, and not less for its distinguished, a bit conservative culture. But owing to Switzerland's peaceful setting among belligerent countries Zürich had emerged from its reserve and in a trice had become the most important city of Europe, a meeting place of all intellectual trends, to be sure, it had become equally a center for every sort of trafficker, speculators, spies, propagandists who, for their sudden affection, were eyed by the native population with quite justifiable suspicion. Every language was to be heard in restaurants, cafés, streetcars and on the street. Everywhere one ran into acquaintances, desirable and undesirable ones, and whether or no, one was caught in a stream of excited argument.

Stefan Zweig, *The World of Yesterday: An Autobiography* (1943)

In Zürich, in 1915, disgusted by the butchery of World War I, we devoted ourselves to the Fine Arts. Despite the remote booming of artillery we sang, painted, pasted, and wrote poetry with all our might and mania. We were seeking an elementary art to cure man of the frenzy of the times and a new world order to restore the balance between heaven and hell.

Jean Arp, *Arp on Arp: Poems, Essays, Memories* (1969)

When I arrived in Zürich in August 1916, the artists and intellectuals used to meet in the Café de la Terrasse. Only a few months later, we moved to the Café Odéon [opened in 1911]. The waiters at the Terrasse had gone on strike. In sympathy with them, because they often let us sit for hours over one cup of coffee, we punished the Terrasse by permanently withdrawing our custom, although we had been much more comfortable in the big room at the Terrasse than we were in the cramped, ill-lit Odéon.

Hans Richter, *Dada: Art and Anti-Art* (1965)

Zürich in 1916 . . . : orderly but tolerant; hospitable but not overly indulgent; cultured but not pretentious; a university hub renowned for its libraries; the home of Carl Jung; the temporary home of Albert Einstein; a city that kept suspicious foreigners under discreet surveillance; a haven for homeless exiles, but not a charity center. The weather: breezy and pleasant in June and September; blustery, cold and wet in Fall and Winter; hopeful and suicidal (owing to the föhn wind) in the Spring.

Andrei Codrescu, *The Posthuman Dada Guide:*

Tzara and Lenin Play Chess (2009)

"In this house on February 5, 1916, the Cabaret Voltaire opened and Dadaism was founded" appears in a circle, gold letters on white marble. The plaque was placed there in 1966 when Hans Arp was asked to commemorate the fiftieth anniversary of the founding of dadaism. He calls it a *Gedenknabel*, or "commemorative navel," to commemorate what had been an art historical navel of the world. Dadaism had become the city's most important cultural heritage since Zwingli's Reformation (1519). The plaque still hangs on the Spiegelgasse, where Goethe visited Lavater, Georg Büchner died of brain fever, and Lenin waited until it was time to board the sealed train that would take him back to Russia and the revolution. I return to it like a pilgrim in search of a holy site, although the entrance has returned to Münstergasse 26. An empty room that became the Cabaret Voltaire has been reopened as the Dada-Haus.

Five men and two women, eventually married to two of the men, meet in Zürich in 1916. Sometimes there are only four men—two Germans (Hugo Ball and Richard Huelsenbeck), one Romanian (Tristan Tzara), and one Alsatian (Hans Arp), which in 1916 means German; after the war, as Jean Arp, he opts for France. Sometimes there are two Romanians, Tzara, who has escaped growing up in the shadow of German humanism, and Marcel Janco. Sometimes there are three brothers, Marcel, Georges, and Jules, formerly Iancu, now Janco, to make it sound more French. The two Germans are friends. They have known each other since they met in Munich in 1912. When Ball leaves, first Berlin and then Zürich, Huelsenbeck follows. The two Romanians are also friends, raised in wealthy Jewish families in Bucharest, the "Paris of the Balkans," now strolling down the Balkanstrasse, nickname for the Bahnhofstrasse. "Tzara, whose real name was Sami Rosenstock, had only lived with this name for a year, having previously tried S. Samyro, Tristan Ruia, and Tristan. 'Tristan' was taken from Wagner's opera, and 'Tzara' or 'tarra' in Romanian meant 'land' or 'country'" (Melzer, *Dada and Surrealist Performance*). *Trist en tara*, then, means "sad in his own country." Was he sad or just bored? Rosenstock wasn't his real name either, since Jews had been ordered to take German names in eighteenth-century Austria-Hungary. As soon as he arrives in Zürich, he begins to write in French.

The two women become friends. Sophie Taeuber-Arp is born in Davos-Platz, to a German pharmacist who dies of lung disease when she is two and a mother from Appenzell who subsequently advertises "lessons in embroidery" to the English colony. Sophie is the only native of Switzerland and the only one to earn a steady income. She is professor of textiles at the Kunstgewerbeschule; her sister is secretary to C. G. Jung. She lives on the outskirts of the city with Arp, whom she meets at his first exhibit in Zürich in 1915. She makes pillowcases and purses as well as paintings, their titles always in French. Emmy Hennings is a cabaret singer who sometimes sings in Danish and writes poetry and eventually a book about her life with Hugo Ball. She is the star of the Cabaret Voltaire: "Years ago she stood by the rustling yellow curtain of a Berlin cabaret, hands on hips, as exuberant as a flowering shrub;

today too she presents the same bold front and performs the same songs with a body that had since then been only slightly ravaged by grief" (Ball, *Flight Out of Time*). When Sophie Taeuber-Arp has her first retrospective in North America in 1982, my godmother, who also attended the Kunstgewerbeschule, will write an article, also in French, to announce its arrival in Montreal.

> Switzerland is a birdcage, surrounded by roaring lions. (Ball, *Flight Out of Time*)

Ball and Hennings arrive in Zürich in 1915, having met at the Café Simplizissimus in Munich in 1913. Hennings sings and sells postcards of herself to supplement her income. When she refuses to sing songs considered patriotic, she loses her job. Ball volunteers three times for military service and is rejected three times on medical grounds but never discharged. He secretly visits the war in Belgium; he openly protests the war in Berlin. His close friend Hans Leybold commits suicide in 1914 after being diagnosed with syphilis, although officially he died of a war wound. Hennings has been accused of forging passports for those seeking to avoid military service, and she spends time in prison. They escape to Zürich under assumed names. Ball is caught receiving mail under two names, including that of John Höxler, a painter from Hannover. They flee to Geneva. On their return to Zürich, Ball spends time in prison. The Swiss authorities only seek to establish his true identity. Avoiding German military service does not concern them. Pimping and prostitution are a different matter.

> The Balls came to Zürich without a cent and left their fate to chance. They had nothing to eat and sat on the shores of Lake Zürich, envying the well-fed swans for their feed. (Heulsenbeck, *Memoirs of a Dada Drummer*)

According to Heulsenbeck: Ball would like to work as a waiter, given that he has a black suit and white shirt. Failing to find a job, he considers throwing his suit into the Lake of Zürich. Hennings thinks it might be better to sell it, perhaps to a waiter in the Niederdorf. The main arterial street of this Vergnügungsviertel is the Niederdorfstrasse, which has twenty-three bars in one hundred houses. In the side alleys, the concentration is even higher: seven out of ten buildings house a public bar. Known as *Animierkneipen*, they were essentially "drinking clubs in which the waitresses provided female company and encouraged the (male) customers to buy as many drinks as possible. Prostitution was common in these establishments, which had flourished since the criminalization of brothels" (Pichon and Riha, *Dada Zurich*). When Hennings enters one of the bars, they ask if she sings. She will sing and Ball will play the piano, sometimes dance music, sometimes Brahms and Bach.

According to Hennings: She and Ball are sitting on the banks of the Limmat, enjoying the sight of the other shore. One evening they decide to sell Ball's suit, which they have been carrying everywhere in a cardboard box. They look for a shop in the Niederdorf, and enter one with, among other things, a broken typewriter, several umbrellas, and a musical clock, but no clothes. Emma will buy the musical clock if the shop owner buys the suit. Will he take it on commission? Will he put the clock aside if she leaves a deposit? They hear the sounds of a *varieté* escape from a neighboring building. Maybe one of the performers needs a suit. Ball waits for Hennings outside, until he hears her voice. She is auditioning, agrees to accept an advance, and Ball is hired as pianist, for which he needs a suit.

They approach Jan Ephraim, the owner of the Holländische Meierei Café, and apply for a permit to open a *Künstlerkneipe* at Spiegelgasse 1. In the Holländische Stübli behind the restaurant, in what was briefly the Cabaret Pantagruel, Zürich's first literary cabaret, they open the Cabaret Voltaire. The room has a small stage and a piano. The walls are painted black and the ceiling blue. Fifteen or twenty round tables seat forty to fifty people. It will be good for his business. It will be good for their morale. There is no admission charge, only a coat-check fee. There is no dressing room, only a canvas with holes as big as fists. There are readings, including texts by Wassily Kandinsky and Blaise Cendrars, French chansons, a balalaika orchestra, and Gottfried Keller anecdotes. Every night except Friday, and then, later, including Friday. There are French evenings and Russian evenings and *poèmes simultanés* in French, German, and English and *Verse ohne Worte*, or "poems without words."

> There were almost no women in the cabaret. It was too wild, too smoky, too way out. (Huelsenbeck, *Memoirs of a Dada Drummer*)

The Laban school for modern or "New German" dance moves to the Seegartenstrasse in Zürich. Rudolph von Laban, born in Bulgaria and brought up in Bosnia, where he was inspired by the dances of the dervishes, summers with his students from Munich on a dance-farm in Ascona, in the Tessin, between 1912 and 1914. There they live collectively and dance in the open air. Shoes are discarded, storytelling is discarded, limbs are exposed. Dancers move to the beat of a gong rather than to a piece of music. Sketching lessons are obligatory, and dance notations resemble the patterns of abstract art. When Laban opens a school in Zürich in 1916, Sophie Taeuber becomes one of his pupils. She performs abstract dances set to poems by Ball and masks by Marcel Janco, at the opening of the Galerie Dada in 1917. She has been asked to do so under a pseudonym, G. Thäuber, to mask her professorial identity. Mary Wigman will become Laban's most famous student, dancing to Nietzsche at the Café des Banques on the Bahnhofstrasse. Eventually, Laban's school moves to Mainaustrasse 32. This is the house where my mother grew up in an apartment on the third floor. This is where I now stay, in a hotel originally just for women, one block closer to the lake.

> If the Odéon was our terrestrial base, our celestial headquarters was Laban's ballet school. (Richter, *Dada*)

The Dada men discover the "ladies of Laban." They are frequent visitors to the school in the Seefeld, allowed into "this nunnery" only at fixed times. With few exceptions, they develop emotional ties, some fleeting, some permanent. One of the dancers, Maja Kruscek, becomes Tzara's girlfriend, although their rows are frequent and noisy; Maria Venselov is often seen with Georges Janco and later marries Hans Richer; Marcel Janco, an architecture student at the ETH, marries Lily Ackermann, a Laban dancer and impoverished Catholic. Four years later, he marries Clara Goldschlager, then returns to Bucharest, and eventually lands in Tel Aviv. Sophie Taeuber "danced to the 'Song of the Flying Fish and the Sea Horses,' an anomatopoetic lament. It was a dance full of flashes and edges, full of dazzling light and penetrating intensity. The lines of her body broke up, each gesture decomposed into a hundred precise, angular and sharp movements" (Arp, *Arp on Arp*). While Hennings's "little voice was so meager and boyish that we sometimes had the feeling it might break at any moment" and "the light of our dim cabaret lamps shone through her thin dress, revealing her boyish figure" (Huelsenbeck qtd. in Melzer, *Dada and Surrealist Performance*), "Sophie was as quiet as we were garrulous, boastful, rowdy and provocative" (Richter, *Dada*). Hennings, a professional cabaret performer, a melancholic poet, converts to Catholicism the day she marries Ball. Taeuber, committed to abstraction in art and dance, explores the limitless expression of a body not necessarily beautiful, not necessarily feminine, even if Hennings remembers it as both. The men's observations outnumber the reminiscences of the women. Sophie's modesty and independence, her calm temperament and pure forms are preferred to the restlessness of Emmy, a vagabond, an artist's model, never financially secure. The two women are reunited the year of Sophie's death. Emmy remembers the walk they had taken together, to Salerno, holding hands. Sophie is trained in art and dance; Emmy retains her connection to the popular, the folksong, the mystics.

Tzara keeps on worrying about the periodical. My proposal to call it "Dada" is accepted. We could take turns editing, and a general editorial staff could assign one member the job of selection and layout for each issue. *Dada* is "yes, yes" in Rumanian, "rocking horse" and "hobbyhorse" in French. For Germans it is a sign of foolish naïveté, joy in procreation, and preoccupation with the baby carriage. (Ball, *Flight Out of Time*)

Richard Huelsenbeck will be drafted into the German military any day now. He tells his parents he wants to study medicine in Zürich. He tells himself he wants to join the Cabaret Voltaire, Ball having summoned him via postcard. He tells his draft board he wants to go to Switzerland. *Why does he want to go to Switzerland?* To study and to rest. He has a certificate from a doctor claiming mental exhaustion. *How long does he plan to stay in Switzerland?* Three months, even though a semester lasts six. The first official is called away. An hour passes, and a second official appears. He grants permission for a six-month stay. The official has a brother-in-law in Switzerland and tells Huelsenbeck to look him up.

Huelsenbeck arrives in Zürich by train, asks for directions to the Spiegelgasse, and enters the cabaret for the first time. When later he appears on stage, he recites his "Negro poems," the ones that met with such success at the "Expressionist evening" in the Harmoniumsaal in 1915 in Berlin. He is told by Ephraim, the landlord who has traveled to Africa and the South Seas, that they are not authentic. Ball encourages something authentic, which Ephraim provides. But "the dada drummer" insists on ending each refrain with "Umba, umba," just as he has always done, much to the disapproval of the seafarer. At one in the morning Huelsenbeck and Ball step out onto the Spiegelgasse. Huelsenbeck has not given a thought to where he will sleep. Ball puts him up in his old room, up a steep set of stairs, in a garret looking down on the city Heulsenbeck has fallen in love with at first sight.

The word Dada was accidentally discovered by Hugo Ball and myself in a German-French dictionary, as we were looking for a name for Madame le Roy, the chanteuse at our cabaret. Dada is French for a wooden horse. It is impressive in its brevity and suggestiveness. Soon Dada became the signboard for all the art that we launched in the Cabaret Voltaire. (Richard Huelsenbeck, "En Avant Dada: A History of Dadaism" [1920], in Motherwell, *The Dada Painters and Poets*)

I was standing behind Ball looking into the dictionary. Ball's finger pointed to the first letter of each word descending the page. Suddenly

I cried halt. I was struck by a word I had never heard before, the word dada.

"Dada," Ball read, and added: "It is a children's word meaning hobby-horse."

At that moment I understood what advantages the word held for us.

"Let's take the word dada," I said. "It's just made for our purpose. The child's first sound expresses the primitiveness, the beginning at zero, the new in our art. We could find no better word. . . ."

And so it happened that it was I who pronounced the word Dada for the first time. (Richard Heulsenbeck, "Dada Lives!" [1936], in Motherwell, *The Dada Painters and Poets*)

Hans Richter is drafted into the German military on September 15, 1914. Several friends, including the two poets Ferdinand Hardekopf and Albert Ehrenstein, throw a farewell party. Not knowing when they will meet again, Ehrenstein suggests the following: "If the three of us are still alive, let us meet at the Café de la Terrasse in Zürich in exactly two years from now, on 15th September 1916, at three in the afternoon" (Richter, *Dada*). Richter is not familiar with either Zürich or the Café de la Terrasse. Eighteen months later, he is severely wounded, discharged, and married to the nurse who saves him in the military hospital. They spend their honeymoon in Zürich. On September 15, at three in the afternoon, Richter is at the Café de la Terrasse, and there waiting for him are Hardekopf and Ehrenstein. He is introduced to Tristan Tzara, and to Marcel and Georges Janco, sitting just a few tables away. A few days later, he is taken to the Cabaret Voltaire, where he remembers having met Hennings, Hardekopf's former girlfriend.

In 1918, in the Hotel Limmatquai, Tzara introduces Richter to a Swedish painter, Viking Eggeling, with whom Richter will make the first abstract films.

In 1918 Francis Picabia, also in a Zürich hotel room, smashes an alarm clock, dips its inner workings into ink, and presses them onto paper.

The City: Public Histories

I hereby declare that Tristan Tzara found the word on 8 February 1916 at six o'clock in the afternoon: I was present with my twelve children when Tzara for the first time uttered this word which filled us with justified enthusiasm. This occurred at the Café de Terrasse in Zürich and I was wearing a brioche in my left nostril. I am convinced that this word is of no importance and that only imbeciles and Spanish professors can take an interest in dates. What interests us is the Dada spirit and we were all Dada before Dada came into existence. (Jean Arp, "Dada-au-grand-air" [1921], in Motherwell, *The Dada Painters and Poets*)

Hans Arp speaks Alsatian with his boyhood friends, German in school, and French with his parents. His first poems are written in Alsatian, but as an artist he dreams of going to Paris. When his father is forced to close his cigar and cigarette factory in Strasbourg, they move to Weggis, on the shores of Lake Lucerne. When Arp returns to Paris in 1914, Germany has declared war. His money has become worthless, and he is forced to return to Switzerland. The draft board at the German consulate in Zürich wants to send him back to Germany. When asked to tell his age, he writes the date of his birth several times in a column:

16 September 1887
16 September 1887
16 September 1887
16 September 1887

Then he draws a line underneath, adds up the numbers, and puts down the figure. They reject him for medical reasons. They think he is insane.

Five men. Five venues. The Cabaret Voltaire opens in the Holländische Meierei Café on Spiegelgasse 1 from February to June 1916. Jan Ephraid is losing money, and Ball and Hennings move to the Tessin, ostensibly for medical reasons. Ball returns to direct the first Dada soirée, which takes place at the Zunfthaus zur Waag (Münsterhof 8) on July 14, 1916, on the bourgeois or commercial side of the Limmat, with music, dance, poems, paintings, and masks. Ball's manifesto, or the "First Dada

Manifesto," announces his final break with Dadaism. The First Dada Exhibition opens in January 1917 at the Galerie Corray in the Sprüngli-Haus on the Paradeplatz (Bahnhofstrasse 19/Tiefenhöfe 12), followed by the Galerie Dada on March 29. According to Ball: "The gallery has three faces. By day it is a kind of teaching body for schoolgirls and upper-class ladies. In the evenings the candlelit Kandinsky room is a club for the most esoteric philosophies. At the soirées, however, the parties have a brilliance and frenzy such as Zürich has never seen" (Ball, *Flight Out of Time*). Ten weeks and three exhibitions later, their landlord, the famous chocolatier, forces them to close. On July 23, 1918, Tzara stages his own Dada soirée (the seventh) in the Zunfthaus zur Meise (Münsterhof 20) reading from his own works, including his "Dada Manifesto 1918," which becomes the most widely distributed Dada text. The eighth, final, and most successful Dada soirée is held at the Kaufleuten Saal (Pelikanstrasse 18) on April 9, 1919. This is where in 2006 I am introduced to the Swiss author Robert Walser by a group of panelists whose discussion I am invited to by my friend C., a writer whom I met in an obligatory Latin class at the university and now works in the theater.

In 1906 Bergman and Company, a maker of perfume and soaps, patents the label "Dada" and launches its Dada products, the most popular of which is lily-milk soap.

By 1921, the year my parents are born, one in Zürich and the other in Moscow, Dada has ended. In 1951, the year I am born in New York City, the origins of "Dada," as a word that only later acquires content, become a source of controversy.

A word was born no one knows how DADADADA *we took an oath of friendship* on the new transmutation that signifies nothing, and was the most formidable protest, the most intense armed affirmation of salvation liberty blasphemy mass combat speed prayer tranquility private guerilla negation and chocolate of the desperate. (Tristan Tzara, "Zürich Chronicle" [1915–19], in Motherwell, *The Dada Painters and Poets*)

With so many languages in such a small space during such a troubled time, it only makes sense that the word to describe what is happening makes no sense. Or has too many meanings. Or a different one in every language. Or is just a meaningless sound. A word found in a dictionary. A word borrowed from a brand name, or from a Romanian saint. A word born "no one knows how," signifying nothing. A word that reminds people of what they said before they entered a national language. Before the nation conscripted them, rejected them, and failed to discharge them, or sent them into exile, or changed their nationality. They speak each other's languages only imperfectly. Their common denominator: the sound of the languages of the countries at war spoken simultaneously.

Poetry beyond paper, paintings without objects, dance without music, collage without glue. The ephemeral, the suggestive, the simultaneous, the spontaneous. Religious incantation and ecstasy. Potential ego disintegration, in the case of Ball. Protest without a program. War waged against the intoxication with death, against personality, against sentimentality. War in art as opposed to art as an antidote to war. A world in disorder, international and antinational, cloistered in Zürich. Individuality against the masses, against the cannon, against the Kaiser, against the mechanized, the commercialized. The trauma of noncombatants: improvisation, intoxication, cultivated and feigned insanity. Leave it to chance, the words in a poem, the squares on a grid. It refuses; it confuses via disorder. It rejects social illusions; it rejects art as illusionistic. It mistrusts traditional community and refuses an alternative community of consensus. It mistrusts the collective. Except for the cabaret, where the time is now, the performer is himself or herself and the stage is no-place. The cabaret destroys the ideological potential for speech through semantic overload. It relies on masks and the shots of revolvers. The human form disappears from painting, reappears in dance, the face hidden behind a mask, absurd, perishable, unattractive. Outrage the public through diversion; reject both contemplation and commercial transaction. Displacement and dissonance. Make the passive spectator a hostile participant. Dada requires poverty. It never grows old. It has no adepts in England. Its critique flaunts its own futility. It fosters mistaken ideas about itself. It becomes a historian's nightmare.

Dada cannot understand itself until it is over, or at least moves on to other venues: Berlin, Hannover, Cologne, Paris, New York. The last manifesto is written at the end of the next world war. The same anecdotes are circulated and recirculated. They repeat themselves in a way that Dada endlessly repeats the same sound, the same shape, the same story: how Walter Serner places artificial flowers at the foot of the dressmaker's dummy to which he recites his poems with his back toward the audience at the Kaufleute; how Auguste Giacometti, no longer young, but wearing a bearskin cap supposedly concealing a fat bankbook, makes the rounds of the bars on the Limmatquai, carefully opening and closing each door and saying, "Long live Dada!" a false report submitted to the newspapers by Serner of a duel between Tzara and Arp on the Realp, with the Swiss poet J. C. Heer as second, although both fire in the same direction and Heer has spent the day in St. Gallen. Anxious that they will become historically incomprehensible, they are eager to self-historicize.

> Dada never really existed in America. This is true despite the many references to it in books and magazine articles. Dada, the laughing, weeping, half-cynical, half-blustering theorem, devoid of system and even substance, a mixture of clownery and religion, half writing, half art, dada, which wants to destroy itself in order to survive, this last *bon mot* that was sucked up along with leftover coffee in Zürich's Odeon and Bellevue—has pathetically little to do with a way of life that aims at material perfection. (Huelsenbeck, *Memoirs of a Dada Drummer*)

Dada returns to New York in the summer of 2006, "the most comprehensive museum exhibition of Dada art ever mounted in the US." It arrives from Washington, D.C., and before that Paris. The global network of artists and the use they make of new media makes it seem timely. I return to New York, alone, for the first time since I have moved to the Midwest. I eat lunch on the balcony that looks down on the sculpture garden I remember from my childhood visits from Leonia, a suburb across the George Washington Bridge.

Once exposed to film footage from World War I, visitors to MOMA are invited to enter one of two doors, leading to one of two cities, Zürich or New York. Dada may have begun simultaneously in two places, just as the word "Dada" may have been invented by two or more people. But only in Zürich are the conditions right in 1916 for the birth of a movement that extends itself beyond this city, whether those conditions are attributed to the claustrophobic atmosphere of a neutral country in the middle of Europe at war, to Lenin at the other end of the Spiegelgasse, or to the Swiss who are in particular need of *épatement* of their *bourgeosie*.

New York is where I was born and Zürich is where I grew up. Zürich is the city whose dialect I speak, whose streets I know better than any other, whose university I attended. It is the city I inhabited while growing up in suburbs and university towns outside of New York, Chicago, San Francisco. New York is where I was born, and yet I never say I am from there, in part because after I was born we moved to New Jersey; in part because Flower Fifth Avenue Hospital no longer exists; in part because friends with whom I stayed moved to the other coast, and for the longest time I didn't return. When I tell people I'm from New Jersey, they don't believe me. They wonder whether they detect an accent. When I tell them I in part grew up in Switzerland, they wonder whether the accent they detect is foreign.

The choice is simple, not because the etiological or ontological conundrum has a simple solution, but because I am never in a position to choose.

I choose Zürich. Not because I know it best, but because I barely know it at all. I know so little of its history, have read so little of its literature. I was taught how to live there, but I was never taught where that there is, except as the birthplace of my mother, the place that perfectly coincided with that of her upbringing, which is what made her so homesick. She has no interest in a plaque on a seedy side street, no need to know that a dance school once resided in the building she long ago vacated. Which is why I have no fellow pilgrims. I want to know that this city has a history other than a personal one.

What a contrast between the Marcel Janco masks, made of paper, board, burlap, paint and twine, including a portrait of Tzara, and the Dada heads by Sophie Taeuber, oil on turned wood, smooth oval shapes without holes or protrusions, including portraits of Arp. The first inspire movement; the second serve as hat stands. Are the masks reminiscent of gas masks, hiding deeply convulsed faces? Are they based on masks from Romanian folk celebrations? Are they symbolic of the hide-and-seek assumed of the assimilated Jew? Or do they simply serve to separate the performer from the audience, in a space too small for so many patrons? In her self-portrait with the Dada head, Taeuber is wearing the hat she might later place on the hat stand. She is using the head as a mask, masking the side of her face not already hidden by a veil. The photographic self-portrait of the female artist with two heads, herself and her art, as opposed to the female artist, Hennings, who sells images of herself on postcards.

I walk by the plaque that says this is the birthplace of Dada, knowing that Zürich is neither my birthplace nor my place of citizenship, which should be my father's birthplace, although even he was not born in Basel. What, then, is Dada but a here here for those for whom there is no longer a there there? This was true for me, who didn't know that anything had been born in Zürich, apart from my mother.

What was once a seedy, smoky bar has been reopened as a brightly lit café, a Graceland, a Goethe-Haus to Dada. In 2000 an insurance company buys the house, with the intent of creating luxury apartments on the upper floors and a gallery on the street level. It is left empty until 2002; squatters occupy the building, an artist's collective that seeks to commune with the *genius loci* in the hope that it might be recognized as a UNESCO world heritage site. Although the city council fails to raise the funds, and gentrification begins, the insurance company eventually agrees to a work-stoppage and the CEO of Swatch Group offers to sponsor a *Dada-Haus* for five years. The city of Zürich and Swatch create a joint company, and in July 2003 four architectural firms are invited to submit plans within three weeks for a project not exceeding CHF750,000 to be completed by September 30, 2004. The idea is to create a space that commemorates historical Dada (documentation), supports contemporary art influenced by Dada (transformation) and includes a café-bar (experimentation). Four rooms are to house a museum shop and rotating exhibits on the first floor, and a café-bar with library and performance space for readings, film screenings, and symposia, on the second.

Rosetti + Wyss, both trained as architects in Zürich, win the competition. Their idea is to leave the four rooms in a state of incompletion, with wall paintings left from the artist's collective and patchwork re-plastering begun under the insurance company, leaving intact the many transformations the building had undergone since it was first sited on a city map of 1576 as two houses, becoming one house a year later. Between the main rooms they insert three boxes made of fiber cement slabs, polished and placed millimeters apart. The counter for the museum shop is dark gray, the library with Internet access is yellow, and the bar of the café is red. The effect is both highly artificial, as though these were foreign bodies taking up permanent residence, and somewhat archaic, given the polished cement. It has a feeling of being unfinished. The chairs in the cafe are aluminum with nylon webbing. The café has always seemed uninviting. It's not clear whether one is entering an exhibition space or a store, whether one is expected to pay an entrance fee or buy something, or whether one has accepted a role in a historical reenactment. It is often closed when I arrive. How to commemorate a place inhabited by exiles, who left nothing except an empty room? How to avoid a museum, given that Dada knows no birth, and no death? How to invite people into a cultural heritage site that the city itself at times feels indifferent toward, at times refuses, and at times displays sympathy with, given that in so many ways Dada is so not Swiss? And yet the seemingly seamless solution to a problem initiated by squatters, addressed by a work stoppage and solved by Swatch, seems like the ultimate Swiss compromise.

Ball reconverts to Catholicism in the Tessin, writes the first book on Hermann Hesse, and dies young. Tzara moves to Paris after the war, in order to make himself, and Dada, more famous. He is the only one to end up in a play by Tom Stoppard. Huelsenbeck, a founder of Berlin Dada, lives in New York for thirty-four years as Charles R. Hulbeck, psychiatrist and cofounder with Karen Horney of the Association for the Advancement of Psychoanalysis. He likewise retires to the Tessin. In 1928 Sophie and Hans Arp settle near Meudon-Val Fleury, France, in a house designed and decorated by Sophie. Hans Arp fails to acquire Swiss citizenship, because they worry he still might go crazy.

> Not even "a man without qualities," the Dadaist is a man without a man; the opposite of the Super-Man, he is an Un-man. The Dadaists virtualized this figure of dehumanization as a form of defense — against world war, brutal industrialization, nationalist madness, repressive government. (Foster, "Dada Mime")

And the women? Hennings works in a factory by day and writes poems at night, alone in a house she shared with Ball in the Tessin. She dies in 1948. Sophie Taeuber-Arp dies in her sleep in 1943, as the result of a malfunctioning gas stove in Max Bill's house in Zürich. She is the only woman and the only Dadaist to appear on a Swiss banknote. Since 1995, the fifty-franc note has been called the "Green Sophie."

I enter the Café de la Terrasse for the first time with my friend C. She is not joining me as a fellow pilgrim; I am joining her for a pot of Ayurvedic tea. It is late afternoon. The patrons are almost all women, talking in pairs. They too have arrived from elsewhere. Most of them are speaking English.

The City

Personal Histories

Freiestrasse 103, Zürich

Paris is a big city, in the sense that London and New York are big cities and that Rome is a village, Los Angeles a collection of villages and Zürich a backwater.

Edmund White, *The Flâneur: A Stroll through the Paradoxes of Paris* (2001)

The most sincere compliment you could pay Zürich is to describe it as one of the great bourgeois cities of the world. . . . Consequently, for about the last 200 years, few places in the Western world have been quite as deeply unfashionable as the city of Zürich.

Alain de Botton, "The Discreet Charm of the Zurich Bourgeoisie" (2005)

I

We arrive by train in Zürich's *Hauptbahnhof* and find ourselves in what in 1871 was considered one of Europe's largest and most elegant railroad stations. An enormously large and colorful woman by Niki de Saint Phalle hangs suspended from the ceiling of a seven-thousand-square-meter pillarless hall. Emerging from the underground labyrinth on several levels known as the regional rapid train transit center, we face the Bahnhofstrasse, the most beautiful commercial street in the world. Behind us is the Bahnhofplatz with a statue of Alfred Escher, the man who brought trains to Switzerland, financed by his commercial bank, Credit Suisse, and below it the Shopville, the place that brought

Sunday shopping to Switzerland, available only in train stations. Why not go for a stroll? The Bahnhofstrasse is only a mile and a half long, lined with linden trees, and free of traffic, apart from the streetcars, known as "Tram." The weather is pleasant, the pedestrians peaceful, the street agreeable. We pass department stores and banks, jewelers and chocolate makers, Franz Karl Weber, where my brother and I once coveted the toys, and Och, where my mother once bought her skis and tennis racket. Before we know it, we've arrived at the Paradeplatz, where I insist we indulge in a *truffe du jour* (its cream so fresh, it must be consumed that day) at Sprüngli's and admire the Georgio Armani clothes in what used to be the main seat of the Kreditanstalt, now Credit Suisse. Banks, after all, no longer require such spacious palaces. Is that the Zürichsee, you ask? The city, which once viewed the lake as a geographical liability as well as a source of fish, rebuilt its shores in the 1880s as a site of recreation. Now there are promenades on either side where in summer the entire city gathers on Sundays, to play Hacky Sack, push a perambulator, barter in languages from other continents, drink a glass of wine. On a clear day, you can see the snow-covered Alps. If there is *Föhn*, a warm wind blowing down from the mountains, known to cause headaches and make people irritable, even suicidal, the distant landscape will look even closer, close enough to touch. At the Bürkliplatz, where steamships offer tramlike transportation for those living along the lake, we cast a glance into the garden of the Hotel Baur au Lac. Charming, isn't it? After crossing the Limmat where it flows out of the lake at the Quaibrücke, we head in the direction of the Bellevue and arrive at its right bank.

We could, instead, turn off the Bahnhofstrasse at the Rennweg, having decided to forego the enticements of commerce for a piece of urban history. Why not treat ourselves to the world's best Butterbrezel, which we find at Honold's, walk up to a bench on the Lindenhof, where in 1292 women who dressed as men surprised the enemy army and saved the city, to enjoy a view of the Limmatquai and the forested hills above it, known as the Zürichberg? We'll make a brief detour to Kirche St. Peter, whose clock is said to have the largest dial in Europe and whose square has the city's oldest bookshop. Why not walk down the tiny alleyways of what was once the medieval city to the Limmat, where on the left we will find the Schipfe, the old ferryman's quarters, and on the right the Wühre, where small steamers used to dock. We walk past the Wasserkirche, where my parents were married and I was baptized, and past the Café Select, where my parents discussed politics with their university friends during the war (it has since been acquired by a pizza chain), to the Bellevue, home to the Café Odeon, where Lenin, Hemingway, and Joyce gathered, next to, but not yet displaced by, a Starbucks.

Either way, we have been making our way to the Stadelhofen, where we decide not to take the Forchbahn into the countryside beyond the city but rather continue up to the Kreuzplatz. From there it is just a few blocks up Klosbachstrasse to Freiestrasse and 103 is one house in on the left.

We decide to take the tram after all, considering the weight of our bags and that with climate change, the summers are no longer cold and rainy but surprisingly hot. We cross the bridge and try to catch the number 3 at the Central, but just miss it, because I've forgotten the fare, no longer remembering whether it is fewer than six stops. We choose not to wait and begin wandering through the Niederdorf, beneath the old city walls and the university buildings, past the library shaded by chestnut trees, past the bars and nightclubs, to the Heimplatz, which everyone has always called Pfauen. This is where the art museum and the theater are. This is where I used to meet my godfather, who came by train from Rüschlikon on the other side of the lake via the railroad station in the Enge. My godfather, who had only enough money for a train ticket and a cup of coffee, after spending all day in the library working on his book about the war.

You notice the many fountains and wonder whether the water is fit to drink. You won't remember the communal stone cups dangling on chains or the lemons left behind after cleaning a syringe. But yes, the water is perfectly safe. From here we can take either the number 3 or the number 8 tram to Hottingerplatz, where I suggest we buy a slice of *Wähe* (a cross between a pizza and a pie, my favorites being apricot, plum, rhubarb, and spinach and onion) for dinner, before walking

Strasse Façade (West)

Neubau an der Freiestrasse von F. Righini, 1889 (Stadtarchiv Zürich)

down Freiestrasse, past the ballet school that still exists, on the right, and the retirement community, once an orchard, on the left, to number 103. We could continue one more stop to the Römerhof, but we decide not to take the Dolderbahn up to the Hotel Dolder, open again after years of renovation, resisting the temptation to play a round of golf or take a walk in the woods, and instead walk down Klosbachstrasse to Freiestrasse, where 103 is again on the left. So far we have not left the map of the central part of Zürich provided by the standard guidebook.

II

Freiestrasse: "the 'free street,' presumably originally in the sense of an open street, that is, not built up."

Sebastian Brändli, Hottingen

In 1889 Francesco Rhigini built two nearly identical houses on two almost identical lots, Freiestrasse 103 and Freiestrasse 105, in the municipality of Hottingen, located at the foot of the Zürichberg. It was a desirable site, sheltered from the north wind, sunny, with a view of the city. The plans indicate two detached apartment buildings with a vaulted cellar, an apartment on the ground and first floor, and a second floor with two maids rooms, two guest rooms, and a *Plunderkammer*, or lumber room. Each apartment has four rooms, a kitchen, a WC and a bathroom, plus a veranda with a wrought-iron railing. The plans are signed by Rhigini, suggesting that he may have been not the client but the builder. The plan is simple, the architecture plain.

In a map from 1883, Freiestrasse between Klosbachstrasse and Konkordiastrasse has no houses, only an isolated farm. In the 1890s an area of once scattered settlements consisting of farms, hamlets, and country estates becomes urbanized. Streets crisscross the steep slopes of the Zürichberg; villas with gardens appear on its terraced inclines; streams and rivers, like Klosbach and Waldbach, are paved over. In the 1830s, when the old part of the city is freed of its medieval walls and moats, the municipalities offer places for growth. They are fiercely independent. People stay in their neighborhoods and join shooting, singing, and athletic clubs. Access to the city is by carriage through the city gates or by foot over the Hottingerpörtli, today's Pfauen. Until the beginning of the nineteenth century, agriculture dominates, specifically vineyards, although Hottingen continues to attract tradespeople and small-scale manufacturers, as well as home workers for the textile industry. Until 1890 goatherds come down daily from Fluntern and Oberstrass to the Altstadt, their milk directly dispensed into the pitchers of consumers. By 1910 agriculture has become a tourist destination.

The Escherhäuser, built between 1837 and 1840 on the Zeltweg, are the first apartment houses built in Hottingen for the haute bourgeoisie, making it the first Biedermeier, or early Victorian, suburban street. A building boom takes place in the 1870s; some streets are placed at right angles and one- and two-family houses begin to creep up the Zürichberg. In 1893, when the city incorporates eleven adjacent municipalities, Hottingen attracts more and more members of the educated and commercial bourgeoisie, in particular those connected to the polytechnicum and university. When the electric tram reaches the Römerhof in 1894 and the Dolderbahn, with its neo-Renaissance station at the Römerhof, opens a year later, agriculture, interspersed with an increasing number of villas, still predominates on the upper slopes, while below them it looks and feels like a city.

Behind the main railroad station, in the flat valley of the River Sihl, is the Aussersihl, where the presence of industry, the working class, and newly arrived foreigners provides fertile ground for socialism. The red flag flies for the first time on May 1, 1891. Beginning in the 1850s it has the largest increase in population growth of any area in Switzerland. People with little money move into quickly and cheaply built rental barracks. They service the necessary but unsightly functions required by an urban environment: locomotive repair, animal slaughter, incarceration, and salt and gasworks. Taxes are low, social services few, and there are many more children here than in other parts of the city. On Sundays, inhabitants of the Aussersihl participate symbolically in urban life by strolling with everyone else down the Bahnhofstrasse.

Zürich has never had a court. By protecting itself against dandies and femme fatales, it has upheld the traditions of bourgeois industry and efficiency. Being receptive rather than productive, it seems provincial.

By 1907 Hedwig Bleuler-Waser—one of the first Swiss women to receive her doctorate from the University of Zürich and the wife of Eugen Bleuler, the director of the Burghölzli, who, by hiring C. G. Jung, introduces psychoanalysis to the city—calls Hottingen the Quartier Latin of Zürich. She is writing a Festschrift for the twenty-fifth anniversary of the Lesezirkel Hottingen, a literary society founded in 1882 at Gemeindestrasse 51 (torn down in 1932 and now a Reformhaus and restaurant), by two brothers, Hans and Hermann Bodmer, descendents of Johann Jakob Bodmer, the Enlightenment reformer, and Karl Bodmer, the painter of Native Americans. Hans, who becomes president in 1900, begins as a mechanic, studies engineering at the polytechnicum, and eventually completes a doctorate at the university. The literary society provides an education for those whose further learning is mostly a matter of chance, members of the striving *Bildungsbürgertum.* It is a melting pot for bookbinders and bakers, tailors, and professors, and *Berufslosen*, those without a profession, mostly single women. They want to feel a social bond by having read the same things; having read the same thing they hope to encounter a conversation partner. Part of their reading material arrives at their doorstep through *Lesemappen*, portfolios of illustrated magazines, circulated on foot by maids and errand-boys, who pick up the portfolio on Tuesday and deliver it on Wednesday with new material, within a month or two of the periodicals' appearance, for two-thirds of the price of a regular subscription. Members are invited to literary evenings, where authors are selected based on the quality of their writing and are asked to speak on subjects of their own choosing. Members participate in festivals where historical events and literary worlds are presented with utmost realism carried through from invitation, to room decoration, to costume, to stage performance.

Gottfried Keller, who lives in Hottingen between 1882 and 1890, is the writer most often invited by the *Lesezirkel* to appear at its literary evenings. In a collection of short stories titled *Die Leute von Seldwyla*, he describes Seldwyla as a small city somewhere in Switzerland,

143

surrounded by city walls, half an hour from a river, "beautifully situated in the middle of green hills, where the sun, but no coarse air, enters after noon." The club identifies with this pre-urban idyll and imagines that by re-creating Seldwyla during one of its festivals, Hottingen might preserve itself against the encroachments of the city. By the 1890s the *Lesezirkel* has over one thousand members, half of Zürich's *Bildungsbürgertum*. Until 1913 it holds a virtual monopoly over literary and cultural evenings, author celebrations, and large festivals. World War I divides the Germans from the German-Swiss and makes the Swiss-Germans more interested in being Swiss. By the 1930s radio threatens books, films are cheaper than festivals, and interest in German literature diminishes: Nazi authors are unsuitable and nonpolitical authors are immaterial. The *Bildungsbürgertum* has been displaced by "the American way of life": cars, bars, jazz, and weekends. By 1940 the *Lesezirkel* has come to an end.

Francesco Rhigini arrives in Zürich in 1880, a scene painter for the theater. The urban scene is changing all around him, and he changes his address several times, always within a few blocks of the houses he builds on the Freiestrasse. His brother, a painter, lives with him for a while, but it is not until Francesco dies and leaves a widow that we know he was married. He lives briefly on the Englischviertelstrasse, in an "English" neighborhood with detached houses built closely together and close to the street, neither villas nor tenement buildings. It is a garden community, based on the English model, a kind of stage set for the bourgeoisie.

Rhigini does not live in the houses he builds, apart from a brief period between 1895 and 1902, when he lives at Freiestrasse 105. My grandfather, Emil Rütschi, who receives his medical degree in 1906, moves to Freiestrasse 103 in 1907, the year his first child, Emil, is born. His wife, Anna, is twenty-one years old. In 1918 Emil the father reappears at Freiestrasse 103, having served as an officer, one presumes, in the army medical service during World War I. Between 1907 and 1918, Anna, my grandmother, is listed as living at Freiestrasse 103, while my grandfather, now assistant municipal doctor, lists three additional addresses between 1912 and 1918, in three distant and disparate parts of the city, Aussersihl, Oberstrass, Wollishofen, for his medical practice. Could it be that he practices medicine as a form of social service, or is he simply moving up in life? From 1918 until 1925, my grandfather lives in the house owned by his wife's two brothers, who bought the house from Rhigini shortly after it was built. Heinrich Keller, or Heiri, is a businessman who marries Rosalie Corrodi, with whom he has two children. Heinrich lives at Freiestrasse 103 until his death in 1919, while Rosalie lives on as a widow until 1938. It is her portrait that hangs on my dining room wall: "Christmas 1890." Hermann Keller is an engineer, unmarried, who supposedly travels to America and whose address is Freiestrasse 103 until 1948. In 1925 my grandfather becomes the owner of a similar house in the Seefeld, closer to the lake, at Mainaustrasse 32. He lives there for three years, until his death in 1928, at the age of fifty-one. In 1948 Anna, who has been a widow for twenty-three years, returns to the Freiestrasse. My mother, Elisabeth, born in 1921 at Freiestrasse 103, moves to Mainaustrasse 32 when she is four and loses her father at the age of seven. It is the company of her aunt Rosalie she seeks at Freiestrasse 103, in preference to that of her mother.

My parents live at Freiestrasse 103 in 1949, the year they leave for America.

My uncle leaves the Mainaustrasse in 1939, at the age of thirty-two, when he marries a woman named Bichsel. He returns just five years later, after she has taken her life. He remarries in 1945 and in 1958 resides again at Freiestrasse 103, this time as its owner. My uncle Emil, my aunt Alice, and my grandmother Anna are now its inhabitants, while my uncle has had his dentist's practice around the corner on Asylstrasse, just below the Römerhof, since 1935.

At my grandfather's funeral on September 17, 1928, the city alderman commends him for his many years of service to the city of Zürich, first as assistant to the municipal doctor, then, for the final two years, as municipal doctor, or *Stadtarzt*. The alderman mentions that he was the son of a farmer who came to the city to study medicine at the university. The day of his death, the Apollo Cinema and Variety Theater, the largest in Switzerland, with two thousand seats, announces its grand opening. In news from America, tornadoes have destroyed five schools in Nebraska, South Dakota, and Iowa, and in San Juan four-fifths of all houses in a ten-kilometer radius have been razed by a hurricane. Citizens of Zürich are encouraged to drink lots of cider and are reminded that grapes, chestnuts, and plums are in season at the market.

III

Schneebedeckte Dächer in Zürich, oil painting by Emil Rütschi, 1968

Christmas card for *Kinder in Not* (Children in need), 1998

Between 1889 and 1890, the house that Franz Rhigini builds on Freiestrasse 103 has doubled in price. What will he do with this money? By 1910 the verandas with wrought-iron railings have been partly encased by windows with etched glass. By 1945 the empty lot on the corner of Freiestrasse and Klosbachstrasse has been filled in by a large apartment building whose apartments all have two balconies, one off the living room and another off the kitchen. From my room on the second floor, the former bathroom that has been converted into a bedroom, I see across to the kitchen balconies, where the husband's suit saturated with last night's cigarette smoke has been hung out to air. My single wooden shutter slams against the dirty stucco wall to let the light in, but domestic dramas rarely spill into spaces where they could be observed by neighbors.

At some point, the second floor or attic is made into another apartment, identical to the ones below it, apart from lower ceilings. The front door, which in Rhigini's plans faces the open lot, moves to the back. The metal sign on the garden gate alerts passersby to my uncle's dental practice, which is on the ground floor. On the first floor, my aunt keeps the apartment immaculate, the poodle's eagerness at the door not a sign that one is encouraged to enter. My grandmother occupies the second floor, where three rooms in her apartment remain unoccupied in anticipation of our yearly return.

I arrive in Zürich for the first time in 1952 from New York City, when I am six months old. My baptism in the Wasserkirche is presided over by my two godparents. My godfather will never marry, never leave his parental home in Rüschlikon, and never finish his book, which is published posthumously as *Politische und militärische Entscheidungen des Zweiten Weltkrieges*. Having contracted tuberculosis during the war, which included a stay in a sanatorium in Davos, converted into a hotel I frequent years later to visit my father, he completes his doctorate in political economy only after the war. Eventually he will write a biweekly column for *Finanz und Wirtschaft*, Switzerland's equivalent of the *Wall Street Journal*. He will make a single trip to America, shortly after the death of my mother, whose bedside he has attended as her lifelong friend and admirer, and visits me in New Haven. The battery once again stolen from the Mustang parked outside my apartment building means I will be late for his train.

My godmother studies art in Zürich at what was then known as the Kunstgewerbeschule, before it became Schule für Gestaltung, then Hochschule für Gestaltung und Kunst, and finally Zürcher Hochschule der Künste, and meets my mother during the war, when they both volunteer for the women's auxiliary. She will marry a Canadian journalist and shuttle back and forth between England and Canada. The paths of my mother and godmother will cross again, in Montreal, before I am born, where my parents first land in North America, and in London, when I am in fourth grade and my father works for the navy. Once I arrive in New Haven, I regularly visit them, first in Toronto and then in Lyme Regis, where my godmother and her husband retire. She will make pen-and-ink drawings of native grasses and a color diary that travels to the provinces, and write about artists like Christo.

In my grandmother's living room, at a large table that occupies most of the space, we eat breakfast but never lunch and dinner. I fetch milk in a metal pail from the grocer across the street. It is unpasteurized and requires boiling and inevitably acquires a skin. I am advised to mask the taste of the skin with Ovaltine, a taste I dislike almost equally. My grandmother eats Swiss honey, which my mother considers too expensive, so for her children she buys honey from multiple Latin American sources. For dinner, my parents go out with the many university friends they have left behind, while my brother and I eat

Bleitibrötli and play guessing games on the veranda with my grandmother until the clock on the Catholic church tower strikes eight. My grandmother sits in the wicker chair designated as hers, which we never occupy, even when she's not there. We never enter her bedroom, which is across from mine, even after she vacates it in the morning with her chamber pot. We never use the bathroom with the bathtub, which has been cut out of the kitchen to make room for my bedroom, as opposed to the WC, which is communal and has only cold running water. My mother washes my hair in the kitchen sink and tells us to take a shower after swimming in the lake at the Strandbad.

Most days we eat lunch in the cafeteria of a *Frauenferein*. In 1894 Susanna Orelli-Rinderknecht founds the Frauenverein für Mässigkeit und Volkswohl, renamed in 1910 Zürcher Frauenverein für alkoholfreie Wirtschaften. Her project is to provide nourishing food, in well-lit rooms, with educational reading material and no alcohol. For the female servers, she reduces the workday to a maximum of nine or ten hours, offers medical and accident insurance, and a pension. The giving and receiving of tips is strictly forbidden. The idea for such an eating establishment emerges out of the temperance movement, whose leaders include Hedwig Bleuler-Waser and her husband, Eugen Bleuler, and whose adherents include Marie Heim-Vögtlin, Switzerland's first woman doctor. Temperance is treated as a public health issue (raw and cooked fruit is better for one's health than fermented fruit) and as an economic issue (less money needs to be spent on meals). Run as a profitable business offering a social service, the alcohol-free restaurant provides youth, women and children, and those who prefer not to eat by themselves an alternative to the tavern. The enterprise is enormously successful, so much so that by 1909 there are nine such restaurants, including one in the Zürichberg. The Frohsinn, the smallest of them, is a short walk down the Freiestrasse, at Gemeindestrasse 48. All of us, including my grandmother, my uncle, and my aunt, select our dishes and carry our trays into the shade of the garden, trying not to swallow a wasp lured by the sweetness of our unfermented apple juice.

Sometimes we go to the Kurhaus Zürichberg, in those days also a *Frauenverein*, at the end of the tramline near the zoo, just past the cemetery where James Joyce is buried. When it opened in 1901, the response of many was dismay that the city's most beautiful piece of land had been sold to the teetotalers. There was no access road; no sewage, gas, or electricity; only a fountain with drinking water. Horses transported the necessary building materials up the hill. High above the fog, away from the dust and fumes of the city, the Kurhaus offered a terrace with a view of the lake as well as forty rooms for tired workers and exhausted housewives who needed a rest from urban life. Today it is the Hotel Zürichberg, a four-star hotel with a modern addition that has won an architecture prize. It last served sparkling cider on New Year's Eve in 2000. The restaurant has recently been renovated to accommodate the lone business traveler, who might prefer eating with others at a long, communal table.

My aunt Alice, who eats only vegetables for lunch, in an attempt to diminish a body considered too large, has a room on the first floor facing the back. It looks out not onto the Freiestrasse, like the verandas, but the garden, filled with flowers and fruit trees, traversed by gravel paths. It faces the back, where rugs are beaten and clothes are hung out to dry, where pine trees and rhododendrons thrive in the shade. The room is unlike its counterpart upstairs, the one my parents share: cluttered, in disarray, filled with acrimony. Apart from a single bed, her room contains an antique armoire lined with Provençal fabric and shelves lined with books, most of them in French.

French is the language of aristocratic aspirations on the part of a grocer's daughter who served as governess in a château before marrying into a family of medical professionals. It is the language of Provence, where she drives every summer with my uncle in their Peugeot, accompanied by their poodle, Le Vent. It is the language of the landscapes my uncle paints, oil on canvas: a solitary building, the color of baked clay, whose only reason for existence, apart from a visual one, is marked by the word "*Boulangerie*." It is the language of the books she reads while my uncle listens to the radio in High German, before he falls asleep after lunch, before she begins to prepare dinner.

The fabrics my aunt brings back from France are fashioned into garments that cover an oversized body, in excess of what can be bought off the rack. She buys food only at specialty stores, never from the

149

supermarket. Although she barely eats, her cupboard is filled with tidy rows of chocolate and *Konfekt,* which she periodically opens and shares with us. Childless, my aunt moves between the kitchen, which as a skilled cook she prohibits others from entering, and my uncle's dental practice, where she keeps his books for years without pay. An excess that looks away from, that covers up, deprivation. When she dies, my uncle shows me the closet of clothes that can be worn by no one else and replaces her clerical skills with those of an old flame.

Speaking the Schwyzerdütsch not of Zürich but of eastern Switzerland, with its broader vowels, my aunt has come from elsewhere. My uncle's second wife. (The first one is never mentioned. She lost her mind; she took her life; she has been forgotten.) Her class origins, her size, her sterility make her a stranger. French is the first language I learn in school, the second Swiss national language I learn to speak. It is foreign, but not strange, like English. I once imagined that if I ever had to live in Switzerland, I would live in Geneva. My aunt's francophilia is something I fail to share, but her exclusion, figured by her allegiance to a foreign language, is similar to my own.

This is the room where she dies, in her bed, her glasses still on her nose, her book still in her hand. She dies reading, a book in French, no doubt. This scene, unannounced, so unanticipated, as neatly arranged as the books on her shelves, as the clothes in her closet, at that moment reveals the perfection I imagine I have been striving for. It is like the stillness of a corpse. A stillness, I realize, available only in death. That perfection, whether of temporal precision or spatial order, is what foreigners think of as Swiss. When perfection falls short, the result is embarrassment. Embarrassed, the Swiss come across as unfriendly.

On the ground floor, my uncle practices dentistry and paints pictures. Sometimes he invites me in and encourages me to choose one of his canvases. I pick the ones with two women: two women in hats; two women on the road somewhere, traveling together. I'm never confident I've picked the right one. Like my grandfather, whose only surviving oil painting is of a large ship on an unruly sea, my uncle is both doctor and painter. He gets up early and goes for a walk with his dog in the Zürichberg. He does the *vitaparcours* in his shirt and tie. He paints in his studio before crossing the corridor to work at his dental chair. One of his paintings—a surrealist scene of two soccer players, a piece of fence and a rose lying on a sheet of tissue paper—hangs in each of our living rooms in America. Occasionally, somebody organizes an exhibit or the city buys one of his paintings. I admire his work. I wonder at his ability to earn a living and still make art. I envy the independence that comes from self-employment. He worries he will run out of space for the canvases that accumulate in his back room. I worry that when he comes up the stairs, having had a few too many and I am alone in the apartment, he will become overly familiar. He has spent his entire adult life living and working in a house he inherited, in the city where he was born, around the corner from his first workplace. He never visits his sister, to whom he has been a surrogate father, whom he encouraged to attend the *Höhere Töchterschule*, with whom he will co-own Freiestrasse 103. She has spent her whole life in America, recognized only as an act of betrayal.

At night I lie awake, listening to a single car zooming down Klosbachstrasse, the clicking of high-heeled shoes scurrying down the pavement. The number 15 tram ends its infrequent run by early evening, silencing its screeching breaks. I count the fifteen-minute intervals chiming from not one but three church towers, until they become so cacophonous that I lose track of time. The insomnia that begins with jet lag continues into most of the summer, the sadness that comes from returning to the place intended to cure my mother's homesickness permeates most of adolescence.

My grandmother dies. My brother and I live in her apartment while attending the university. My mother comes to visit, but it's not clear whose apartment it has become. My mother, who has never enjoyed cooking, suggests that I prepare meals for my brother. Positioned as the interloper, I dream of studying in Germany, of leaving Zürich for Freiburg-im-Breisgau.

My uncle dies and leaves my share of Freiestrasse 103 to my brother. A woman without a man, a Swiss living in America, can't be trusted with a piece of Switzerland. My brother inherits everything in all three apartments. He tries to sell the paintings, but with little success. When he opens a private practice as an ear, nose, and throat specialist, just above the Römerhof, every wall is covered with my uncle's paintings, including the one titled *Boulangerie*, on the back of which is written "This belongs to Anne."

My brother moves up the lake, to the town in Switzerland with the highest concentration of millionaires. The Freiestrasse apartments have all been rented. When I visit, I stay in a hotel on the Mainaustrasse, a block from where my mother once lived.

My brother abandons his private practice to join a private clinic closer to where he lives. The paintings have all disappeared. The only trace is a large poster once in my uncle's possession for winter sports by Alois Carigiet, whose reds match the rest of the decor.

The birch tree in the front yard, barely visible in a photograph from 1908, is no longer standing.

My brother eventually sells the house to the dentist who has been renting my uncle's former practice and his wife, who practices acupuncture.

When I think of Zürich not in terms of family members who view women and Americans as traitors or intruders, I think of the lake. Four generations of women swimming: my grandmother, who tried to swim across and was rescued by the boat moving alongside her; my mother, who claimed that without the lake she never would have made it through adolescence; my niece, who convinces me to jump off the diving board and swims with me to the float. Like my mother, she is studying law at the university, but unlike my mother, she is at ease traversing a transnational landscape. As the fourth generation, she will no longer be poorly educated; she will not have to renounce her profession; she will not feel compelled to write a book. She happily inhabits five languages; she continuously crosses borders; she has myriad ways to stay in touch.

Something does not suddenly appear out of nothing.

Basel

Basel is the city of culture, as opposed to commerce. It is located on a river, not a lake. The streetcars are green, as opposed to blue.

In Basel there is Fasnacht, which is world famous. The dark, cold, silent streets; the 4:00 a.m. sounds of the fife and drum of the Morgestraich; people dressed as *Waggis*, Alsatian peasants, or *Alte Tante*, old aunts. Leaflets on brightly colored paper distributed with limericks in a Swiss-German only the people of Basel can read, satirizing political situations only they can understand. Zürich has the Sechseläuten, the ringing of the Grossmünster bell at 6:00 p.m., and the burning of winter in the form of the Böögg, a giant snowman. But few outside of Switzerland have heard of it.

In Basel, my grandmother stores her extra pans in the oven of a one-bedroom apartment across from the railroad tracks. This is where she has landed, after a life in Kiev, St. Petersburg, Moscow. This is how she has landed: things collected in a space too small to neatly store the multitude of memories.

In Basel, we spend one night in the *Mansarde*—not like in Zürich, where we spend several months in an apartment where we each have a room. The room in the attic is filled with more things, including photographs signed by musicians like Rachmaninoff.

My grandmother leaves Basel a child prodigy, to play the piano at the Russian court. Eventually she plays for experimental theater performances at the Bolshoi, where my father spends evenings in his reserved seat. She marries a Russian who practices law, whose voice she trains as a form of cover from the Revolution. When he confesses to having had an affair with the leading lady while on tour in America, she divorces him. His singing barely audible on an old LP, he dies before I am born.

In Basel she speaks Russian with my father, who never thinks to translate. Unlike my brother, for whom Norwegian secures the nuclear family against the possible incursion of a sibling, my father reestablishes the only bond that endures from his family of origin. She left her soul in Russia, she says, forever regretting the divorce from the country she first adopted, which then forced her into exile. A single mother, she smuggles her son out of a Soviet Union that considers it a crime not to have him raised by the state. In a train station at the border, he loses sight of her and imagines it will be forever. They arrive in Switzerland, and she never plays again, claiming it was not something she had ever enjoyed doing. While someone else practices the piano in the apartment next door, she suffers from perfect pitch.

She remarries into an old Basel family and moves to Agno, in the Tessin, with her cats and a pergola and a terrace with a view that stretches across the distant valley. When my parents take trips without us, we receive postcards from places with names we can barely pronounce, with messages neatly printed in English, which only we are able to read. My grandmother cuts our fingernails, records our behavior with red and black marks in a hardbound book, and teaches us to play short pieces on one of her grands. I excel at black marks, but neither of us demonstrates a particular aptitude for music. When the nights are hot, my grandmother sleeps outside on her cot; when the days are hot, she closes the shutters and encourages the night to come in.

She is the only relative who visits America. Does it remind her of that fateful trip to that other enormous country that led to a decision she always longed to reconsider? She lives with us for a month in the Midwest. Every evening, I sit with her at the upright piano in the dining room before dinner. I make progress, but not enough. I begin to understand how progress could be made, but my teacher has arrived too late.

She is the only relative to convert to Catholicism. They say she refused to baptize my father because at the time she was an atheist.

Basel

My grandfather has my father baptized in secret, something that later will ratify his Russianness. The metropolite, now patriarch, who presides over my father's funeral at the Russian Orthodox church in Zürich, claims him as a member. I claim I never knew him to believe in God.

I am a citizen of Basel because hereditary citizenship could only be inherited from the father, even though the language I speak is Züridütsch, my mother's tongue. I know how to swim in a lake, not a river with a strong current, like the Rhine. I know how to reach my grandmother's house on a tram that is bright blue, not one that is dusky green. I know that the people of Basel think they are more politically progressive, but they also form cliques, like the Fasnachtsclique, that someone like me has no chance of joining.

For my mother, Basel was like a foreign country. When she was at a total loss, she would say I had inherited my grandmother's artistic temperament; this provided her the only explanation for my tearfulness that she considered shameful, like her own.

I know about the city's illustrious inhabitants: Erasmus, Burckhardt, Nietzsche. But even my father left Basel for Zürich to be trained in a subject too modern for a place so steeped in tradition.

Swiss Colonies
in America

Nueva Helvetia,
California (1839)

"An Area as Vast as
the Little Canton of Basle"

Land. Far removed from the City of Mexico, the inhabitants of the northwest corner of the Republic of Mexico cling to a ribbon of land along the Pacific Coast, consider themselves Spanish, with Castilian blood purer than other Mexicans have, and dream of independence. Indians, mostly Nisenan and Miwok, inhabit the vast interior of the Department of Alta California. The governor, Juan Batista Alvarado, is stationed in the capital, Monterey. Alvarado's uncle, Commandante Generale Mariano Guadalupe Vallejo, has been ordered to establish a military post at Sonoma to check the Russian-American Company at Bodega, twenty miles north of the bay of San Francisco. Although outlawed by the Mexican government, fur trappers make their yearly forays into the interior, where they catch up to thirty-nine beavers a night. Beaver hats are in high demand, and beaver skins, along with cowhides, are principle mediums of exchange. The *californios* are cattle ranchers whose hides twice circle Cape Horn so they can buy shoes made in Boston. Unlike Alvarado, a native of California, Vallejo prides himself on having come directly from Spain. Without a single newspaper, news can be as much as a year old.

Swiss Colonies in America

Johann Augustus Sutter arrives in California hoping to become an *empresario de colonización*. Alvarado advises him to travel into the interior, select any suitable tract of land, except what is under the jurisdiction of Sonoma, and at the end of a year he will receive his naturalization papers and a land grant from the Mexican government. He must settle twelve families, and after ten years the land belongs to them. Alvarado hopes inland settlement will serve to check his uncle. In 1839 Alvarado grants Sutter eleven square leagues of land, the equivalent of 48,418 acres, or "an area as vast as the little canton of Basle, his homeland" (Cendrars, *Gold*). Johann Augustus Sutter becomes Don Juan Augusto Sutter, *naturilizado de México*. He becomes *Católico Apostólico y Romano*, since Protestants are not tolerated. He is named *representante del gobierno y encargado de la justicia en las terrenas del río Sacramento*. He calls his land Nueva Helvetia, or New Switzerland.

Mexican land grants have no exact surveys. Does the land grant exclude land inundated by water?

Homeland. Johann Augustus Sutter's father manages the paper mill for the Häussler family of Basel in Kandern, in the Margravate of Baden, thirteen miles north of the city. Johann's father, who has inherited the position from his father, is a citizen of Rünenberg, Basel, in the northwest corner of Switzerland. His ancestors, peasants and ribbon-weavers, can be traced to the sixteenth century. His name—"*sutor*," or cobbler—refers to one of the oldest crafts brought north by the conquering Romans and one of the oldest names to indicate a person's trade. In the middle of the eighteenth century, the first Suters immigrate to Basel, where all prosperous trades are closed to those who are not native born.

In 1803 Johann is born at the mill, a Swiss enclave, which even during the Thirty Years' War had been respected as neutral territory. He is a citizen of Rünenberg.

In 1803 Napoleon sells Louisiana to the United States to finance his military campaigns and Jefferson sends Lewis and Clark with a Corps of Discovery to explore the Louisiana Purchase in search of a waterway to the Pacific. In 1814 Czar Alexander I of Russia, Emperor Joseph II of Austria, and King August Wilhelm of Prussia establish their headquarters in Basel to prepare their campaign against Napoleon. Kandern is a few miles from one of the only bridges Napoleon can use to cross the Rhine.

At fifteen, Sutter is sent to a school in Neuchâtel to learn French, where he reimagines himself as *Souter*. After a failed apprenticeship with the firm that acquires his father's paper mill, he works as a clerk in a draper's shop in Aarburg. There he meets Anna Dübeld and follows her to Burgdorf in the canton of Bern, thirty miles from Rünenberg, where political rights and commercial opportunities are reserved for the native born. Anna's mother operates the bakery and restaurant of her late husband, and her house occupies the most prominent corner of the town square. In 1826 Rünenberg and Anna's mother grant Johann permission to marry Anna. Their son, named after his father, is born the following day. Two years later, Johann Sr. embarks on his own venture, Johann August Sutter and Company, a draper's and dry goods store. He lives beyond his means. He acquires debts. He buys not less but more, including the complete works of Walter Scott. He pays off only those creditors willing to extend him further credit. His coworker, who has been caught embezzling, dies of consumption, leaving Sutter to assume his debts. He sells his house to his mother-in-law, who runs Sutter and Company. She sells the house he is living in, for which he can no longer pay rent.

In 1834 Sutter liquidates his assets and disappears. He acquires a passport, written in French, on which his destination is noted as America, along with those of thirty-four thousand other Swiss who leave that year for the United States and Canada. He escapes via France rather than down the Rhine, where he might be intercepted for not having completed his military service or be inducted into the military forces of some German prince. Two weeks later, from Le Havre, he notifies Anna that he intends never to return. Bankruptcy proceedings are initiated, and one of his chief creditors issues a belated warrant of arrest. When Anna's mother dies half a year later, the substantial fortune she has left pays for only half of Sutter's debts. Anna and her five children move into the *Stöckli*, or grandparents' retreat, of an old farmhouse outside of Burgdorf. There she lives, dependent on her sisters and entrusted to Martin Birmann, a pastor in charge of the local poor, for the next sixteen years. Sutter takes all his clothes and books and leaves behind "a few bolts of cloth, aprons, slippers, handkerchiefs, neckties, gloves . . . a trumpet, a piano and a sign reading '*Joh.Aug.Sutter Tuchhandlung*'" (Zollinger, *Sutter*), as well as a journal in which nothing is written and many pages have been cut out.

Overland. Sutter arrives in New York in 1834. The city has recently surpassed all others in size. One-third of its inhabitants are from the Germanies. John Jacob Astor, the wealthiest man in America, is an immigrant of Germanic origin. Louisiana and Missouri are the only two states west of the Mississippi, so Sutter heads for the German colony in St. Louis. He travels with two Frenchmen and two Germans through Pennsylvania and Ohio to Cincinnati. There they separate, because otherwise they will never learn English.

Sutter is thought to have read Gottfried Duden's *Bericht über eine Reise nach den westlichen Staaten Nordamerika's*, published in 1829 and reprinted unofficially in 1832 by the Swiss Emigration Society in St. Gallen. Duden's thirty-six imaginary letters from America contain passages such as the following: "It is unusually tempting to settle in regions where nothing hampers one's choice and where, with a map in your hand, you may roam through beautiful nature for hundreds of miles, to study to your heart's content the condition of the soil and its vegetation in woods and meadows. Here, if anywhere, it is possible to combine pleasure with utility. . . . And what is more, you can have your choice of climate." The Duden farm in Warren County, Missouri, becomes the intellectual center of Duden disciples, an elite group of immigrants who attempt to become farmers but eventually drift back to the city. *Lateinische Bauern*, or "Latin farmers," they are called.

Nueva Helvetia, California (1839)

Sutter appears in St. Louis and lodges at the Hotel Schwyzerland. From Johann August Laufkötter, a newly arrived Westphalian whom Sutter reencounters in California, we learn that the Swiss in particular are almost paralyzed by homesickness. When Sutter suggests founding a settlers' colony of his own, people are dubious about "a man who had never handled an implement save the yardstick" (Zollinger, *Sutter*).

Sutter joins a trading expedition to Santa Fe. Stolen mustangs are purchased from Apaches and sold to German farmers in Missouri. Able to speak fluent French, although one assumes with a heavy *accent bâlois*, a group of French merchants agree to take him along. The expedition is a financial failure. When Sutter returns, he moves to Westport (Kansas City) and begins building The Far West Hotel. Again on the verge of bankruptcy, he leaves behind "a long black silk velvet circular coat, satin lined; some knee-breeches, a silk vest or two." He departs as "Captain John A. Sutter, formerly of the Royal Swiss Guards of Charles X of France," which turns out not to have been possible (Zollinger, *Sutter*). He is headed west. He has heard about a place called California from a French-Canadian priest in Taos who has become a naturalized Mexican citizen and alcalde. Only two white women, riding sidesaddle the entire way, have completed the overland journey.

At the rendezvous at Popo Agie (Wyoming), Sutter buys an Indian boy. Because the boy speaks English, Sutter pays more for him than he thinks he should.

Islands. From the Willamette Valley, Sutter arrives at Fort Vancouver (Oregon) in 1838. It has taken him more than four years. The impending onset of winter and the hostility of the Indians discourage him from making his way south along the coast. He takes passage on one of the Hudson Bay boats that ply between California and the Sandwich Islands. Twenty-eight days later, he lands in Honolulu, where his letters of introduction make him a minor celebrity and he is greeted by King Kamehameha III. His arrival is announced in the *Sandwich*

Islands Gazette under the name "Shuiter," and he remains for four months.

Vessels from the islands to California are not as frequent as originally indicated, and Sutter is offered a free trip to Sitka, a Russian colony, if he agrees to take the *Clementine* from there to California. About Sitka, Sutter writes: "With the chief clerk I had to speak Spanish, with the storekeeper German, and with the Governor, his lady and officers French. I was obliged to dance Russian dances which I had never seen before" (Zollinger, *Sutter*). He leaves with three white men, ten native islanders, or Kanakas, provided by the king as indentured laborers, two of them women—one of whom, Manuiki, Sutter will father several children with—and a bulldog.

One month later, on July 1, 1839, he anchors the *Clementine* in the bay of San Francisco, then called Yerba Buena, which is named after the Spanish *hierba buena*, or "wild peppermint," that covers the surrounding hills, consists of half a dozen huts, and is not a port of entry. Sutter sails to Monterey.

> Imagine a strip of land running from London to the oases of the Sahara and from St. Petersburg to Constantinople. This strip of land is entirely coastal. Its land-mass is considerably larger than that of France. The North is exposed to the most rigorous winters, the South is tropical. A long, deep canyon, which cuts through two chains of mountains and divides this strip of land into two exactly equal parts, connects a great inland lake with the sea. This lake would accommodate all fleets of the world. Two majestic rivers, which have irrigated the regions of the interior to the north and to the south, come to pour their waters into it. These are the Sacramento and the Joaquin. (Cendrars, *Gold*)

Landscape. The Indians have kept the oak savannahs free of underbrush through controlled fires. This encourages the growth of grasses when food is scarce, in late winter and early spring. These sustain antelope, elk, and deer, which will in turn sustain them. They encourage the production of acorns on live oaks and blue oaks. Food is primarily meal ground from acorns and grasshoppers, captured in pits and baked before the fire or dried in the sun. The native perennial bunch grass gradually loses ground to herds of horses and introduced grasses on the hooves of European grazers.

Trappers collect over one hundred thousand beavers a year. Dams disintegrate, ponds empty, meadows dry up. Large and small animals dependent on the succulent grasses of the flooded lowlands starve or move on. Indians, dependent on the small and large animals, starve or move on. In Paris hats are now made of silk, which in 1834 induces John Jacob Astor to sell his American Fur Company.

The first night, clouds of mosquitoes make it impossible for Sutter and his crew to rest. Six out of nine men have decided to turn back to Yerba Buena. The three remaining are from Germany, Belgium, and Ireland. Hudson Bay Company trappers from Oregon have brought malaria to Sacramento's alluvial plain, which becomes prime habitat for its transmitter, the *Anapheles* mosquito.

> It is scarcely possible to imagine a more delightful temperature, or a climate which is more agreeable and uniform. The sky is cloudless, without the slightest film of vapor apparent in all the vast azure vault. In the middle of the day the sun shines with great power, but in the shade it is nowhere uncomfortable. At night, so pure is the atmosphere, that the moon gives a light sufficiently powerful for the purposes of the reader or student who has good eyesight. There is no necessity of burning the "midnight oil." Nature here, lights the candle for the bookworm. (Bryant, *What I Saw in California*)

Inland. Sutter wants to settle on a navigable river. It takes him a week to find the mouth of the Sacramento. He imagines building a fort like the Russian Fort Ross at the confluence of the Sacramento and American Rivers. He wants to trade with Indians and *californios*. He wants to defend himself against Indians and *californios*. He wants to cultivate Indian lands. He wants to live beyond Mexican law. He wants to be a law unto himself. He wants to establish a colony of Swiss compatriots. He wants to be a farmer, but for two years he has made no attempt at agriculture.

Sutter's Fort begins as two houses roofed with thule grass, built by Kanakas. Four years later, it will have adobe walls eighteen feet high and two and a half feet thick. It will be a trading post for mountain men, trappers, and Indians. An Indian army wearing green and blue uniforms with red trim acquired from the Russians will march to cadence called in German. A half-hourglass in the guardroom marks the "all is well" call every thirty minutes during the night.

Sutter settles in Nisenan country near villages of the Pusane and Momol Indians, north of Miwok territory, on the borderland between the Miwok and Nisenan. The Nisenan have been decimated by the malaria epidemic of 1833. The Miwok have learned to plant and harvest crops, ride horses, build irrigation systems, and make adobe bricks, at the Franciscan missions begun in 1769. They have been Hispanicized and Christianized, before the missions are secularized in 1834. Sutter provides rancheros with Indians for pay and sells Indian orphans. Indians are issued metal disks, to be worn as pendants on necklaces. Holes are punched, representing a monetary value that can be redeemed only at Sutter's store. Like Sutter, they are always in debt.

In 1841 Sutter acquires all the movable property of Fort Ross from the Russians, a debt, owed over four years primarily in wheat, that he finally pays off in 1849. Included are two cannons, taken from Napoleon after his defeat in Moscow.

In 1841 the first overland immigrants arrive from Oregon and Missouri. To these Americans he offers free shelter and supplies. He treats them as guests in the hope that they will become customers, even coworkers. He tries to extract the Swiss and Germans, but few agree to stay.

Nueva Helvetia, California (1839)

In 1845 the Mexicans attempt to buy Sutter's Fort to prevent further immigration, to prevent further Americanization of California by a Swiss. In 1846 the war begins between Mexico and the United States; at the end of it Mexico will have lost half of its territory.

In 1847 there are ten to twelve Swiss living at the fort; all of them are unmarried men, including Heinrich Lienhard of Glarus.

> Sutter's letters had to travel north to the Columbia, thence with the couriers of the Hudson's Bay Company through Canada, from there to England and to Switzerland. Later the Russian agent who came to collect the wheat in autumn would take a letter to Sitka, where it traveled to the coast of Siberia, across the Continent of Asia to Russia, Germany and Switzerland. (Zollinger, *Sutter*)

No-Man's-Land. In 1842 Micheltorena, the last of the Mexican centralist governors, becomes governor of California. Alvarado, who considers him a foreigner, leads a group of insurgents against him. Sutter leads his men against Alvarado by marching toward what is now Hollywood and Universal City. Micheltorena surrenders but promises Sutter another twenty-two square leagues of land, bringing the total to 229 square miles. John Frémont captures Sonoma and raises the flag of the Bear Republic, which lasts twenty-six days. The United States arrives to conquer California and discovers it has declared itself a republic. Mormons arrive, hoping to escape persecution, only to discover that the so-called uninhabited Pacific coast has become U.S. territory. In 1846 the U.S. flag is raised on Sutter's Fort, and the fort is renamed Fort Sacramento. "Don Juan Augusto Sutter" is now "John A. Sutter." That autumn, the first members of the Donner party arrive. Two Indians whom Sutter has sent as part of a rescue mission succumb to members of the party who prefer not to starve. In 1847 the Mormons are on their way to Salt Lake, but there is nothing for them to eat, they are told, so they stay. For Sutter they are like Swiss: skilled, diligent, trustworthy. John Marshall of New Jersey, who has been at Sutter's Fort for several years, is sent to build a sawmill at Coloma, another of Sutter's follies.

Swiss Colonies in America

Marshall discovers gold. Sutter looks it up in the *Encyclopedia Americana* to make sure it is indeed gold. Sutter has leased the land that is not in New Helvetia from the Indians for three years. It is against the law to mine on Indian lands, which belong to the U.S. government. Gold is discovered nine days after the signing of the Treaty of Guadalupe Hidalgo, which is the day Sutter visits his sawmill, so California is U.S. territory. The day Sutter contracts for his sawmill, the government in Washington, D.C., signs contracts for three steamship lines: New York to Liverpool; New York to Chagres, Panama; Panama City to California and Oregon. The largest voluntary migration in history will have to figure out how to get from Chagres to Panama City. California is a conquered Mexican province ready to be penalized. U.S. laws do not apply. It takes four years for California to be admitted to the union. It takes another year for Congress to pass a law to settle private land claims in California. No land can be owned until confirmed by a U.S. court of law. In the massacre of Indians at Coloma, the Oregonians enact their rage, as members of a system of free labor, against a system of proprietors and peons. From 1848 to 1860, the number of "Digger Indians" drops from 150,000 to 30,000. The Foreign Miners Tax Law is passed in 1850 to exclude foreigners from the gold diggings, primarily aimed at Mexicans from Sonora. Why should foreigners be allowed to take gold from the God-given property of the American people? Outlaws and desperadoes lay down the only law. Sutter's Fort is no longer the center of New Helvetia. In 1854 Sacramento becomes the capital of California.

> For the first time in history, gold lay scattered on the ground, unclaimed, free, and plentiful, within the reach of anyone with the will to go after it. Argonauts came from distant shores: Europeans fleeing wars, plagues and tyrannies; Americans, ambitious and short-tempered; blacks pursuing freedom; Oregonians and Russians dressed in deerskin, like Indians; Mexicans, Chileans, and Peruvians; Australian bandits; starving Chinese peasants who were risking their necks by violating the imperial order against leaving their country. All races flowed together in the muddy alleyways of San Francisco. (Allende, *Daughter of Fortune*)

Landing. In 1848 Sutter's son August arrives from Switzerland, not knowing that gold has been discovered. He is twenty-two years old and speaks little English. Six hundred ships lie abandoned in the bay of San Francisco by sailors who have deserted them for the mines. To save his father's finances, he founds the city of Sacramento, a bustling waterfront that outfits miners. The city is plotted on a grid, with thirty-one numbered and twenty-four lettered streets, like the geometrically planned Washington, D.C., he saw on his way from Europe. He gives to the city twelve public squares, of one block each, and a cemetery. To escape the sedatives prescribed by his doctor and the land speculators who have sold Sacramento lots twice or three times, he settles permanently in Acapulco. His father never forgives him for founding a rival city to Sutterville, a phantom city that is never built, and for renaming Nueva Helvetia as Sacramento City. When Sacramento is flooded, the fort and Sutterville stay dry.

August sends Heinrich Lienhard to bring his mother and four siblings from Switzerland. They stay in a hotel that has been shipped in sections from Baltimore, cotton blankets partitioning the rooms. San Francisco is still charred from the last fire. Their father takes them to Hock Farm, forty miles north of the fort on the Feather River, where he has kept his livestock dry. He builds a new house. He builds, along with eight other Swiss, a six-hundred-acre horticultural showcase. He has a three-acre peach orchard and two acres of roses. He builds Eliza City for his daughter, who falls in love with her brother's Swiss piano teacher, a marriage he refuses to condone. The city is eventually eclipsed by Marysville.

In 1865 a discharged soldier who has been caught stealing sets fire to Hock Farm. "A large library in four languages, 'pictures, busts, curiosities, and everything he has been accumulating for the last forty years, excepting a medal or two and his family portraits'" (Hurtado, *John Sutter*), goes up in flames. Two months later, a fire destroys the house where Sutter once lived in Burgdorf.

After ten years in California, Sutter spends the next fifteen seeking reparations. He who enriched the nation is himself in ruins, the gold seekers and squatters having robbed him of everything he had. In 1855 the Land Commission says yes to his land grants; in 1857 the District Court for the Northern District of California says yes; in 1858 the Supreme Court of the United States says yes to the New Helvetia land grant but not to the Sobrante one. It was never registered. It was compensation for military participation. Two-thirds of what he owned was never his.

For four years, Sutter lives at Charles Modes's Pennsylvania Hotel in Washington, D.C. It is the end of the Civil War, and the Supreme Court is in the hands of former slaveholders. California is the only state of the New West to outlaw slavery. When Indians are so cheap, there is no need for slavery, Sutter always said. Gold gave the Union the necessary resources to fight the war. The transcontinental railroad will restore unity to a divided nation. California needs history and prestige, and Sutter is willing to provide it.

Sutter moves with Anna to Lititz, Pennsylvania, home to the Moravian Brotherhood, an offshoot of the Czech Reformation, hounded across Europe, now a German-speaking community. Anna, who has never learned English, must adjust to the Pennsylvania Dutch who say *du* even to strangers. They live in the only brick house apart from the hotel, today General Sutter's Inn. Their granddaughter attends Linden Hall, the first boarding school for girls in the United States. Sutter subscribes to eight newspapers, in which he reads about California in order to feel less homesick, and he has given up the alcohol that has fueled a lifetime of fiscal mismanagement.

> More and more often, he returns in thought to his distant homeland; he dreams of that peaceful little corner of old Europe where all is calm, well-ordered and methodical. There, everything is in its appointed place, the bridges, the canals, the roads. The houses have been standing forever. The lives of the inhabitants are uneventful: they work, they are content with their lot. He sees Rünenberg, as if in a painting. (Cendrars, *Gold*)

Nueva Helvetia, California (1839)

At his funeral in 1880, someone suggests that California has made more progress in the last ten years than Europe in the last fifty.

Landmine. Sutter's Fort is located in Midtown Sacramento between K and L Streets and 26th and 27th Streets. The Mexican flag flies above the nation's oldest re-created historic fort, although only one of the buildings is original. In 1890 the Native Sons of the Golden West purchase the fort, which has served as a hotel, saloon, and pigsty. They donate it to the state of California in 1891 as a memorial to Anglo-European pioneers, with a provision that it be managed by a board of trustees appointed by the governor. Between 1891 and 1893 the organization rehabilitates the central building and begins reconstruction of the exterior walls and interior shed structures. An oval pond excavated to represent a slough is cited by the City of Sacramento as a mosquito hazard and has to be filled in again. In 1921 the governor disbands the board of trustees, and in 1927 Harry Peterson, the curator of the Stanford Art Museum, is hired to complete the fort as a pioneer museum. He creates house museums by furnishing rooms with rustic furniture; he creates display museums by housing artifacts in bleached oak cases made for the 1939 Centennial. In 1947 the fort becomes part of the state park system.

Sutter's Fort is a third smaller than the original, based on the Kunzel maps that Sutter prepared to lure German-speaking immigrants to California, published in Darmstadt in 1848. The original 1841 three-story adobe building is built in the Swiss style, with the third floor projecting over the second floor on all sides.

In 1976 the 1853 portrait of Sutter by William S. Jewet, which had hung in the state capitol building since 1869, was removed and stored in the flood-prone basement of the State Museum Resource Center.

The United Swiss Lodge of California, founded in 1981, is the umbrella organization for Swiss clubs in Sacramento. One of its main purposes is to spread the word that Sutter, the founder of New

Helvetia/Sacramento, was Swiss. In 1987, to pursue this goal, they sought to erect a monument on the grounds of Sutter's Fort. But public objections prevented it from being placed on state property. He was, after all, a buyer and seller of Indians. It now stands across the street, on the grounds of Sutter General Hospital. The plaque reads:

General John A. Sutter
February 15, 1803–June 18, 1880
Swiss Immigrant
Founder of New Helvetia
The Beginning of Sacramento
Builder of Sutter's Fort
A Man of Vision and Compassion
Who Deserves the Respect
and Gratitude
of Americans and Swiss
Donated by
The People of Switzerland
Swiss Americans and Friends

Landmarks. Frédéric Sauser, better known by his pseudonym, Blaise Cendrars, is born in 1887 in La Chaux-de-Fonds, Neuchâtel. An incessant traveler, he later chooses as his birthplace the address of his first hotel in Paris, 216 Rue Saint-Jacques. There in 1910 he meets the sculptor August Suter, Sutter's great-grandson. The following year he changes his name first to Blaise Cendrart and then to Cendrars. In 1925, having had his poetry solicited by every avant-garde journal in Europe, he publishes his first novel, *L'Or, ou la merveilleuse histoire du General Johann August Sutter*. It becomes an instant bestseller and is translated into thirty-four languages. Stalin is thought to have kept a copy on his night table, and Eisenstein is said to have wanted to turn it into a film. The fictional biography imagines Sutter a solitary adventurer, a Swiss mercenary who swears allegiance to whatever state happens to have jurisdiction over California. At the very moment gold is discovered and the entire world is enriching itself, Sutter loses everything. His name is circling the globe, but New Helvetia has disappeared. Anna dies the moment she sets foot on the Hermitage, that is, Hock Farm, leaving Sutter to turn to the Book of Revelations: how could the gold that belongs to him bring him such misfortune? Is he to blame, or is it part of God's design? In a letter to Martin Birmann, the surrogate father of his children, he wonders whether he should return to Switzerland or take on the world in a lawsuit. If gold digging and drinking are signs of the Antichrist, only the community of Herrenhüter can clarify his rights before God. His journey eastward is not toward open land but into the labyrinth of the law.

Caesar von Arx, the most important Swiss playwright of the twentieth century prior to Max Frisch and Friedrich Dürrenmatt, writes *Die Geschichte vom Johann August Suter* in 1929, in part based on the fabrications of Cendrars's biography. Arx, the son of a poor typesetter from Basel, begins writing plays in the *Gymnasium* and in 1924 is appointed director of the Zürich Schauspielhaus, a position he loses within hours due to a quarrel over staging. He inherits his mother's house but remains so sensitive to his quiet surroundings that he begins to write at night with three mattress-like cushions fitted tightly into the windows of his study. Following his wife's death, he takes his own life. If Cendrars portrays gold as the Antichrist and imagines Sutter suing the world, Arx portrays the law as the biggest lie, misused by the few against the many. Sutter is again the failed father, mistaking his daughter for his wife when they arrive sixteen years later, but this time his son Emil, ready to abandon sole responsibility for the lawsuit, stands up to his father and claims that Mexicans stole the property his father is suing for. Sutter exits the stage disguised in his son's clothes, fumbling with the tie, to escape the angry mob that eventually burns down the office and all its legal documents. Whether Sutter lost everything he owned or never owned anything in the first place, no one will allow him to singlehandedly throw the existence of the state of California into jeopardy. For Cendrars, Sutter is suing not for money but for justice; for Arx, Sutter inflates prices to rob miners of their gold and seeks to fleece California of its assets.

Landward. After many years, a friend and I return to northern California, where we both attended college. We drive to Sutter Creek in the car that belonged to my father, recently deceased, a citizen of Basel whose name kept changing and who kept moving west, until, like Sutter, he landed in California. We learn that Sacramento, where together with schoolchildren we visit Sutter's Fort, is now part of the greater Bay Area and that Amador County, with over thirty wineries, is supplanting Sonoma. When I mention Sutter, I am asked whether I mean Sutter Home. The winery, founded in 1874 by a Swiss-German man, John Thomann, still advertises "a fair product for a fair price." The most recent Swiss biographer of Sutter first encounters his biographical subject on a bottle of Sutter Home in the Sutter Grill in a hotel restaurant in the Zürich airport. Although there are Sutter County, Sutter Creek, Sutter Buttes, General Sutter Inn, Sutter Grill, and Sutter Home, there is no mention of Sutter in the *Oxford History of the American West.*

New Glarus, Wisconsin (1845)

"Switzerland's Tiniest, Most Distant Canton"

Herbert O. Kubly (1915–96)

Herbert Kubly, the grandson of Swiss immigrants, was born on the Kubly Family Farm in New Glarus. A noted author and playwright, Kubly's first book, *American in Italy*, won the National Book Award in 1956. Kubly also authored ten other books and countless short stories, travel articles and plays and served as *Time Magazine* music editor from 1945–47.

Wisconsin Historical Society marker,

erected in front of New Glarus City Hall, 1999

ANNE HERRMANN (AH): When I first discovered your Swiss American memoir, I thought, "I am not alone. I have found a precursor."

HERBERT KUBLY (HK): You have brought me back as a ghost.

AH: It was pure chance.

HK: You have brought me back although I never wanted to come back. Not once I left New Glarus in search of what I thought was America. My first stop was Pittsburgh, where I am tempted to say I was born.

AH: That is before you discovered that your actual birth in New Glarus had been recorded in Glarus, Switzerland.

HK: I join the police beat for the *Sun-Telegraph* and end up the art critic. I eventually do the culture beat, which means attending concerts, interviewing opera singers, and accompanying painters on their weekends in the mountains of Pennsylvania.

AH: And yet, you remain the Wisconsin farm boy, you retain "the soul of a peasant" (Kubly, *An American in Italy*).

HK: I grow up speaking Swiss-German in a village where 90 percent of the inhabitants are Swiss or of Swiss descent.

AH: I grow up speaking Swiss-German because that is the language my parents, recent immigrants, speak to one another.

HK: I resign my position at the *New York Herald Tribune* to have one of my plays produced on Broadway. I begin teaching at the University of Illinois as an associate professor of playwriting, which becomes the occasion for my first novel, *The Whistling Zone* (1963). I volunteer for Adlai Stevenson, who fails to win the 1952 presidential election.

AH: In 1951, the year I am born, you take your first trip to Switzerland. For the first time in four generations, someone in your family returns to Elm. In seventy-four years, your father has never left the farm. "Who walks on his own land walks with God" is one of his favorite Swiss sayings.

HK: My ventures into anonymous group journalism, the commercial theater, marriage, all end in defeat. I suffer a profound sense of failure. I am urged to write and encouraged to live abroad. I decide to move to Italy.

AH: In 1956 Carl Van Vechten takes your photograph. In 1996 the *New York Times* publishes your obituary. The Wisconsin Historical Society has erected a commemorative marker.

HK: All markers of ghostliness.

AH: In December 2010 I find a "Book in Time Book Review" of *An American in Italy* for an online travel magazine. The reviewer appreciates the book's historical specificity concerning the years following World War II, about which, he confesses, he knows very little. He considers the book's pejoratives and political opinions somewhat outdated. He finds the imagined conversation between

Herbert Kubly, photographed by Carl Van Vechten, 1956 (courtesy Carl Van Vechten Trust and Department of Special Collections and University Archives, Marquette University Libraries)

your American self and your newly found Italian self a bit strained, although significant. He rates it "one of the top travel books of all time."

HK: I call him Esposito, that Italian self, "the name given by Neopolitans to foundlings." I wonder whether to leave him in Italy or to take him back to America. He insists on coming with me. He claims I will be lonely without him, that we understand each other, in spite of the fact that he is a "citizen of a land that is Latin, pagan, Catholic and poor," and I am from a "country whose culture is Anglo-Saxon, puritan, Protestant and rich." He convinces me that Americans, as the "world's greatest humanitarians, but as very poor humanists," need Italy, and thus him (Kubly, *An American in Italy*).

AH: The book, considered too sympathetic to communism, is banned from libraries by the U.S. State Department. The pastor of the church you attend as a boy declares all of your books "immoral."

HK: You're resurrecting me as some kind of renegade, my books long forgotten, out of print, no longer read.

AH: I'm introducing you as my literary precursor. *Native's Return: An American of Swiss Descent Unmasks an Enigmatic Land and People* chronicles twenty-five years of visits to Switzerland, including the centenary re-creation of Thomas Cook's first group tour—published as *Miss Jemima's Swiss Journal* in 1963—which you join as a representative for *Life*.

HK: I return to several places numerous times. I see myself as the wanderer "who comes back periodically and sees only change" (Kubly, *At Large*).

AH: This book is also a "chronicle of confrontation" (Kubly, *Native's Return*), not with a newly acquired Italian self but with a Swiss self you struggle to make peace with.

HK: It is difficult to be a guest in a country that is one's ancestral home.

AH: To speak the language, with hesitancy, even archaisms.

HK: To see one's name carved on tombstones in a place one has never been.

AH: To penetrate, as an introvert, the isolation of the Swiss.

New Glarus, Wisconsin (1845)

HK: According to Yolande Jacobi, a Jungian psychoanalyst I meet in Zürich, the greatest obstacle to a life of the imagination for a Swiss is the sin of self-indulgence, the fear of wasting one's time, the compulsion to work.

AH: Your *Varieties of Love* is republished in 1960 as a mass paperback, "an uncensored abridgment," with a scantily clad woman on the front cover and a tantalizing offer on the back:"an unforgettable gallery of women gripped by every kind of passion known to the human heart."

HK: At that point I am a freelance writer and have to make money.

AH: The recurring object of desire in these stories, for both men and women, is the young man. The only one set in Switzerland is "The Wasp," about a music teacher who agrees to take on a sixteen-year-old pupil, a gifted musician who plays "football like a fox" and looks like the Belvedere Apollo. Together they admire the wasp that on sunny days awakens between the window panes and which together they name Wolfgang. The pupil imagines bicycling through the Alps with his teacher; the teacher imagines traveling with his pupil to Sicily. Intoxicated by this friendship with a boy who has no father and a mother who has no time, the teacher seeks to make a gift of the Stradivarius he has so far only lent him. The mother, once she discovers the violin's value, is unable to accept either the gift or future lessons. The teacher cuts the wasp in two with his nail scissors in front of the pupil, who doubles over in the snow, emptying the port wine they regularly share. The teacher departs for his yearly sojourn in Sicily, his heart once again "weary and heavy with loneliness."

HK: A condition that is all too familiar: "the fear of loneliness in solitary men who were striving, with the exuberance of drink, to cross an unbridged human gap; and I knew the silent, remorseful solitude into which each would be withdrawn in the morning" (Kubly, *Native's Return*).

AH: "Nothing was so gloomy as Zürich in a winter storm, nothing such a trap for the human spirit" (Kubly, *Varieties of Love*). This line resonates.

HK: And yet, wouldn't we agree with Thornton Wilder when he claims that Zürich is "the only city in Europe in which I would like to live?" (Kubly, *At Large*). This is where he drafted the third act of *Our Town*, during a brief affair with Samuel Steward, whom he met through Gertrude Stein.

AH: Clearly the mother, who discusses the situation with a teacher at her son's school, imagines an expensive gift will lead to exchanges even more unacceptable.

HK: The dedicated teacher as fraud, as nothing but "the deception of a barren life," which is what I learn when I begin to teach.

AH: His indeterminate marital status as a form of queerness.

HK: The boy's name, Taugerwald, a permutation of Taugwalder, a family of professional guides from Zermatt, about whom I am told, "There will always be a Taugwalder on the Matterhorn." And yet the twenty-one-year-old son is deciding between becoming a mountain guide and leaving the valley to become an artist. When I return two decades later, he has become a locksmith near Neuchâtel.

AH: We return to Switzerland recognizing that the qualities the Swiss bring out in us are ones we would rather repudiate. We forget to say *Sie*, because the Swiss in America are all *du* to us. We are afraid to laugh in public, because it will make heads turn. We fail to understand why the Swiss don't invite us into their homes.

HK: I spend twenty years living in the cities of the world before returning to William Tell Farm in Wisconsin.

AH: The first time I visit New Glarus is on Labor Day weekend in 1962, the summer we move from New Jersey to Illinois. We attend the William Tell performance, produced every year since 1938, in Swiss-German, in the outdoor amphitheater of Elmer's Grove, before it moves to your family farm. For someone who regularly returns to Switzerland, "little Switzerland" seems less Swiss than American, a transplanted Swissness rooted in the rural Midwest.

HK: I return to New Glarus as the *Wunderlicher*, the "odd one." "We have never had anything like him in the family before," says my grandfather. I am a reader in a community where reading is frowned on. I fail as a farmer on a farm where no one but a Kubly has ever lived. When my father tells me he plans to paint "Nic H. Kubly and Son" across the barn, I tell him, in that case "you shall have to have another son" (Kubly, *At Large*).

AH: The Swiss do not welcome back their prodigals: they fear them, and in some way they can't acknowledge, they envy them. Those who do not have the courage to leave do not approve of those who have chosen not to return.

HK: Inasmuch as we come back, Americans speaking Swiss-German, they marvel at us.

AH: We return as natives to a place we have never lived.

HK: I return to Switzerland as the professor who rents an apartment in the Niederdorf, who makes hay with other farmers. These things are simply "not done."

AH: I live in a hotel; I fail to renew contact with my brother.

HK: "I discover my Americanism by leaving America" (Kubly, *At Large*).

AH: And yet Italy allows you to triangulate the unbearable heaviness of being that comes from both Switzerland and America.

HK: I apply for a Fulbright, which we sometimes forget is an educational exchange program funded by the sale of U.S. military equipment in storage depots all over the world after World War II. There were sixteen of us on our way to Italy in 1951, "to study the use of humanities in the democratization of a former totalitarian people" (Kubly, *An American in Italy*). My project involved "the use of the theater in international communication."

AH: You meet a Swiss guard in Rome with whom you share a mountain patois and who takes you into the guards' quarters, which you describe as "a tiny twenty-third canton," where the language, food, newspapers, and calendar photos decorating the cells of the celibate are all Swiss. You meet a schizophrenic Swiss baroness in Milan and a wealthy vintner from Glarus on Capri and a woman who presents a Lambretta motor scooter from her Lucerne charities to an orphanage in Naples.

HK: It was "as if I had been suddenly liberated into a sunlight of freedom from the stifling cocoon of Swiss Calvinism and American

Puritanism" (Kubly, *An American in Italy*). And yet, every day I am asked whether I can help someone go to America, an America of Hollywood films and the McCarran Act that limits immigration to 5,645 Italians a year.

AH: In Switzerland you find the possible Italian origins of Kubli, who are latecomers to Glarus, that is, they arrive in the fourteenth century. They are thought to be peasants or anti-papal political refugees named Capelli, the Italian word for hair. The first Kublis in the archives are *Kubli genannt Zopfi, "Zopf"* in Swiss-German, meaning a braid of hair that seems to refer to the custom of Kubli men wearing their hair long. The sons of the first Glarner Kubli distinguish themselves as soldiers by fighting against their ancestral Italy. In America, Kubli is anglicized as Kubly.

HK: My cousin Kap prefers to see us as descendants of the Walsers, the nomadic Alemanic tribes pushed out of Germany in the sixth century, who were poor and sought free land, the land in the Alps that was highest and least fertile. In the ninth century, they settled in the Valais, thus their name, and in the fourteenth century they climbed over the Segnes and Panixer Passes and settled above Elm.

AH: You negotiate your outsider status in Switzerland by identifying with the marginalization of women.

HK: I am made an honorary brother of the tailors' guild for Sechseläuten in Zürich, the festival that celebrates the public burning of winter; I attend the Landesgemeinde of Glarus, the annual outdoor legislative assembly of voters, which includes only men; when I am invited to the *Bähnli-Abschied*, or "farewell to the little train" that has taken people the eight and a half miles up the Sernf River from Schwanden to Elm since 1905, I notice that only men are invited as distinguished guests.

AH: You make a point of meeting a *Fräulein Pfarrer*, to see how one of the 120 "lady pastors" manage in such a patriarchal country; you ask for an appointment with Elisabeth Blunschy when she is elected the first female president of the Nationalrat six years after

women received the vote; you invite the governor's wife to join
you on the final journey of the "little red train," which you think
you can get away with as an American.

HK: As someone whose unorthodox social conduct might be tolerated.

AH: I'm telling you, it's still that way.

Intermission

AH: The founding of New Glarus remains a singular case in the history
of Swiss emigration. The town of Schwanden invites interested
communities in the canton of Glarus to discuss the possibility of
participating according to their means in leading a group of immigrants to a specified destination in the western part of the
United States. All except two communities, who join later, create
Der glarnerische Auswanderungs-Verein or the Emigration Society, with instructions for the *Experten*, or leaders, who are sent
ahead to buy land and statutes regulating the rights and responsibilities of the immigrants.

HK: The stipulation is to create a community in Illinois, Missouri,
Indiana, or Ohio, somewhere with a healthy climate, available
springs, good soil, sufficient timber, and a potential market. The
leaders, neither of whom speak English, are instructed to seek the
assistance of Wilhelm Heinrich Blumer, a Swiss who has settled
in Allentown, Pennsylvania. They are to buy twelve hundred acres
of land all in one piece, provide initial shelter and food, and guide
the early settling.

AH: Of the two leaders, Nicholas Dürst is to keep a detailed journal
and return to Switzerland once their instructions are fulfilled,
while Fridolin Streiff is to remain with the colony for three years
and regularly report back.

HK: The instructions for the emigrants are equally elaborate: They are
to choose their leaders for the voyage and pay for their trip, unless
they belong to a community able to extend a twelve-year interest-
free loan. They will each be given twenty acres of land, which

they are not allowed to dispute and have to pay for within ten years. They are not allowed to leave the colony for three years, except to return to Switzerland.

AH: They are to build a church and school and at all times provide for the ill, the widowed, and the orphaned.

HK: On April 10, 1845, a group of 193 emigrants—the majority weavers, textile workers, slaters, and laborers—depart under the auspices of the Emigration Society. They travel by wagon via Zürich and Basel to Rotterdam, from Rotterdam to Baltimore by forty-nine days at sea, from Baltimore to Columbia, Pennsylvania, by rail, with canal boats to Pittsburgh, via barges to Cincinnati, and by steamboat to St. Louis. From there they travel to Galena, Illinois, and then through trackless country to New Glarus, where 108 emigrants arrive on August 15, sixteen miles north of Monroe, twenty-five miles southwest of Madison, on the west bank of the Little Sugar River, in what was then Wisconsin Territory.

AH: The textile industry in the 1840s has displaced skilled and semi-skilled artisans; by 1844 there is an overproduction of manufactured goods, leading to a reduction in labor; crop failure has led to a rise in the price of potatoes. Since grain cannot be grown at such high altitudes, breadstuff is imported from Italy, Hungary, and Russia and becomes unaffordable.

HK: Repeatedly, land that has not been spoken for either has insufficient water or forest or is deemed unhealthy or too small. Vast swaths of prairie are still available but judged undesirable.

AH: The land has been stolen from Indians like the Sauk and sold to settlers and speculators. No Indian settlements remain in this area after the defeat of Black Hawk in 1832, although in the summer small groups return to camp and beg for food.

HK: In spite of the organization, instructions, statutes, even constitution of the colony, the voyage itself remains the most intimidating aspect of the entire enterprise. One of the leaders of the emigrant group, Matthias Dürst, a tinsmith who provides many of the emigrants with dishes, has also left us a diary. He describes how the travelers have never been to sea and curse the Emigration

Committee for their ignorance. The emigrants are not told they need to pay for food and lodging during the several-month voyage; food on the transatlantic ship is insufficient and eventually inedible, including potatoes in the hold so rotten that one "could believe [oneself] to be lost in a swamp or morass because one's feet sink in over the top of one's shoes" (Schelbert, *New Glarus 1845–1970*); on shore they are repeatedly overcharged, especially for excess baggage, not knowing what to bring.

AH: In the Clements Library I read in *Fraktur* the original report of the Committee of the Emigration Society, published in Glarus in 1847. It includes the diary of Joshua Frey, whom Blumer chose as his replacement to accompany the leaders out west and provides a detailed record of their itinerary, which takes them by train from Detroit to Marshall, Michigan, passing through Ypsilanti, Ann Arbor, and Dexter, which is where I currently live.

HK: Once they arrive: "America is no Glarus land. For there, there is only one, but a good road, and villages every ¼ league, or houses where one can speak to people; but here, there are very many and bad roads which often cross each other, running over prairies taking ½ day to cross, or through equally long stretches of timber in which there are many by-roads and other roads leading sometimes to settlements—such roads are often better than the chief roads; then again 10 to 20 miles with no house, and when finally one reaches a house we cannot understand each other; often we meet people who give little or nothing for good money. All these things one at home cannot imagine" (Schelbert, *New Glarus 1845–1970*).

AH: And your ancestors?

HK: Nicholas and Verena Elmer leave the canton of Glarus in 1847, taking with them four children. Two more children are born in America; the youngest, Anna Marie Elmer-Elmer, becomes my grandmother. Oswald and Barbara Kubli leave Glarus in 1853, taking four sons, Hans Ulrich, Paulus, Jakob, and Oswald. Paulus and Jakob die of cholera the first year. Hans Ulrich loses a leg in the Civil War. They have three more children, two of them also named Paulus and Jakob, stonemasons who lay the foundations of most of the houses in New Glarus built before 1930. Oswald becomes my grandfather. Maria Elmer and Oswald Kubli marry in New Glarus in 1874 and their son, Nicholas, my father, is born in 1882.

AH: None of them have spent a night away from Elm, the village at the end of the Sernftal, also known as the Kleintal or Chlital, the smaller of two small valleys, the second highest village in the canton, a canton with a population of forty thousand, less than twenty-five miles long, where they burned the second to last witch in Europe and staged the first industrial strike.

HK: In spite of the fact that differences between the Grosstal and Kleintal are transplanted to the new world in the form of a brief secession by a twenty-five-person faction to the other side of the Little Sugar River and that none of the original settlers are farmers, much less wheat farmers, 450 more immigrants join the colony by 1860.

AH: By 1856 official ties with Glarus have been dissolved, and by 1879 young men begin to leave to create their own colonies in Minnesota, the Dakotas, California, and Oregon. Twenty acres, as they learn on arrival, turn out to be nothing.

HK: Thirty of the original settlers return to Switzerland, but only six remain: "Everything in the old country appears close and contracted by comparison; and, as some have expressed it, that there seemed hardly room to breathe there" (Luchsinger, "The Planting of the Swiss Colony at New Glarus, Wis.").

AH: New Glarus becomes the wealthiest farm community in Wisconsin.

HK: After the Civil War, when wheat growing moves to the Great Plains, New Glarus turns to cheese-making, which is not transplanted from the old country, since the cheese-makers who join the colony are primarily from Bern, but nevertheless signifies Swissness. Because the original cheese-maker has been trained in Holland and New York, most of the cheese produced here is Limburger and cheddar. Emmentaler, or "Swiss cheese," brings a higher price but has a much smaller market. In 1905 there are twenty-two cheese factories; by 1915 only three remain. By then the Helvetia Milk Condensing Company, later known as Pet Milk, has opened a plant in New Glarus and pays each farmer a few cents extra for every gallon of milk. In 1962 it ceases operations.

AH: At which point, what option is there but tourism?

HK: In 1965, for the 120th anniversary of New Glarus's founding, the Heidi Festival is inaugurated as a way to cash in on the success of William Tell, and in 1969 the Hall of History is built, the first joint venture between Glarus and New Glarus.

AH: When the *New Yorker* sends Calvin Trillin to New Glarus on assignment, in 1975, he quotes one resident as saying: "We're trying to keep our heritage, but we're trying to make it a salable commodity too." Unlike the "Danish" town of Solvang, California, New Glarus relies on the historical fact of its Swiss immigrants, while the descendants of those immigrants see the Swissness being promoted as increasingly less about the heritage of Glarus.

HK: Since then, the links between old and New Glarus steadily have become stronger, in part promoted by the Friends of New Glarus in Glarus.

AH: In *Heritage on Stage: The Invention of Ethnic Place in America's Little Switzerland*, Steven Hoelscher makes the case for "Swiss-scapes," or what he calls "the efforts to create a recognizable themed place, in landscapes deliberately contrived to appeal to the outsider."

HK: New Glarus becomes the global guardian of Swiss heritage and values that no longer seem to exist in Switzerland, such as yodelers, men's choirs, and Swiss wrestlers.

AH: By the 1990s, "much of the impetus for the New Glarus memory work came not from the village itself, but from Switzerland" (Hoelscher, *Heritage on Stage*).

HK: I belong to the last generation to speak Swiss-German at home. By the time I return to New Glarus in the late 1960s, the identity I had sought to escape by leaving has become a commodity that people want to sell.

AH: You write that it is not until the governor of Wisconsin, Warren Knowles, arrives in Elm in 1970 and the Swiss and American flags are flying side by side against the Zwölflihorn that "it seemed that the whole Swiss and American duality was coming together in a meaningful unity" (Schelbert, *New Glarus 1845–1970*).

HK: Elm and New Glarus: the preservation not just of an invented tradition, but of rural cultures.

AH: Rip van Winkle, who seeks to escape familial duties by drinking with a group of ghosts a liquor that makes him fall asleep for twenty years, becomes a kind of model.

HK: "Having propelled myself out of the world into which I was born and never achieving the world toward which I aspired, I have been no place, belonged nowhere" (Kubly, *At Large*).

AH: You belong to your readers, still.

HK: Guilt from turning my back on my roots and paranoia from seeing myself a lonely outcast, fueled by a feeling of inferiority, what I call "the dilemma of the feeling man" (Kubly, *Native's Return*).

AH: The legacy of, as Kay Boyle puts it, the mountain man, "the restlessness, the loneliness, the uneasiness."

HK: Zwingli was, after all, from Glarus.

AH: As is Elmer Citro, the most popular soft drink in Switzerland.

HK: And Schabziger (Sapsago), the only fat-free cheese, flavored by a local herb and pressed into a cone, that literally keeps forever.

Americanizing
Swiss Stories

Swiss Family Robinson (1812);
or,
"The Most Famous Robinsonade"

Since we must have books, there is one book which, to my thinking, supplies the best treatise on education according to nature. This is the first book Emile will read; for a long time it will form his whole library, and it will always retain an honoured place. . . . What is this wonderful book? Is it Aristotle? Pliny? Buffon? No; it is *Robinson Crusoe.*

Jean-Jacques Rousseau, *Émile; or, On Education* (1762)

To girls this species of reading cannot be as dangerous as it is for boys; girls must soon perceive the impossibility of their rambling about the world in quest of adventure; and where there appears an obvious impossibility in gratifying any wish, it is not likely to become, or at least to continue to torment the imagination.

Maria Edgeworth, *Practical Education* (1798)

I could lecture to you now on *The Swiss Family Robinson* and it would be a glowing lecture, because of the emotions felt in boyhood. . . . That is my eternal summer, that is what *The Swiss Family Robinson* means to me.

E. M. Forster, *Aspects of the Novel* (1927)

I have recently reread *The Swiss Family Robinson*, some 65 years after my last reading, to see what I make of it now. I must

191

confess that I have been as enchanted, or almost, as I remember
myself being at my first reading, at about the age of ten.

J. Hillis Miller, "Reading: *The Swiss Family Robinson* as Virtual Reality" (2004)

About six weeks ago Gertrude Stein said, it does not look to
me as if you were ever going to write that autobiography. You
know what I am going to do. I am going to write it for you. I
am going to write it as simply as Defoe did the autobiography
of Robinson Crusoe. And she has and this is it.

Gertrude Stein, *The Autobiography of Alice B. Toklas* (1933)

Crusoe is a corruption of Kreutznaer, the name of Robinson Crusoe's
father, who emigrated from Bremen first to Hull and then to York, in
Daniel Defoe's *Robinson Crusoe* (1719).

There is a female Crusoe and a Catholic Crusoe, a Sachsen Robinson
and a Danish Robinson, a Robinson of the wilderness and a Robinson
of the prairies. There are false Robinsons, where the likeness to the
original appears only in the title, but there is no Swiss family by the
name of Robinson.

J. D. Wyss (1743–1818), a mercenary and then military chaplain, served
as rector of the Protestant cathedral in Bern. He was an outdoorsman
and avid reader of travel narratives, and sought to educate his four
sons by having them found a colony in the South Seas. By 1859 his
name appeared nowhere on the title page of the seventh edition in
English of *The Swiss Family Robinson*. He has no entry in most Swiss
books of literary reference.

J. R. Wyss, a professor of philosophy and author of the Swiss national
anthem, organized his father's unwieldy 841-page manuscript for
publication. Sometimes called *Charakteristik meiner Kinder in einer*

Swiss Family Robinson (1812)

Robinsonade (Qualities of my children in a Robinsonade), it includes sixty illustrations by his brother, J. E. Wyss. It was originally published in Zürich in two parts in 1812 and 1813.

William Godwin's second wife, Mary Jane Godwin, is the first to translate *Der Schweizerische Robinson; oder, Der schiffbrüchige Schweizerprediger und seine Familie; Ein lehrreiches Buch für Kinder und Kinderfreunde zu Stadt und Land* (The shipwrecked Swiss clergyman and his family; or, an instructional book for children and the friends of children in both city and country) into English. She may have used the French translation, rather than the German original. *The Family Robinson Crusoe; or, Journal of a Father Shipwrecked, with his Wife and Children, on an Uninhabited Island* joins the list of the Juvenile Library, published by M. J. Godwin and Co. in 1814. William Godwin, also an educational theorist, believed, like Rousseau, that children should learn directly from nature, rather than from books. Not until 1849 was there a standard edition in English.

Madame la Baronne Isabelle de Montolieu (1751–1832), the daughter of a vicar of Huguenot descent who grew up in Lausanne and at an early age made the acquaintance of Jean-Jacques Rousseau, is best known as the author of *Caroline de Litchfield* (1813). The first translator of Jane Austen's *Sense and Sensibility* and *Persuasion* into French, she is the first to provide a translation of *Le Robinson Suisse, ou, Journal d'un père de famille naufragé avec ses enfants*. Given her imperfect mastery of English and German, her translations more closely resemble free adaptations. Is it she who invents the English girl, Emily Montrose, sometimes Jenny Montrose (a Walter Scott heroine), rescued by the oldest son? Early editions end with an English ship that discovers the family but fails to rescue it because a storm sends it back out to sea, taking only the manuscript. In later editions, the family is divided into those who want to remain on the island and those who seek to be repatriated. In my edition, Fritz rescues Emily, Fritz and Francis return to Europe, and Emily returns with them, hoping to once again reach England.

Americanizing Swiss Stories

The first edition of *Robinson Crusoe* abridged specifically for children is published in 1768. Between 1719 and 1819 there are approximately 150 abridgements for children. The first German version aimed at young people is written by Joachim Heinrich Campe in 1779. Campe translates *Robinson der Jüngere* as *Robinson the Younger* in 1781. Robinson is no longer eighteen years old, but twenty-eight.

Frederick Marryat, the captain of Virginia Woolf's *The Captain's Deathbed*, writes *Masterman Ready; or, The Wreck of the Pacific* (1841) in response to his children's request for a sequel to *The Swiss Family Robinson*. Mr. and Mrs. Seagrave, their four children—one of whom is Caroline—and a black servant, Juno, are bound for Australia. Masterman Ready, the only crew member to survive, provides a practical education by recounting his conversion from a life of rebellion to one of filial responsibility, even though he has never heard of Robinson Crusoe. In addition, Marryat seeks to correct the many errors found in *The Swiss Family Robinson* having to do with seamanship, flora, and fauna. But, as James Joyce points out, what about the errors in the original: "How could Robinson Crusoe have filled his pockets with biscuits if he had undressed before swimming from the beach to the stranded ship? . . . How could the Spaniards have given Friday's father a written agreement if they had no ink or quill pens? Are there bears or not on the islands of the West Indies?"

By the time R. M. Ballantyne writes *The Coral Island* (1858), the parents have disappeared and only three boys remain, to endure dangers but above all to have fun. One boy becomes the leader, and together they enjoy the bounty of the island and their newfound freedom, even as they begin by establishing a daily regimen. Being stranded on a South Sea island has now become a boy's adventure story.

The Swiss Family Robinson is made into a Hollywood film in 1940 and remade by Disney in 1960. When the story comes to America, the boys, of whom there are only three, are turning into teenagers. The only thing missing on the bountiful island is girls. The only reason to explore the island is to look for a potential mate. When they find an Englishman with a fourteen-year-old boy held captive by pirates, Fritz and Ernst decide he's not the right kind of boy, but rather a sissy who has never used his hands. When the boys reminisce about Switzerland, besides "real mountains" and "snow in the air," they wax nostalgic about the girls on the Marktgasse in Bern, where "you look and they look." When they discover the boy is actually a girl, Roberta, the brothers become rivals for her, since the island, in all its bounty, has produced only one girl for three sons. Will she return to London with Ernest, so he can continue his studies and wear a tall hat, or will she remain with Fritz, who instead of working in an office wants to build a new country with his own hands? When the pirates return during the "first national holiday in the history of New Switzerland," Roberta imagines a third option, giving herself up for the safety of a family (of all boys). Once her grandfather saves them from pirates, he offers to take the family back to Europe or on to New Guinea. The parents decide to stay on the island with Francis, and Ernest decides to leave for England, to become someone not quite a sissy, not quite an adventurer. When Roberta asks "what it is one really wants," for a girl there is only one answer: to stay "alone" on the island with Fritz, who already is someone, that is, a dependable provider.

Two years after the release of the film, Disney re-creates the story as the Swiss Family Treehouse in Yesterland, California, nestled in the branches of a banyan tree belonging to the species *Disneyodendron eximus*, or "out of the ordinary Disney tree." The giant artificial tree is made out of steel and concrete, with "roots" forty-two feet into the ground, fourteen hundred branches, and three hundred thousand polythene leaves, although draped with real Spanish moss. The furnishings, "an intriguing combination of European goods and primitive jungle products," is most noted for its "clever and functional" (American) plumbing system, which provides "clean, running water to every room" (Yesterland, "Swiss Family Treehouse"), so no one has to share. All of this is accompanied by the theme tune "Swisskapolka." In 1999 Disneyland evicts the Swiss Family from their tree house to make room for Tarzan, just as *Tarzan* premiers in movie houses. The giant tree receives a massive makeover, including replacement vinyl leaves. The old gramophone still plays "Swisskapolka," for those nostalgic for the old country. Those nostalgic for another adventure can find the evicted family in several other Disney locations, including those in Florida, Japan, and France.

What Is an Island?

If an island isolates species, is it like a schoolhouse without walls, or like a curiosity cabinet?

Is it an ideal scene of instruction, or an imaginary solution to a social contradiction?

Does it have an educational purpose, and if so, what is it teaching besides an imperial fantasy?

Is the Swiss pastor a precursor to Lord Baden-Powell or to J. H. Pestalozzi?

The pastor, his wife, and their four sons are bound for Tahiti, with plans to go on to Port Jackson (now Sydney, Australia). Shipwrecked, they establish "New Switzerland" somewhere near New Guinea. Eventually their colony will be absorbed into the British Empire.

Many of the Protestant missionaries in the British Empire, by way of the London Missionary Society, founded in 1795, were German (Hermann Hesse's grandfather), or Danish (Olive Schreiner's father), or Swiss. It is said *Robinson Crusoe* was among their favorite reading.

Although the pastor emigrates due to financial distress, ostensibly because of losses incurred during the Napoleonic wars, he does not abandon his family in Switzerland, like J. A. Sutter. Rather, the family is a model of piety, hard work, and collective effort. It is a hierarchy organized by birth order, where youth feminizes but intellectual as well as manual labor represents an acceptable form of masculinity. The sons must compete with each other in athletic games but only inasmuch as mens sana in corpore sano.

Swiss Family Robinson (1812)

"The Piece of Land Entrusted to Each Is the Soul"

They have lost their way but not their things.

They have everything they need to found a colony.

The colony will be established elsewhere.

> Human creatures . . . are the colonists of God; we are required to perform the business of probation for a certain period, and, sooner or later, are destined to be taken hence. Our final destination is Heaven, and a perfect happiness with the spirits of just men made perfect, and in the presence of the bountiful Father of us all. The piece of land entrusted to each is the soul; and according as he cultivates and ennobles it, or neglects or depraves it, will be his future reward or punishment. (Wyss, *The Swiss Family Robinson*)

God, not the empire, demands a colony, which leaves the Swiss off the hook. The soul is that piece of land that has been entrusted by God, not appropriated by stealth or murder. It is perfected only in heaven, which requires labor on earth. Labor conquers idleness in order to banish ignorance. Those who are averse to labor, as all German-Swiss know, are the Italians. The island is paradise, but not Eden. It is too insular, too isolated. It is uninhabited by other Swiss.

"A Native of Switzerland"

Swiss Family Robinson is about being at home in a strange land. Its strangeness lies in the fact that it is surrounded by water, unlike Switzerland, a landlocked island dotted by lakes. Homesickness for the homeland makes salt water turn into tears.

> The lake was situated in a deep and abrupt valley. No one who is not a native of Switzerland can conceive this emotion which trembled at my heart, the faithful miniature of so many grand originals, which I had probably lost sight of for ever [*sic*]. My eyes swam with tears! Alas! A single glance upon the surrounding picture, the different characters of the trees, the vast ocean in the distance, destroyed the

momentary illusion, and brought back my ideas to the painful reality, that I and mine were — strangers in a desert island. (Wyss, *The Swiss Family Robinson*)

The lake, in the middle of the island, is like an island in the middle of the ocean. It is like Switzerland in the middle of Europe, which has acted like an island for much of its history, living in splendid isolation with a strong sense of self-determination and an idealized sense of its past. It relies on the immutability of its mountains, rather than the waywardness of the sea. One might lose one's way, but one can't get lost. There are storms, but one will never be cast away.

"New Switzerland"

Animals replace natives as those who threaten and those who can be tamed. Some are hunted and others are killed and catalogued in the cabinet of natural history. The liminal figure is the monkey, between man and animal, both pet and prey.

I even thought it might be practicable to erect a sort of farmhouse on the soil, which we might visit occasionally, and be welcomed by the agreeable sounds of the cackling of our feathered subjects, which would so forcibly remind us of the customs of our forsaken but ever-cherished country. (Wyss, *The Swiss Family Robinson*)

In the absence of natives there are untutored Swiss children. They will be taught to govern themselves, and their learning will take the form of an adventure. Fritz, the oldest, plays the role of the savage, dressed up in costume to look like a Malay. Friday is the girl dressed up as a boy who has lived on an island of her own, a future girl Friday.

"English was the Language of the Sea"

The Swiss family is a multilingual microcosm.
English will mediate between the major continental languages.
Malay remains useless.

Swiss Family Robinson (1812)

We all knew a little of French, for this is as much in use as German throughout Switzerland. Fritz and Ernst had commenced to learn English at Zurich, and I had myself paid some attention to the language, in order to superintend their education. I now urged them to continue their studies, as English was the language of the sea, and there were very few ships that did not contain some one [*sic*] who understood it. Jack, who knew nothing at all, began to pay some attention to Spanish and Italian, the pomp and melody of these two languages according with his character. As for myself, I laboured hard to master the Malay tongue; for the inspection of charts and maps convinced me that we were in the neighborhood of these people. (Wyss, *The Swiss Family Robinson*)

The father is the source of all book knowledge. He must eradicate not just idleness but ignorance. Everything they discover is recognizable because of what he has learned in books. Knowledge is taxonomic. He has always already read the world. The book they read together is *Robinson Crusoe*. In contrast to the solitary castaway, the family is still intact, smug. They each contribute to the written journal, the only proof that they were really there.

The Female Castaway

Together with *Heidi*, *The Swiss Family Robinson* maintains its position among the ten most popular children's books in the world.

The family has no daughter. Emily/Jenny, the adopted daughter, is born in India of English parentage and receives a boy's education from her father, a colonel. As a girl, because she is not allowed to board a battleship in time of war, she is to return to England on a ship whose passage her father arranges, a ship eventually thrown off course by a storm. On her island, she accomplishes in three years what the Swiss family accomplishes in ten.

Over sixteen German *Robinsonaden* appear between 1720 and 1800 with female castaways. Most of them are "well-educated, moral, competent and headstrong young women" (Blackwell, "An Island of Her Own"). They refuse to marry. They put on men's clothes. They encounter other women living on the island. Eventually they will be rescued and return to Europe, reintegrated into a social order that makes them forget they had ever wished for adventure.

"No Man Is an Island"

In Muriel Spark's *Robinson* (1958), Robinson is the name of an island where Miles Mary Robinson lives, reluctant to host the three guests who land when their plane crashes. January Marlow, "My name is January, because I was born in January," is the only female survivor. A journalist, as well as a single mother, she is mandated by Robinson to keep a journal: "Keeping a journal would be an occupation for my mind, and I fancied that I might later dress it up for a novel." According to Robinson, it will also keep her mind off Jimmie, the man she has singled out to protect her from the other two. Robinson counsels her to "stick to the facts," which initially means his story and the history of the island, but when Robinson disappears, January uses the journal to decide which of the two men has murdered him. When Robinson re-appears unharmed, the prime suspect steals the journal and claims to have burned it. January eventually retrieves her journal intact, and when the pomegranate boat finally rescues them, she realizes, "my journal . . . was my only baggage."

"The World Is Full of Islands"

In J. M. Coetzee's *Foe* (1986), Susan Barton lands on Cruso's island: "My name is Susan Barton, and I am a woman alone. My father was a Frenchman who fled to England to escape the persecutions in Flanders. His name was properly Berton, but, as happens, it became corrupted in the mouths of strangers. My mother was an Englishwoman." Cruso lives with Friday, who is unable to speak because he has no tongue. When Cruso dies on the way to England, Susan asks Daniel Foe to write her story: "There has never before, to my knowledge, been a female castaway of our nation. It will cause a great stir." But whose story will he tell, hers or his, the story of how dull it was on the island or the one he will invent that will reduce the island to a single episode? What about Friday's story, the story that can't be told, the hole in the narrative, "a buttonhole, carefully cross-stitched around, but empty, waiting for the button?" Passing as Mrs. Cruso, Susan fails to free Friday by sending him back to Africa because she is afraid he will be resold. She fails to recognize her daughter, Susan Barton, whom she claims is not hers, but Foe's.

"Rural American. Cheap and Cheerless."

In Fiona Cooper's *Not the Swiss Family Robinson* (1991), Monica Robinson, a young woman who has grown up in middle America, learns that the only way to leave home is with a beau. Yearning to join the rodeo, she instead meets the rodeo rider Terrible Tess, who renames her Sonya, insisting on her royal Russian heritage. Once Monica overhears her father saying he adopted her, "given me his name, had he, like I was a dog he rescued," she strives to attend college. Her English teacher, Margaret Courtland, who is English and "had this marvelous English voice and she talked like a book," teaches her about courtly love and encourages her to compete for a scholarship that will take her to England, the home of her birth mother. Provided with her birth certificate, Monica learns that her mother's name is Smith and that her father remains nameless. For her scholarship she will have to write an essay on Jane Austen: "I hadn't been happy with the nit-picky little world of *Pride and Prejudice*, and couldn't put my heart into it." The adopted daughter, neither American nor straight, becomes a castaway in her own family. Monica begins by having tea with Margaret, moves into her spare room, and eventually shares her bed, but her teacher's religious fervor prevents her from naming the romantic friendship as anything other than a perversion. When Margaret decides against accompanying her to New York City by plane, Monica takes the bus. When the bus breaks down, she meets her first out lesbian, who gives her a ride to the airport on her motorcycle. There she meets a man in a frock who tells her to call him Bubbles: "I knew what he meant about names. A shame I had Noreen Jane Smith and Monica Robinson to choose from. And of course, I had once, briefly, been Sonya Dumbassova, the fool who admitted to being seventeen at just the wrong moment." Although children are to learn from nature rather than from books, Monica will win her scholarship by learning what to say about Austen, and to *Swiss Family Robinson* she says: "Eat your heart out, Pastor Robinson, with your little wife and pretty, handsome, spirited, bold, thoughtless, intelligent, well-informed Franz, Fritz, Jack and Ernest! Mom gave me a deal-with-you-later smile." Although her mother was unable to tell Monica the story of her birth, Monica recalled, "Mom's stories weren't the kind you read in children's books. They were all true and no endings, happy or otherwise."

For Stein and Toklas, expatriates in Paris, America is not the mainland but a desert island, where lesbian lovers, like the lesbian with two mothers, have been shipwrecked.

To be Swiss not in New York or San Francisco is to be stranded, in the middle, shipwrecked between two oceans, landlocked in a monolingual wilderness, or so they imagine in Switzerland.

"Switzerland and Other Islands"

Aleksandra Mir was born in Communist Poland in 1967, grew up in socialist Sweden in the 1970s, spent fifteen years living in capitalist New York City, moved to Palermo, on the island of Sicily, and is currently living in multicultural London. She studied media and communications in Gothenburg, Sweden, received her BFA in Media Arts from the School of Visual Arts in New York, and studied cultural anthropology at the New School. A citizen of Sweden and the United States, she says, "I wear all my national identities like second-hand clothes: loose old T-shirts, baggy jeans and borrowed sneakers. They all kind of fit, but not really" (Sgualdini, "How to Do Something with Nothing").

Swiss Family Robinson (1812)

Mir is best known for *The First Woman on the Moon*, a project that took place in 1999 on a Dutch beach where ten bulldozers created a crater in the sand and Mir planted an American flag. She was interested in the manmade nature of one of the widest beaches in Europe, as well as the thirtieth anniversary of the moon landing as both media event and as coinciding, more or less, with her lifetime.

In 2006 the Zürich Kunsthaus commissions Mir to think about Switzerland as a political island in the heart of Europe, for which she produces thirty-two drawings, four by six meters in size, that represent political, geographical, and mythological islands, including a series of undiscovered islands. *Switzerland and Other Islands*, curated by Marjam Varadinis, represents Mir's first solo show in a major art museum. "The . . . show was conceived on the urban jungle island of Manhattan, produced on the fertile island of Sicily, and exhibited at the political island of Switzerland" (Sansone, "Interview with Aleksandra Mir"). Islands for her represent the impossibility of isolation, "marked by the relationship between borders and boundaries as points of awareness that need to be transcended" (Schmidt, "Interview with Aleksandra Mir"). Switzerland for her represents friendships, research into photographic archives, and a helium-inflated airplane sculpture suspended in a permanent state of landing at the Zurich airport. "Switzerland is used as a hypothesis," she says, as "a point of departure to study more general phenomena" (Schmidt, "Interview with Aleksandra Mir").

Mir calls her mapmaking "naïve cartography," which means drawing from existing maps, "so my freehand translations inevitably become naïve renderings of modern cartographic technologies: they resemble the maps made by the early explorers of our world" (Mir, "The World from Above"). She likes the idea that people who live there can complete the drawing with their own references and so the maps are never finished.

The drawings are all made with Sharpies—thick, indelible, felt-tip pens—on paper. She calls these "an unpretentious tool" in her immediate

Aleksandra Mir, *Insula Svizzera*, marker on paper, 360 x 600 cm, Kunsthaus, Zürich, *Switzerland and Other Islands*, 2006 (courtesy Aleksandra Mir)

environment and in the environment of the general public, allowing her access to a "vernacular present." The maps are simple line drawings, minimalist in their representation, outlined by Mir and filled in by her assistants in varying shades of grey, depending on how new or used the Sharpie is.

The exhibition poster *Insula Svizzera* refers to a tradition of early-modern map-making that places the island in the middle of the sea surrounded by four continents as a way to represent its place in the world. Elaborate ornamentation depicts a series of sea monsters but also foregrounds an icon from another island nation, namely Hello Kitty, where the sea monster becomes the domestic feline and historical iconography takes the form of popular culture.

Insula Svizzera shifts the detail from what we imagine about the sea to what we know about the land through voyages of discovery. Three ships sailing toward an island whose interior has been mapped suggests that what Switzerland discovers is ultimately its own isolation.

"Lac Suissy" suggests that the ships are not external but internal, sail-boats on Switzerland's many lakes that serve as among its main tourist attractions, surrounded this time not by ornamentation that threatens from the unknown but by what contains the inside through infinite domestic labor. The ornamental border references the lace doily as a kind of island on the surfaces of the bourgeois interior.

In "Asteroidus Svizzerus" Switzerland the island is shown as an asteroid, living in the splendid isolation of outer space, where the insignificance of the country is remarked on by the impossibility of it ever having a space program. But inasmuch as there are millions of asteroids, Switzerland will become one of many in the infinite rather than alone at the continental center.

As Russell King observes in "Geography, Islands and Migration in an Era of Global Mobility," "islands are good at emigration but bad at immigration, especially those that see themselves as small islands with a high population density." The boat quickly becomes too full. Switzerland's own islandness, as a non-EU country, as the site of so-called offshore banking, and as a model in miniature of the very thing it refuses to belong to, namely a unified, multilingual Europe, results in an unwillingness to join but also a fear of invasion. Islandness leads to insularity, to a kind of geopolitical fortress that refuses the in-migration of minarets. Tourism, unlike colonization, relies on a stay that is always temporary.

Heidi (1880)

<<<<<<<<<<<<<<<<<<<<<<<<<<<<<<<<<<<<<<<<<<<<<<<<<<<<<<<<<<<<<<<<<<<<<<

"Switzerland's Most Famous Girl"

Dear Johanna Spyri,

A 2006 ad campaign for *Heidiland*, the mineral water, uses the slogan *"Call Me Heidi!"* But who is calling, in English, no less? Not a girl with blond braids or even dark curls, but a young man with kinky brown hair and an extraordinarily wide smile. He is wearing a blue polo shirt, where instead of bearing a logo such as Lacoste's alligator, it has the words *FrauenPower pur.* The sound of *FrauenPower* reminds me of "flower power," but that could just be me. At the bottom of the ad, in the tiniest print, comes the punch line: *Funktioniert sogar für Männer!* "It even works for men!" He is tilting back the bottle, ready to take his first sip. Should we warn him? In the drawing on the bottle's label, a little girl in a red dress is looking out over an alpine scene: jagged snowcapped mountains, a winding stream flowing past a solitary chalet, a stand of alpine flowers: Edelweiss, Enzian, Alpenrosen.

How has Heidi, barely five years old, come to embody "woman power"? What aspect of "woman power" makes this man so radiant?

Anne

Dear Johanna Spyri,

When I mention Heidi, people ask me whether I am referring to the "Heidi game." What, you may ask, and so did I, is the "Heidi game"? It is November 17, 1968, and the NFL playoffs between the Oakland

Raiders and the New York Jets are being broadcast on national television. There are fifty (or was it sixty-five?) seconds left to play and the
Jets are ahead by three points when *Heidi* (the 1968 U.S./German co-
production with Maximilian Schell and Michael Redgrave) is scheduled
to begin at 7:00 p.m. Twenty minutes into the movie, a ticker along the
bottom of the Swiss alps announces that the Raiders have won, 43–32.
Raiders fans are outraged because they have failed to witness the final
two touchdowns; Jets fans are enraged because had the referee's call
not taken players off the field, they might not have lost. Thousands of
distressed viewers call the New York City Police, the New York Telephone Company, the *New York Times*. The phone lines are snarled for
hours, and NBC's switchboard breaks down. NFL television contracts
are changed forever: games are now broadcast to their conclusion.

If we assume, correctly or incorrectly, that the distressed viewers
were mostly men, we might also assume that they were drinking something other than water.

Anne

Dear Johanna Spyri,

The Swiss have been cracking down on *Bergkäse* as a label to
certify cheese made from milk produced by cows grazing on grass at
an altitude high enough to be called alpine. This has affected, most
specifically, the line of milk products produced by Migros under the
Heidi label. As the largest retailer in Switzerland, Migros is unlikely to
acquire all of its milk from the same source, and so will it still be able
to market its products as *Bergmilch*? The drawings of Heidi on the
labels for milk, butter, and *Rahmquark* are similar to those on the
mineral water, but she is younger, her hair shorter, and she is wearing
pants, all of which make her more boyish. There are short quotes from
Heidi on each product, illustrating different scenes from the book.

Anne

Dear Johanna Spyri,

My father has agreed to introduce me to friends of his who live in
Maienfeld, the only place mentioned by name in your book, even

though he considers my topic a bit trashy for a literary critic, for an established academic. Although the family includes three grown daughters, the father volunteers to take me on a tour of Heidiland.

Heidiland, I learn, was invented in 1999 as a tourist region in eastern Switzerland, renaming what was once referred to as "Sarganserland— Walensee—Wartau—Bündnerherrschaft" and now comprises thirty-two villages within twenty-four square miles. The name "Heidiland" was originally coined in St. Moritz in 1977, to mark the place where the twenty-six-episode television series *Heidi* was filmed. Trying to do for summer tourism what skiing does for winter tourism, the enterprise failed. St. Moritz has since called itself "Top of the World," but only after registering the trade name "Heidiland." It collects license fees from the Mövenpick restaurant and rest stop along the Autobahn; the "Heidiland Express," part of a cantonal train system; and "Switzerland East." "Switzerland East" is now "Heidiland—The Heart of Switzerland."

Do you remember the week you spent in Jenins in 1879 with your friend Anna von Salis-Hössli? She was one of four sisters you met while in Yverdon, in the French-speaking part of Switzerland, where, like many young women, you were sent at seventeen: part language school, part finishing school, part year abroad, mostly polishing-up for the marriage market. From Jenins, the two of you walked to the town of Rofels and farther up to the Ochsenbergalp, encouraged by a tale Anna's grandfather told about a crusty old mercenary who had settled there. On the way to Rofels, a little girl with short black curls crossed your path.

Because this is the first story not based on your childhood memories, people are obsessed with finding the origins of the novel you finished in four weeks, has been translated into fifty languages, and has sold over 50 million copies.

They have finally given up thinking you are Heidi.

Anne

Dear Johanna Spyri,

I remain somewhat perplexed by the two competing Heidiweg leading to two different Heidi alps in two different cantons on two sides of the Rhine. One leads from Bad Ragaz to the Alp Schwarzbüel in the canton of St. Gallen; the other from Maienfeld to the Ochsenberg in the canton of Graubünden.

On the western side of the Rhine is Bad Ragaz, the spa resort with luxury hotels, where your mother took the waters and Heidi's aunt Dete worked as a chambermaid. From the train station, a brief walk through a residential neighborhood brings us to the bottom of the Pizolbahn, four-person gondolas built to transport skiers up to the Pizol hut at 2,227 meters. The ride takes about half an hour and drops us off at the bottom of the chair lift, which operates only in winter.

A sign indicates the way to the Schwarzbüel hut, subtitled the Heidipfad. The walk takes about twenty-five minutes on a gravel path, level enough to make it wheelchair accessible. The path is punctuated by signposts with excerpts and illustrations from *Heidi*, placed too high for children to read. The story is a retold version of your novel, ending with Heidi falling asleep at the dinner table her first night in Frankfurt, which is hardly the end of your story. But it is the end of the path. We arrive at a picnic spot with a snack bar where Heidi's grandfather will be serving local specialties. Grandfather seems to have the day off. The picnic spot is swarming with children unwilling to share the few available seats with the childless.

Maienfeld, on the other side of the Rhine, was unwilling to sacrifice its identity as part of a wine-growing region in order to buy into destination tourism. Part of the Bündnerherrschaft, it wants to be the Napa Valley, not the Disneyland, much less the Legoland, of Switzerland. But Heidiland needed an alp, making the top of the Pizol Bahn the logical choice. A Heidipfad is more likely to produce revenue during the summer months than a multi-lake hike, the other featured attraction, requiring a commitment of four to five hours on the part of those more likely to bring, rather than buy, their lunch.

Anne

Dear Johanna Spyri,

I'm not sure why I'm dragging you up another alp.

A five-minute cab ride for a set fee takes us across the channeled Rhine from Bad Ragaz to Maienfeld, past the recently constructed

Swiss Heidi Hotel. Shunned by locals as a new eyesore, it positions itself against both the luxury hotels such as the Meierhof in Bad Ragaz, for an international clientele seeking physical rehabilitation, and the Heidihof above Maienfeld, for those, especially Japanese visitors, seeking Swiss hospitality while visiting the Heidi Village. There is also a Heidi-Hof Hotel in Hakuba, Japan. The Swiss Heidi Hotel is not meant to attract primarily Heidi enthusiasts but rather also hikers, mountain bikers, and wine tasters. Leisure activities once associated with childhood are now marketed to adults who find themselves either not wanting to grow up or not wanting to grow old. You can still "check-in" twenty-four hours a day, but the originally advertised "Convenience-Food" in the cafeteria and the "Chill-Out" music in the bar have been replaced by a restaurant with a panoramic view and meeting rooms for more than "business as usual."

The cab drops us off at the Heidihof, which makes it possible to visit the Heididorf, in particular Heidi's House—The Original. The three-hundred-year-old house, located in an original Walser settlement, was de-modernized in 1997 to recreate a rustic household of 1880, the year, more or less, you walked past it. Heididorf, otherwise known as Ober-Rofels, is where you imagined Heidi lived. The house was never built as the set of a film, nor was a film ever made on its site, except for one scene in the 1955 *Heidi and Peter*. This endows it with an authenticity that allows it to be marketed as "the original."

The Heidihaus, at a time when the postal system is threatening to eliminate post offices in many small villages, has secured its own postmark and stamps my "passport" to confirm that I have been here. (B. decides to pass.) "This is where Heidi lived," proclaims the taped loop, in German and English, "Switzerland's most famous girl." "Authentic furnishings arranged in a natural and realistic manner" indicate Heidi's room, which we know she never had. The closet holds a fancy dress, which we know she never brought back from Frankfurt. Heidi's bed is covered with a "leaf-filled duvet," somewhere between the hay you have her sleep on and the down-filled duvet visitors will find on their hotel beds.

Anne

Heidi (1880)

Dear Johanna Spyri,

At one point you imagine immigrating to Berlin, after you discover, like so many of us, that mothers tend to prefer sons. What are your options? You could immigrate to Argentina, like your favorite brother, Christian, a surveyor, who marries an English woman who speaks no German and returns to Switzerland only twice. You could remain in the parental household, unmarried, like your two younger sisters. Or, like Aunt Regula, your mother surrogate, you could regret not being a man and after two broken engagements maintain a lifelong friendship with a man who immigrates to New York and returns every year to visit you.

Instead, you console yourself with reading, in a small room behind the common sitting room. The book you read over and over again is Goethe's *Wilhelm Meister* (1795–96), from which you borrow the subtitles for your novel and its sequel: *Heidi's Years of Learning and Travel* (1880) and *Heidi Makes Use of What She Learns* (1881).

I seem to be digressing.

We have bypassed the red, or Kleiner Heidiweg, from the train station to the Heidi village, which takes an hour and a half, by taking a taxi. I suggest foregoing the blue, or Grosser Heidiweg, from the Heidi village to the Heidi alp and back through the town of Jenins, which takes four and a half hours, since you've already taken it, or should I say, invented it. Instead, we take the Heidi Erlebnisweg, or "Heidi Adventure Trail," subtitled *Wandere, Spiele, und Lerne* or "Hike, Play, and Learn," advertised as a forty-five-minute walk. Implemented on the hundred-year anniversary of your death, July 2001, the trail consists of twelve stations. Heidi's story is told not chronologically but thematically. Each rest stop offers quotations from the novel, in both German and English, with illustrations by the official Heididorf illustrator and a hands-on exhibit, that is, put your hands in this hole, sit on this bench, drink from this spring, that is, "some activity," according to the tourist brochure, "that children and families might want to engage in to reinforce their experience with Heidi, her story and the surroundings."

What do you think it means "to reinforce one's experience with Heidi"?

Why is reading a book, as an experience, no longer sufficient?

The climb through the woods on a worn path takes us to an access road used by local mountain-bikers. The afternoon is coming to a close, and the path is not particularly picturesque. All those with children have long since descended. Two hours later, we arrive at the final station, but there is only an unmown meadow. We are greeted by another collection box, even though each sign has been financed by at least half a dozen local sponsors. A small hand-painted sign says, "food and drink, three minutes." We follow it to the Heidialp and order—I know you can't guess—a bottle of Heidiland mineral water. This one is on me. The young man portraying Peter takes my money before he and the older bearded man playing Grandfather head down the access road in their car, eager to check on their cows.

Where is Heidi?

I realize I am asking tough questions.

Anne

Dear Johanna Spyri,

Since I haven't heard from you, I'm beginning to think you might be away. I know that once you became a widow, you often traveled. To Montreux, for example, where you spent each fall. They say you preferred *Ferienbekanntschaften*, "acquaintances made while on vacation," to friends.

Is that true?

If it were true, is this something you would recognize, much less reveal?

You did succeed in burning all the letters that you wrote when they were returned to you.

Anne

Dear Johanna Spyri,

Wouldn't you agree that most of your closest friendships were with women? Of the letters we still have, among the most passionate are to Betsy, the sister of Conrad Ferdinand-Meyer, one of the most famous Swiss writers of your day: "Dearest Betsy, I thank you for your love, I thank you for your words, that do my heart good; it is always a comfort to be near you, especially when you are completely with me, but also when I am able to be near you in writing, or you near me; I love your being from the depths of my heart. And yet I can't bring my heart to my lips" (Zeller and Zeller, *Johanna Spyri/Conrad Ferdinand Meyer*). Is this the rhetoric of Pietism, something you learned from your mother, a published poet, or the language of romantic female friendship, something you might have grown comfortable with growing up in Hirzel, a household of fifteen consisting almost exclusively of women?

When Betsy moves to Geneva after her mother, Elisa Meyer-Ulrich, the host of a literary salon and someone you adopted as surrogate mother, drowns herself, Hedwig Kappeler takes her place. She is a boarder attending the *Höhere Töchterschule* in Zürich. She will help you move into your final apartment, visit you until your death, and inherit your desk. She will greet your attending physician, Marie Heim-Vögtlin, the first Swiss female doctor.

You will maintain a lifelong friendship with Henriette Devaley, the oldest daughter of the household where you stayed in Yverdon.

I know you insist that it is better to be a good mother than an educated woman, but you did sit on the board of the *Töchterschule* for almost twenty years, where you were instrumental in hiring the Genevan Camille Vidart, the first female teacher at the school and the first translator, although anonymous and subsequently forgotten, of *Heidi* into French. And you did begin learning Latin at fifty. Biographers are obsessed with explaining the decade-long depression after the birth of your only child, Bernhard, the gifted violinist who studied law and died of tuberculosis at the age of twenty-nine. And your marriage to Johann Spyri, attorney, city clerk, editor of a conservative newspaper, who is more interested in writing his editorials than in conversing with you over either lunch or dinner.

I think we can agree it was his loss.

Anne

Americanizing Swiss Stories

Dear Johanna Spyri,

Considering that you grew up in such a large household, why are forty-seven out of forty-nine of your stories about orphans?

You claim to be homesick for your mother, your aunt, and your *Heimat*, and yet you fail to return to Hirzel for twenty-five years.

Please explain.

Anne

Dear Johanna Spyri,

I'm not sure how to read your continuing silence.

Your first story, "Ein Blatt auf Vrony's Grab," appears in the *Bremen Kirchenblatt*, meant to raise money for the nuns' disability pension. It is not signed.

It is 1871, the height of the Russian colony in Zurich, a hotbed of revolutionary thought.

A collection of stories, "for children and for those who love children," entitled *Heimatlos*, follows in 1887. Only with *Heidi* do you forego your initials "J.S." and for the first time sign your name.

In Bremen, you visit relatives and Pastor Veitor, whose daughter Helene is responsible for pushing the wheelchair of her sister Lina. The youngest sister, Adelheid, is ten years old and nicknamed Alli.

Years later, you will invite the pastor's granddaughter to stay with you in Zürich.

All of your work will be published in Germany, with a family-owned publisher, F. A. Perthes, located first in Bremen and then in Gotha. As a result of *Heidi*'s immediate and immense success, the firm is bought out, goes public, and Emil Perthes is forced out. He spends years in litigation and finally ends up bankrupt.

How do you feel about this?

Anne

Dear Johanna Spyri,

What made you invent a new name? You claim that Heidi is short for Adelheid. This has never been the case, either in Graubünden, where the story takes place, or in Zürich, where you grew up. In

Heidi (1880)

Frankfurt, no one has heard of the name. "It can't be the name you were baptized with. It can't be a Christian name," Fräulein Rottenmeier, the stern housekeeper, scolds the eight-year-old child. Heidi has just arrived from the Swiss Alps to be the companion of Clara, the daughter of a wealthy businessman, four years her senior and confined to a wheelchair. When Clara asks whether she should call her Heidi or Adelheid, the orphan insists that Heidi is all she knows. Adelheid is the name of her mother, whose death precipitously followed her father's, resulting in her orphan status. That Heidi stems from Adelheid she has just learned from her aunt Dete, who is trying to dispose of her unwanted charge by fulfilling the request for a girl "apart, not like the others."

In Frankfurt, Heidi is referred to simply as "the Swiss child." "Swiss" in this case means illiterate, ill-mannered, "barbarian," rather than noble savage, "born of mountain air, never touching the ground." It means not knowing that one does not refer to servants by the informal *du*. When the housekeeper mandates that Heidi call them by the formal *Sie* or the third-person *er*, she uses both simultaneously. When she is told to refer to the grandmother as *Gnädige Frau* (Honored Madam), she does so literally, that is, *Frau Gnädige* (Madam Honor). The servants in turn have been told to call her "Mamsell." Heidi sighs at the thought of having three names.

In 1997 Heidi is found to be the third most popular name in Switzerland.

She joins Cleopatra and Cher, among others, as one-name female stars.

I thought you might find this interesting.

Anne

Dear Johanna Spyri,

In 1931 the copyright to your story expires, and the demand for sequels becomes insatiable. You produced one, to appease your favorite niece, Anna, but apparently that was not enough. You did of course tempt future storytellers by giving your last chapter the title "Parting to Meet Again?"

215

Americanizing Swiss Stories

The first person we meet is Charles Tritten from Lausanne, second translator into French, who begins by adding four chapters to your sequel to justify writing his own sequel, *Heidi Grows Up* (1938). By "growing up," he means being sent to an international boarding school in the French-speaking part of Switzerland, becoming a schoolteacher, and giving up teaching school to engage in eldercare and marry Peter. Then, Tritten claims, he was forced to write a sequel to his sequel, to answer the question posed by hundreds of his readers: do Heidi and Peter have children? This is exactly the kind of question you insisted on never asking. Tritten's second sequel is called *Heidi's Children* (1939).

Heidi has not one but three children, twins she gives birth to, and Marta, whom she adopts, the sister of a schoolmate from Lausanne who has taken her place as schoolmistress. The naming of the twins, one boy and one girl, once again raises the issue of Heidi's name, which is both not one and short for Adelheid, her mother. Because her mother was a sleepwalker, the name "Heidi" is rejected as unsuitable. While the boy twin is named after his grandfather, Tobias, the girl, Martali, is named after Marta, Heidi's adopted daughter who turns out to be her cousin.

Are you still following?

The grandfather dies, and the secret of his wife's identity is revealed when she turns out to be Marta's grandmother. This breaks another of your cardinal rules: orphans never find their biological parents.

My favorite moment? When the grandfather uses pieces of dried apple to signify Switzerland's original three cantons, Uri, Schwyz, and Unterwalden, which unite and swear allegiance: "The men of these three cantons promised to help each other just as a husband and wife do when they take each other's hands in marriage."

I'm surprised these books were available in the university library.

Anne

Dear Johanna Spyri,

I hope this doesn't come as too great a shock, but these sequels are less the successors of your book than of the first film version of *Heidi* (1937), starring Shirley Temple. Most people in the United States have heard of Heidi because of this film. Dörfli is no longer in Switzerland but located south of the Schwarzwald. Germany becomes interchangeable with Holland, when Shirley Temple, now no longer Heidi but the Hollywood child actress, performs a song-and-dance routine in wooden shoes. Holland becomes interchangeable with Austria, when Shirley Temple joins a group of children to perform a courtly dance in powdered wigs and formal dress.

Switzerland has never been a colonial power, like Holland, nor has it ever had a monarchy, like Austria. But why am I telling you this?

Heidi is not homesick for the mountains but sad because she won't be home for Christmas. Grandfather, rather than patiently waiting on the alp, shows up in Frankfurt and makes a nuisance of himself by randomly knocking on doors, ending up in jail, escaping from jail, and leading a chase scene in a horse-drawn sleigh. The scene I have never forgotten from my own childhood viewing is the one where Fräulein Rottenmeier smashes Heidi's Christmas present, a snow globe containing a miniature scene of grandfather in front of his hut, against the fireplace. She also drops Clara's porcelain doll on the stone floor, but that makes less of an impact.

The 1993 Disney version of *Heidi* is filmed in Austria, and the trailer suggests that those who enjoyed this film might also want to watch *The Sound of Music.*

This is probably more than you want to know about the Americanization, via Austria, of Heidi.

Anne

Dear Johanna Spyri,

New Glarus, Wisconsin, known as "America's Little Switzerland," has hosted a Heidi Festival the last full weekend in June for the past forty years. Located on the Sugar River, forty-five minutes south of Madison, two hours west of Milwaukee, and two and a half hours west of Chicago, it's close to a ten-hour drive from where I live.

"Heidi Festival" means a dramatic performance of *Heidi*, combined with garage sales, arts and crafts in the park, ethnic food stands on the sidewalk, and, when night begins to fall on a hot summer day, a street dance with live music. All of this is much more reminiscent of summer festivals in small towns in the Midwest than of Switzerland.

Performances of "your" play begin at 10:00 a.m. in the air-conditioned auditorium of the New Glarus High School, with local actors, including the former owner and operator of the meat market, who has played grandfather every single year. The goats, one young and one old, are cooperative, if not engaged with the action on the stage. The kittens, their eyes barely open, seem a bit too young for dramatic roles. Heidi appears only after the minister and grandfather have discussed her at length, and before she even sets foot on stage, we know that grandfather intensely dislikes women like Dete and doesn't think much of girls in general. But this seems to be the fault of Lucille Miller's 1936 adaptation, *Heidi: English Language Adaptation, Dramatized from the Book of Johanna Spyri*. Heidi seems overly solicitous toward her grandfather's loneliness and overly imperious about what he "must do," making her less the dependent child than the domineering wife.

When the person appears between the acts to entertain specifically "those less than three feet tall," the answer to his question for the audience about where the previous scene has taken place is not Dörfli but "Berkeley."

The California dairy industry has begun an ad campaign against Wisconsin, "America's Dairyland." The artisanal bakery, in continuous operation since the first settlement of New Glarus, has just gone out of business.

The Heidi Festival is modeled on Tellenspiele, reenactments of the William Tell legend, regularly staged in Switzerland since the early sixteenth-century and in New Glarus since 1938.

In 2010 a Swiss newspaper lists the ten most important Swiss people in history. No sign of William Tell. The two women to make the list are Heidi and Helvetia, neither of whom, as you know, existed.

Anne

Dear Johanna Spyri,

The only copy of *Heidi* I find in my possession is in English, published in 1959, part of an "Around the World Treasures" series that boasts a "unique BOOK-WITHIN-A-BOOK." This feature consists of a thirty-two-page introductory section that tells the story in full-page illustrations with captions for those children "still too young to attempt the full story as originally written." In an introductory section titled "About This Book," the life of the author is retold in addition to one "Swiss" custom, namely candles on Christmas trees: "The children were not allowed to become satiated with Christmas delights, for the wax candles on the tree were never lighted for more than one hour, and then not necessarily on Christmas Day, but somewhere in the Christmas week. So the tree when it was lighted, had love and admiration lavished on it, that no tree that blazes away all through Christmas knows." We never spent Christmas in Switzerland; instead we imported candles for the tree and by lighting them, technically broke the law.

When I read *Heidi* again, this time in German, I am struck by how much it is a novel about reading. But then, I was trained as a deconstructionist, which means a certain affinity for scenes of reading. Reading has been mourned for not being a national pastime, in a country where reading competes with climbing and rarely wins.

A persistent reader,

Anne

Dear Johanna Spyri,

In 1974, fifty-two episodes of the anime *Heidi, the Girl of the Alps* are broadcast every Sunday night on television in Japan, as part of a *World Masterpiece Theater* anime series. A former student of mine, T.Y., who has come to the United States to study anthropology, says she can still sing the theme song.

She brings back a 1994 book from Japan, *Haiji kiko* (*Travels with Heidi*) by Man Arai and Noriko Arai, which another Japanese student in sociology, H.S., is kind enough to translate for me. It is part travel diary, part travel guide, written by a married couple, he a well-known novelist, and she a housewife. It is her lifelong dream to travel to Switzerland. Noriko is eight years old when she first reads *Heidi*. She wants to be Heidi, surrounded by nature rather than the factory noise, screams of sirens, and sounds from the sewage canal that flows in front of her family's subsidized house in a small company town. Her children grow up, her parents die, and she is confronted by the unfulfilled dream she has harbored since childhood of retracing the steps of Heidi's author and climbing the mountains above Maienfeld. She imagines that what Heidi felt in Frankfurt is what you felt in the big city of Zürich, after you married and moved from Hirzel. It is what she feels when her husband is relocated to western Japan, farther and farther from Tokyo. She too reads *Heidi* as a book about becoming literate, about education, about the importance of female education, in particular.

Her husband agrees to accompany her to Switzerland as a way of enabling the fulfillment of her dream, of repaying her for having fulfilled her domestic role. Reading *Heidi* in the hotel room, he is reminded of his own favorite childhood story, *Jiro's Story*. For him there are three kinds of men: those who are dead; those who are barely alive; those who have undertaken a sea voyage. Together they undertake a sea voyage by climbing the Alps. They hope to inspire others to undertake their own "travels with Heidi."

On their return, Noriko becomes an author by writing "Three Conditions for Happiness I learned from Heidi." They include waking up healthy; having food for lunch; sleeping peacefully. Noriko discovers a fourth condition for happiness: self-fulfillment, which she achieves by writing. She takes you as her inspiration, a housewife who begins to write in middle-age.

What do you think about Heidi becoming part of "cuteness culture," that is, an idealization of childhood, a resistance to the rigidity of gender roles, and a market that caters to women as girl consumers up to the age of thirty?

I'm just curious.

Anne

Dear Johanna Spyri,

My father's friend who lives in Maienfeld shared the following story: He met a young man from Japan who had finished secondary school with the highest score in English; his prize was a three-week trip to London. His father then sent him a ticket from London to

Heidi (1880)

Zürich, telling him he had to visit Heidi in Maienfeld. His uncle then sent him a ticket from Zürich to Berlin, saying he had to visit the new capital of Europe.

Anne

Dear Johann Spyri,

The Skymetro, or Automated People Mover, is Switzerland's most frequented cable car, able to transport forty-two hundred passengers an hour from Airside Center to Dock E under Piste 10/28 at the Zürich airport. In 2006, light boxes, 160 in all, were installed every hundred meters, showing scenes from two short films, *Heidi* and *Matterhorn*. Diccon Bewes provides the following description: "The yodelling starts as the train leaves, followed by jangling cowbells and deep-throated alphorns, all from the loudspeaker system. And then she appears, as if by magic, larger than life outside the window. She turns her head of golden, braided hair towards us, blows a kiss and vanishes."

This is who greets me now when I return to Switzerland, not my relatives (who don't know I'm coming) and not my friends (who don't have time for a trip to the airport), but Heidi, a bit too friendly, a bit too provocative.

I don't expect you to commiserate.

Anne

Epilogue

"I'm Swiss"

I

In July 2010 McDonald's introduces a new ad campaign, of which there are two versions on the walls of the Zürich train station. Each consists of a bright red background, with a small *Suisse Garantie* and Swiss flag in the bottom left-hand corner and the Golden arches and "I'm lovin' it" in the bottom right. In the center in large white letters is "I'm Swiss," except the "I" in each case is replaced, in one instance with an ice-cream cone and in the other with a french fry. In the case of the french fry, the caption under "I'm Swiss," in much smaller letters, is *"Für unsere Pommes Frites verwenden wir nur Schweizer Kartoffeln"* (For our french fries we use only Swiss potatoes). In the case of the *Soft Ice*—vanilla ice cream topped with chocolate sauce in a plastic cup—the caption is *Für unsere Glacés verwenden wir nur Schweizer Milch* (For our ice cream we use only Swiss milk). McDonald's is coming out Swiss. It is coming out in white letters on a red background, the colors of the Swiss flag. It is coming out in English, to guarantee its ingredients in German, for food items that rely on borrowings from the French, which is how we know the food items are Swiss. Coming out means coming out local in a globalized economy. It means revealing a secret that someone thought we didn't know, even though the secret, in this case, is not shameful. It is meant to mitigate the shame that

223

comes from being a purveyor of fast food whose brand is so ubiquitous it doesn't need to name itself. The multinational becomes conscious of sustainability by revealing the national origin of some of its agricultural ingredients. It once again desires a nationality, in this case, even a multilingual one. Coming out is meant to cater to as yet unconverted customers, possibly Swiss, potentially left. It is meant to sell. Being Swiss in English, which is not an official national language, is a way to become cosmopolitan. The other way is to consume globally available food whose taste remains identical in spite of local ingredients. Are we surprised, or just skeptical?

"Swiss" is not just a word; it has become a logo. It guarantees many things—neutrality, quality, naturalness—but at this moment it also connotes cool. "Swissair" became "Swiss" to save itself after its shameful "Grounding," which proved unsuccessful in as much as it is now an affiliate of Lufthansa. "Swiss," that five-letter word with three "s"es, is so much sexier than "*Schweizer/in*" or "*schweizerisch.*" It is even more hip than "Suisse," recently appropriated by the bank Credit Suisse, which used to be Schweizerische Kreditanstalt, at least in German. A first-person pronoun that is simply a letter of the alphabet capitalized and available for contraction with another letter doesn't hurt either. It was made for a world where everything belongs to me because I have made it mine by calling it "my" something. The golden arches, placed opposite the Swiss flag, remind us that corporations are countries that only need to market themselves, without ever needing to govern, that is, count their citizens, provide them with sidewalks, or make them literate. Maybe what is coming out is that you really are what you eat, including the sign for not just what is yours, but yourself, namely "I."

II

Bill Maher delivers a live performance in Portland, Oregon, on March 26, 2005, titled *I'm Swiss*, subtitled *And Other Treasonous Statements*. The show is a response to the second inauguration of George Bush, where "bullshit issues," in particular gay marriage, have resulted in his reelection. Maher's hatred for Bush leads him to line up the likely suspects: the war in Iraq, tax breaks for the rich, Bush's response to 9/11, his cowboy costume. But these abominations lead to a further litany of what's wrong with the country: reality TV, presidents from Texas, rap lyrics, Rush Limbaugh's oxycontin addiction, fatness, and the politics of food. If the show has a theme, it is "legislating taste," which means taking the opinions of some people and turning them into laws for all people. The church and children function as primary legislators. Only two of the Ten Commandments are also laws; in the name of protecting children, America is "cuckoo about safety," so that "no one can ever die." Maher "gets it"; he just can't believe it, and above all, he doesn't agree with it. When the bounty on bin Laden is raised from $25 million to $50 million to incentivize his capture, he gets the ethnocentrism that would think the goatherd on the border between Afghanistan and Pakistan might find the initial reward insulting. But capturing or killing Bin Laden would have the same effect on terrorism as Ray Kroc's death had on McDonald's—none: "the franchise has been built."

"What country is this? What year are we in? Janet Jackson's milkshake was on the television for one second, and America was permanently traumatized. I tell you, when that was going down I was telling people 'I'm Swiss.' I live here now but I'm actually a Swiss, nationally." Being an American in a country run by right-wing Republicans is so repugnant that it requires changing one's nationality. Maher doesn't hate America; he loves it, but why, he asks, "does it always have to be the stupid country?" Why can't America be a hip country, "where the president has a permanent tan and expensive suits and has a Versace mistress and there's pictures of them fucking on a boat but nobody cares because that's *amore*?" It's anti-gay marriage, and yet Abu Ghraib is so "overwhelmingly gay," "Rumsfeld shouldn't step down, he should come out." "Of course the Catholic church doesn't want gay men to marry: half the priesthood would walk out the door the first day and marry the UPS driver." Maybe people could agree on a compromise: "(1) people who are already gay are okay, but no new gays; (2) there could be gay marriage but no gay mortgage; (3) just let lesbians marry, since marriage is kind of a chick thing anyway and men don't really want to do it, since marriage was something cooked up by women in the Catholic church to stamp out oral sex." Maher supports gay marriage not as a gay man, not as a man who is pro-gay sex, but as a pot smoker. Gay sex, like pot smoking, although widely practiced, makes participants noncitizens. Maher comes out straight by saying that personally he is revolted by "hairy man ass sex" but he would never ask that his opinion be made into law. His straightness involves a speech act and relies on the impersonation of gayness: Daniel Lieb[es]kind's feyness stands in sharp contrast to the 1776-floor Freedom Tower he has been asked to design to replace the World Trade Center. When Maher reports that the president does not believe in evolution, his exasperation leads to the reiteration of "I'm Swiss. Are you Swiss too? A lot of Swiss here." Swissness provides an alternative to both political parties, since even elected Democrats fail to advocate for the legalization of marijuana, gay marriage as opposed to civil unions, and legislation to address climate change. His final message to the terrorists, as well as his audience: "Hate the Dutch! I've been to Amsterdam. If freedom is what bugs you so much, scare the shit out of those pot-smoking, whoremongering motherfuckers and leave us Swiss people alone!"

Coming out Swiss means betraying the United States by engaging in un-American activities, or at least anti-American humor. Maher is not revealing the secret of his Swiss ancestry; he is renouncing his United States citizenship and doing so as a comedic act. But why Swiss? Certainly not because of its visual coolness. Being an American, at least for liberals, progressives, libertarians, even lapsed Catholics and potheads like Maher, is shameful. "Swissness" refers to a disenfranchised minority, represented by, among others, the inhabitants of Portland, who have lost the election and imagine themselves living in a separate country. "Swissness" is also an empty signifier. How many Americans have ever met a Swiss? How would they know how to be Swiss? Finally, Switzerland is the butt of the joke. It is small, insignificant, and interchangeable, and what goes on there can't possibly matter as much as the United States presidential election. If the Swiss really are traditional, reserved, precise, that's not a bad thing, given that Bush makes uninformed decisions based on misinformation that alienate him from just about everybody, but above all, Old Europe, where Switzerland is.

Maher's coming-out scene for the DVD audience is enhanced with background visuals that consist of childlike drawings and captions with arrows pointing to the iconic Matterhorn, Swiss Chalet, and St. Bernard. St. Moritz (137 km), Zürich (68 km), Geneva (53 km), as well as the United States (6500 km) all have signs indicating direction as well as distance. So, where exactly in Switzerland are we? The next shot is a map of Switzerland surrounded on each side by its neighbors—France, Italy, and Germany—just in case anyone needed to be reminded of its exact location. The final shot shows a cuckoo clock superimposed on a Swiss flag that echoes Orson Welles in *The Third Man*: "The Italian Renaissance was full of crimes and excess, and yet it gave us the greatest masterpieces of art. . . . Switzerland had lived in peace for three centuries, and what's she given us? The cuckoo clock." Welles never apologizes for confusing Switzerland with the Schwarzwald in southern Germany, unlike Paul Krugman, the economist. In his August 17, 2007, *New York Times* editorial titled "The Swiss Menace," meaning Obamacare, that is, the perceived attempt to "Swissify America" through mandatory health-care coverage, he describes the Swiss as "lederhosen-wearing holey-cheese eaters." He corrects himself in his next column by recognizing that he has confused Switzerland with Austria.

III

The 2007 film *Helvetica* is a documentary about a typeface. "Nobody doesn't know what Helvetica is." It is the font of governments and corporations. Signs for Greyhound, Toyota, Nestlé, Verizon, North Face, J.C. Penney, Staples, Target, Lufthansa, Crate and Barrel, and New York City Transit, as well United States tax forms, are all written in Helvetica. It wants to look accessible, transparent, accountable; it wants not to look overly authoritarian. It even invites interpretation: to some, American Apparel looks cheeky, while American Airlines looks sober. It is clear, readable, and above all neutral. As one of the designers interviewed put it: "Most people use it because it is ubiquitous. It's like going to McDonald's instead of thinking about food because it's there. It's on every street corner so let's eat crap because it's on the corner." It is beautiful and timeless. It is not damaging or dangerous. It is the "perfume of the city." It is the typeface of capitalism. It is the typeface of socialism. ABH: anything but Helvetica. It is simple, clean, and boring. It is a global monster. It is modern.

> Helvetica is to typeface as Toblerone is to chocolate. (Müller, *Helvetica*)

No one except a Swiss, or the friends of Swiss or Switzerland, would know that it has anything to do with Swissness. It was designed by Eduard Hoffman, the manager of Hass Type Foundry in Münchenstein, Switzerland, who had the idea, and Max Miedinger, a graphic designer turned traveling salesman, who did the drawings. Hoffman wanted to make modern the typeface Akzidenz Grotesk, a traditional nineteenth-century German sans serif, and called the result Die Neue Haas Grotesk. But Haas was owned by D. Stempel AG in Frankfurt am Main, whose marketing director feared that such a name would not fare well in the United States. He suggested instead the name "Helvetia." Hoffman said one couldn't name a typeface after a country, since "Helvetia" is the Latin name for Switzerland, so everyone agreed on "Helvetica," "the Swiss typeface." The name seemed perfect, since Swiss typography in the 1950s was identical with the international typographic style. The world needed a rational typeface that could create order after World War II and itself remain neutral. Once it was introduced, there was nothing like it. There has been nothing like it since. Stempel was bought by Linotype in Bad Homburg, Germany, which still owns Helvetica. The font closest to Helvetica available on my PC is a clone called "Ariel."

> Some years ago a young intern in our New York office, when looking at an old map where Switzerland was named Helvetia, said, "Fancy naming a country after a typeface." (Müller, *Helvetica*)

Epilogue

> The influence of Swiss designers was most strongly felt in the United States. It was heralded by Herbert Matter's arrival in New York in 1935. After his work on the Swiss pavilion at the World's Fair in 1939, Matter had become prominent as a photographer and designer. His house styles for the New Haven Railroad and Knoll furniture in the 1950s are now in the canon of graphic design history. In 1952 he began teaching at Yale. His "Swissness" went unremarked, and his photomontages were too early to be included in the exhibition of "Recent Swiss Posters" held at the Museum of Modern Art in New York in 1951. (Hollis, *Swiss Graphic Design*)

If Swissness is a secret, it is an open one. Helvetica is everywhere, but no one knows it is Swiss. It is the opposite of Swissness as a series of stereotypes: the Matterhorn, the chalet, the St. Bernard. If it is shameful, it is because even "the Swiss typeface" is owned by a German company. That the name is in Latin keeps it a secret. Helvetica comes out by saying not "I'm Swiss" but, in spite of being Swiss, "I'm ubiquitous." Even if it also means sameness, dullness, invisibility, as long as it creates order and conveys information, who cares?

Few topics place Zürich in the same company as Amsterdam, Berlin, New York, and London, the cities featured by the documentary as places to have conversations with designers. Switzerland is the first country to have its passport professionally designed. The Swiss Railway Station Clock, designed in 1955, has replaced the cuckoo clock, at least on the wrists of those who venture into the Schweizer Heimatwerk, which has been selling contemporary Swiss handicrafts since 1930. The "Swiss style" in graphic design has its origins in the 1920s and its heyday in the 1960s, when it reaches its apogee as the international style. It replaces Expressionism with Neue Sachlichkeit. It says, "Out with symmetry, ornamentation and drawing"; it says, "In with white space, plain letter forms, and photography." It is the graphic designer who gives visual character to modern life; he (mostly) is neither printer nor painter, nor simply commercial artist. He is anonymous rather than individualistic; he is mathematical rather than intuitive;

he organizes essential information without provoking emotional sensations. He relies on strength and economy, the square and the circle, typefaces made by machine, such as Helvetica, placed at an angle, interrupting spatial voids. He uses letters in lower case, for simplicity and because their forms are richer than those of capitals. Besides, German nouns are capitalized, and thus it becomes a radical act.

Design organizes, simplifies, creates order. It relies on an austere geometry for clarity and legibility. It is self-explanatory. It unites art and industry in the name of public service, that is, getting people on and off trains, in and out of airports, to the drugs they might need, to the concerts they might want to attend. There is the Geigy (as in the pharmaceutical) style, which comes out of Basel and relies more on the typeface Univers, and the style that comes out of Zürich, insisting on Helvetica, more constructivist and seemingly colder. Every style moves, eventually, from originality to orthodoxy.

"Yet the graphic design and typography developed in Switzerland in the middle years of the twentieth century was a template used and adapted by designers for fifty years. Its origin was pan-European. Its consummation and achievements were Swiss. But now it is justly described as an International Style" (Hollis, *Swiss Graphic Design*). It is everywhere, and nowhere, which is why, occasionally, it needs to come out Swiss, and once again find itself on a map.

Bibliography

General

Works Consulted

Altwegg, Jürg. *Ach, du liebe Schweiz: Essay zur Lage der Nation*. Zürich: Nagel und Kimche, 2002.

Bernard, Paul. *Rush to the Alps: The Evolution of Vacationing in Switzerland*. New York: Columbia University Press, 1978.

Blocher, Andreas. *Die Eigenart der Zürcher Auswanderer nach Amerika 1734–1744*. Zürich: Atlantis, 1976.

Botton, Alain de. *The Consolations of Philosophy*. New York: Vintage International, 2000.

Brendon, Piers. *Thomas Cook: 150 Years of Popular Tourism*. London: Secker & Warburg, 1991.

Gavranic, Cynthia, ed. *Paradies Schweiz/Paradise Switzerland*. Zürich: Poster Collection, Museum für Gestaltung, 2010.

Hendricks, Monique. *Leaving Europe: A Cross-Cultural Memoir*. Bloomington, IN: Xlibris, 2006.

Hürlimann, Thomas. *Himmelsöhi, hilf! Über die Schweiz und andere Nester*. Zürich: Ammann, 2002.

Kreis, Georg. *Schweizer Erinnerungsorte: Aus dem Speicher der Swissness*. Zürich: Neue Zürcher Zeitung, 2010.

Matt, Peter von. *Das Kalb vor der Gotthardpost: Zur Literatur und Politik der Schweiz*. Munich: Hanser, 2012.

Pollack, Eileen. *Woman Walking Ahead: In Search of Catherine Weldon and Sitting Bull*. Albuquerque: University of New Mexico Press, 2002.

Rodriguez, Richard. *Days of Obligation: An Argument with My Mexican Father*. New York: Viking, 1992.

Bibliography

——. *Hunger of Memory: The Education of Richard Rodriguez.* 1982. Reprint, New York: Bantam, 1983.

Sandoz, Marie. *Old Jules.* 1935. Reprint, Lincoln: University of Nebraska Press, 2005.

Sante, Luc. *The Factory of Facts.* New York: Pantheon, 1998.

Schwanitz, Dietrich, and Angela Denzel. *Schweiz: Liebesprobe jenseits der Baumgrenze: Kleine Philosophie der Passionen.* Munich: DTV, 2000.

Steinberg, Jonathan. *Why Switzerland?* 1976. Reprint, Cambridge: Cambridge University Press, 1996.

Stoppard, Tom. *Travesties.* London: Faber & Faber, 1975.

Vavrin, Olivia. *Surviving New Zealand: Ups and Downs of a Swiss Miss.* Victoria, BC: Trafford, 2006.

Wyss, Laure. *Briefe nach Feuerland: Wahrnehmungen zur Schweiz in Europa.* Zürich: Limmat, 1997.

Zimmer, Oliver. *A Contested Nation: History, Memory, and Nationalism in Switzerland, 1761–1891.* Cambridge: Cambridge University Press, 2003.

Prologue

Works Cited

Anderson, Benedict. *Imagined Communities.* London: Verso, 1991.

Hughes, Christopher. *Switzerland.* Nations of the Modern World. New York: Praeger, 1974.

Stein, Gertrude. *Paris France.* 1940. Reprint, New York: Liveright, 1970.

Work Consulted

Brodbeck, Gabriele. "New Look for the Swiss Army." *Swiss Review: The Magazine of the Swiss Abroad* (April 2004): 14–15.

Chocolate

Works Cited

Chocosuisse. *Chocology: The Swiss Chocolate Industry, Past and Present.* Berne: Chocosuisse, Association of Swiss Chocolate Manufacturers, 2001.

Esquivel, Laura. *Like Water for Chocolate: A Novel in Monthly Installments with*

Bibliography

Recipes, Romances, and Home Remedies. Translated by Carol and Thomas
Christenson. New York: Anchor, 1989.

González, Jovita. *Life along the Border: A Landmark Tejana Thesis.* Edited by Maria
Eugenia Cotera. College Station: Texas A&M University Press, 2006.

Harris, Joanne. *Chocolat: A Novel.* New York: Penguin, 1999.

Off, Carol. *Bitter Chocolate: Investigating the Dark Side of the World's Most Seductive Sweet.* Toronto: Vintage, 2006.

Terrio, Susan J. *Crafting the Culture and History of French Chocolate.* Berkeley:
University of California Press, 2000.

Works Consulted

"Chocolate Packaging Comes under Fire." *NZZ Online,* April 15, 2006. Accessed
July 4, 2007. http://www.nzz.ch/2006/04/15/eng/article6630993.print.html.

Coe, Sophie D. and Michael D. Coe. *The True History of Chocolate.* London:
Thames & Hudson, 1996.

Doutre-Rousel, Chloé. *The Chocolate Connoisseur: For Everyone with a Passion for
Chocolate.* New York: Penguin, 2005.

Pennington, Hugh. "In the Chocolate." *London Review of Books,* August 2, 2007, 29.

Wey, Alain. "The Story of Swiss Chocolate." *Swiss Review: The Magazine of the
Swiss Abroad* (December 2006): 8–10.

Young, Gordon. "Chocolate: Food of the Gods." *National Geographic* 166 (November
1984): 665–87.

Gold

Works Cited

Alphen, Ernst van. "Deadly Historians: Boltanski's Intervention in Holocaust
Historiography." In *Visual Culture and the Holocaust,* edited by Barbie Zelizer.
New Brunswick, NJ: Rutgers University Press, 2000.

Bardach, Ann Louise. "Edgar's List: Edgar Bronfman Sr.'s Hunt for Nazi Gold."
Vanity Fair, March 1997, 254–69.

Braillard, Philipe. *Switzerland and the Crisis of Dormant Assets and Nazi Gold.*
Translated by Denys Crapon de Caprona and André Lötter. London: Kegan
Paul, 2000.

Carlyle, Thomas. *Sartor Resartus.* Edited by Archibald MacMechan. 1896. Reprint,
Boston: Atheneum Press, 1902.

Bibliography

Erdman, Paul. *The Swiss Account: A Novel.* New York: Tom Doherty Associates, 1992.

Faith, Nicholas. *Safety in Numbers: The Mysterious World of Swiss Banking.* London: Hamish Hamilton, 1982.

Gumpert, Lynn. *Christian Boltanski.* Translated by Francis Cowper. Paris: Flammarion, 1994.

Semin, Didier, Tamar Garb, and Donald Kuspit. *Christian Boltanski.* London: Phaidon, 1997.

Smith, Arthur L. *Hitler's Gold: The Story of the Nazi War Loot.* New York: Oxford University Press, 1989.

Vilar, Pierre. *A History of Gold and Money, 1450–1920.* Translated by Judith White. 1969. Reprint, London: New Left Books, 1976.

Vilches, Elvira. *New World Gold: Cultural Anxiety and Monetary Disorder in Early Modern Spain.* Chicago: University of Chicago Press, 2010.

Vincent, Isabel. *Hitler's Silent Partners: Swiss Banks, Nazi Gold, and the Pursuit of Justice.* New York: Morrow, 1997.

Wilson, Simon. "Christian Boltanski." Accessed September 7, 2006. hppt://www.tate.org.uk/servlet/CollectionDisplays?roomid=3232.

Ziegler, Jean. *The Swiss, the Gold, and the Dead: How Swiss Bankers Helped Finance the Nazi War Machine.* Translated by John Brownjohn. New York: Harcourt Brace, 1998.

Works Consulted

Beker, Avi. "Why Was Switzerland Singled Out? A Case of Belated Justice." In *The Plunder of Jewish Property during the Holocaust: Confronting European History*, edited by Avi Beker. New York: New York University Press, 2001.

Blood Money: Switzerland's Nazi Gold. DVD. Directed by Stephen Crisman. New York: New Video Group, 2002.

Boltanski, Christian, and Catherine Grenier. *The Possible Life of Christian Boltanski.* Translated by Marc Lowenthal. Boston: MFA Publications, 2009.

Cowell, Alan. "Switzerland's Wartime Blood Money." *Foreign Policy* 107 (Summer 1997): 132–44.

Kimmelman, Michael. "Art View; Dead Reckoning: From Obituary to Art." *New York Times,* January 13, 1991.

LeBor, Adam. *Hitler's Secret Bankers: The Myth of Swiss Neutrality during the Holocaust.* 1997. Reprint, Toronto: Citadel, 1999.

Muschg, Adolf. *Wenn Auschwitz in der Schweiz liegt.* Frankfurt am Main: Suhrkamp, 1997.

Nazi Gold. DVD. Directed by Christopher Olgiati. Arlington, VA: PBS Video, 1997.

Picard, Jacques. *Die Schweiz und die Juden, 1933–1945.* Zürich: Chronos, 1994.

Tracking Nazi Gold. DVD. Directed by Jonathan Martin. New York: New Video, 2006.

Vicker, Ray. *Those Swiss Money Men.* New York: Charles Scribner's, 1973.

Zabludoff, Sidney. *Movements of Gold: Uncovering the Trail.* Policy Study No. 10. Jerusalem: Institute of the World Jewish Congress, 1997.

Heimweh, or Homesickness

Works Cited

Gallop, Jane. *Reading Lacan.* Ithaca, NY: Cornell University Press, 1985.

Hofer, Johannes. "Medical Dissertation on Nostalgia by Johannes Hofer, 1688." Translated by Carolyn Kiser Anspach. *Bulletin of the Institute of the History of Medicine* 7 (1934): 379–91.

Hoffman, Eva. *Lost in Translation: A Life in a New Language.* New York: Penguin, 1989.

Kincaid, Jamaica. *Lucy.* New York: Farrar, Straus & Giroux, 1990.

Kundera, Milan. *The Book of Laughter and Forgetting.* Translated by Michael Henry Heim. 1978. Reprint, New York: Penguin, 1980.

Rütschi, Elisabeth. "Zürcherinnen, denen es schwer fällt, Neuyorkerinnen zu werden." *Zürcher Woche*, August, 23, 1957, 10.

Woolf, Virginia. *To the Lighthouse.* New York: Harcourt, Brace & World, 1927.

Works Consulted

Aciman, André. *False Papers: Essays on Exile and Memory.* New York: Picador, 2000.

———, ed. *Letters of Transit: Reflections on Exile, Identity, Language, and Loss.* New York: New Press, 1999.

Bach, Jonathan. "'The Taste Remains': Consumption, (N)ostalgia, and the Production of East Germany." *Public Culture* 3 (2002): 545–56.

Berdahl, Daphne. "'(N)Ostalgia' for the Present: Memory, Longing, and East German Things." *Ethnos* 64 (1999): 192–211.

Bisky, Jens. "Zonensucht. Über die neue Ostalgie." *Merkur* 58 (2004): 117–27.

Blum, Martin. "Remaking the East German Past: *Ostalgie*, Identity, and Material Culture." *Journal of Popular Culture* 34 (2000): 229–53.

Boyer, Dominic. "*Ostalgie* and the Politics of the Future in Eastern Germany." *Public Culture* 18 (2006): 361–81.

Boym, Svetlana. *The Future of Nostalgia.* New York: Basic Books, 2001.

Bibliography

Chase, Malcolm, and Christopher Shaw, eds. *The Imagined Past: History and Nostalgia.* Manchester: Manchester University Press, 1989.

Cooke, Paul, "Performing 'Ostalgie': Leander Haussmann's *Sonnenallee.*" *German Life and Letters* 56 (2003): 156–67.

Davis, Fred. *Yearning for Yesterday: A Sociology of Nostalgia.* New York: Free Press, 1979.

Finger, Anke. "Hello Willy, Good Bye Lenin! Transitions of an East German Family." *South Central Review* 22 (2005): 39–58.

Huffer, Lynne. *Maternal Pasts, Feminist Futures: Nostalgia, Ethics, and the Question of Difference.* Palo Alto, CA: Stanford University Press, 1998.

Knopp, Lisa. *The Nature of Home: A Lexicon and Essays.* Lincoln: University of Nebraska Press, 2002.

Pickering, Jean, and Suzanne Kehde, eds. *Narratives of Nostalgia, Gender, and Nationalism.* New York: New York University Press, 1997.

Ritivoi, Andreea Deciu. *Yesterday's Self: Nostalgia and the Immigrant Identity.* Lanham, MD: Rowman & Littlefield, 2003.

Rosen, George. "Nostalgia: A 'Forgotten' Psychological Disorder." *Psychological Medicine* 5 (1975): 340–54.

Roth, Michael. "Dying of the Past: Medical Studies of Nostalgia in 19th Century France." *History and Memory* 3 (1991): 5–29.

———. "Returning to Nostalgia." In *Home and Its Dislocations in Nineteenth Century France,* edited by Suzanne Nash. Albany: SUNY Press, 1993.

———. "The Time of Nostalgia: Medicine, History, and Normality in Nineteenth Century France." *Time and Society* 1 (1992): 271–86.

Starobinski, Jean. "The Idea of Nostalgia." *Diogenes* 54 (1996): 81–103.

Stewart, Susan. *On Longing: Narratives of the Miniature, the Gigantic, the Souvenir, the Collection.* Durham, NC: Duke University Press, 1993.

———. "Proust's Turn from Nostalgia." *Raritan* 19 (1999): 77–94.

Sugg, Katherine. "'I Would Rather Be Dead': Nostalgia and Narrative in Jamaica Kincaid's *Lucy.*" *Narrative* 10 (2002): 156–73.

The Alp(s)

Works Cited

Beattie, Andrea. *The Alps: A Cultural History.* Oxford: Oxford University Press, 2006.

Dickinson, Emily. *The Complete Poems of Emily Dickinson.* Edited by Thomas H. Johnson. Boston: Little, Brown, 1957.

Bibliography

Dilwale Dulhania Le Jayenge. Directed by Aditya Chopra. Mumbai: Yash Raj Films Home Entertainment, 2005.

Mitchie, Helen. "Victorian Honeymoons: Sexual Reorientations and the 'Sights' of Europe." *Victorian Studies* 43 (2001): 229–51.

Paris Exhibition reproduced from the official photographs, taken under the supervision of the French government for permanent preservation in the National Archives. . . . New York: Peale (R.S.) Co., 1900.

Sangam. DVD. Directed by Raj Kapoor. London: Yash Raj Films Home Entertainment, 2000.

Stephen, Leslie. *The Playground of Europe*. London: Longmans, Green, 1907.

———. *Selected Letters*. Edited by John W. Bicknell. Columbus: Ohio State University Press, 1996.

Tyrnauer, Matt. "Architecture in the Age of Gehry." *Vanity Fair*, August 2010, 156–67.

Woolf, Virginia. *The Letters of Virginia Woolf*. Vol. 1, *1888–1912*. Edited by Nigel Nicolson. London: Hogarth, 1975.

———. *The Letters of Virginia Woolf*. Vol. 3, *1923–1928*. Edited by Nigel Nicolson and Joanne Trautmann. New York: Harcourt Brace Jovanovich, 1977.

Works Consulted

Annan, Noel. *Leslie Stephen: The Godless Victorian*. Chicago: University of Chicago Press, 1984.

Baldwin, James. *Notes of a Native Son*. 1955. Reprint, Boston: Beacon, 1984.

Barton, Susan. *Healthy Living in the Alps: The Origins of Winter Tourism in Switzerland, 1860–1914*. Manchester: Manchester University Press, 2008.

Bezzola, Tobia, and Cathérine Hug, eds. *In den Alpen*. Zürich: Kunsthaus, 2006.

Fleming, Fergus. *Killing Dragons: The Conquest of the Alps*. London: Granta, 2000.

Graf, Felix, and Eberhard Wolff, eds. *Zauberberge: Die Schweiz als Kraftraum und Sanatorium*. Baden: hier+jetzt, 2010.

Haller, Albrecht von. *Die Alpen*. 1729. Berlin: Akademie Verlag, 1959.

Hollis, Catherine W. *Leslie Stephen as Mountaineer: "Where Does the Mont Blanc End, and Where Do I begin?"* London: Cecil Woolf, 2010.

Kimmelman, Michael. "The Ascension of Peter Zumthor." *New York Times Magazine*, March 13, 2011, 32.

Klucker, Christian. *Adventures of an Alpine Guide*. Translated by Erwin and Pleasaunce von Gaisberg. London: John Murray, 1932.

Le Blond, Aubrey. *The Story of an Alpine Winter*. London: George Bell and Sons, 1907.

Bibliography

Loetscher, Hugo. *Lesen statt klettern: Aufsätze zur literarischen Schweiz.* Zürich: Diogenes, 2003.

Lunn, Arnold. *The Swiss and Their Mountains: A Study of the Influence of Mountains on Man.* London: Allen and Unwin, 1963.

———. *Switzerland and the English.* London: Eyre & Spottiswoode, 1944.

Mathieu, Jon. *History of the Alps, 1500–1900: Environment, Development, and Society.* Translated by Matthew Vester. Morgantown: University of West Virginia Press, 2009.

Mühl, Melanie. *Menschen am Berg: Geschichten vom Leben ganz oben.* München: Nagel und Kimche, 2010.

Netting, Robert. *Balancing on an Alp: Ecological Change and Continuity in a Swiss Mountain Community.* Cambridge: Cambridge University Press, 1981.

Ring, Jim. *How the English Made the Alps.* London: John Murray, 2000.

Schneider, Alexandra. *Bollywood: Das Indische Kino und die Schweiz.* Zürich: Museum für Gestaltung, 2002.

Stephen, Leslie. *Men, Books, and Mountains.* Edited by S. O. A. Ullman. Minneapolis: University of Minnesota Press, 1956.

———. *Some Early Impressions.* London: Hogarth, 1924.

Wyder, Margrit. *Kräuter Kröpfe Höhenkuren: Die Alpen in der Medizin—Die Medizin in den Alpen: Texte aus zehn Jahrhunderten.* Zürich: Neue Zürcher Zeitung, 2003.

Davos, or "How the English Invented the Alps"

Works Cited

Benson, E. F. *The Relentless City.* London: Heinemann, 1903.

Davos as Health Resort: A Handbook. Davos: Davos Printing Company, 1906.

Harman, Claire. *Robert Louis Stevenson: A Biography.* New York: HarperCollins, 2005.

Harraden, Beatrice. *Ships That Pass in the Night.* New York: Putnam, 1894.

Lockett, W.G. *Robert Louis Stevenson at Davos.* London: Hurst & Blackett, 1934.

[MacMorland, Mrs. Elizabeth McDonald]. *Davos-Platz: A New Alpine Resort for Sick and Sound in Summer and Winter by One Who Knows It Well.* London: Edward Stanford, 1878.

The Memoirs of John Addington Symonds: The Secret Homosexual Life of a Leading Nineteenth Century Man of Letters. Edited by Phyllis Grosskurth. Chicago: University of Chicago Press, 1984.

Osbourne, Lloyd. *An Intimate Portrait of R.L.S.* New York: Charles Scribner's Sons, 1924.

Bibliography

Selected Letters of Leslie Stephen. Vol. 2, *1882–1904.* Edited by John W. Bicknell. Columbus: University of Ohio Press, 1996.

Ships That Pass in the Night. Directed by Percy Nash. London: National Film and TV Archive, 1921.

Stephen, Leslie. *The Playground of Europe.* London: Longmans, Green, 1907.

Stevenson, Robert Louis. *Essays of Travel.* London: Chatto & Windus, 1905.

———. *Memories and Portraits.* New York: Charles Scribner's Sons, 1915.

Symonds, John Addington. "Davos English Library: A Letter from John Addington Symonds, February 4, 1886." *Davos Courier,* November 2, 1923.

Symonds, John Addington, and Margaret Symonds. *Our Life in the Swiss Highlands.* 1907. Reprint, Amsterdam: Fredonia Books, 2002.

Symonds, Margaret. *Out of the Past.* New York: Charles Scribner's Sons, 1925.

Weber, J. *Davos, with 20 illustrations by J. Weber.* Illustrated Europe 21. Zürich: Orell Füssli, ca. 1880.

Works Consulted

"Davos English Library." *Davos Courier,* November 29, 1888–April 3, 1897.

Fedin, Konstantin. *Sanatorium Arktur.* Translated by Olga Shartse. 1940. Reprint, Moscow: Foreign Languages Publishing House, 1958.

Ferdman, J. *Der Aufstieg von Davos.* Davos: Davoser Revue, 1990.

Frey-Hauser, Marianne. "Herbsüsse Davoser Kur-Romanze—'British Style.'" *Davoser Revue* 71 (1996): 11–14.

Furse, Dame Katherine. *Hearts and Pomegranates: The Story of Forty-Five Years, 1875–1920.* London: Peter Davies, 1940.

Grosskurth, Phyllis. *The Woeful Victorian: A Biography of John Addington Symonds.* New York: Holt, Rinehart, Winston, 1964.

Gürke, Volker. *Davos Entdecken: Wege zu einem ungewöhnlichen Ort.* Davos: Davoser Revue, 1997.

Halter, Ernst, ed. *Davos: Profil eines Phänomens.* Zürich: Offizin, 1994.

Hauri, Johannes. *Bilder aus dem Davoser Kurleben von einem alten Kurgaste.* Davos: Hugo Richter; Chur: F. Schuler, 1886.

Holdsworth, Annie E. [Mrs. Lee-Hamilton]. *The Valley of the Great Shadow.* Chicago: Herbert Stone, 1900.

Hörner, Unda. *Hoch Oben in der Guten Luft: Die Literarische Bohème in Davos.* Berlin: Edition Ebersbach, 2005.

Lockett, W. G. *The British at Davos.* Davos: Public Interests Association, 1920.

———. "An English-Davos Portrait Gallery: VI. John Addington Symonds." *Davoser Revue,* August 15, 1929, 308–12.

Bibliography

———. "An English-Davos Portrait Gallery: VII. Robert Louis Stevenson." *Davoser Revue*, September 15, 1929, 335–39.

———. "An English-Davos Portrait Gallery: VIII. Stevenson and Symonds: A Comparison and a Contrast." *Davoser Revue*, October 15, 1929, 8–14.

———. "An English-Davos Portrait Gallery: IX. Mrs. R. L. Stevenson." *Davoser Revue*, November 15, 1929, 49–54.

Mann, Thomas. *The Magic Mountain.* Translated by John E. Woods. 1924. Reprint, New York: Vintage: 1995.

Marti, Hugo. *Das Haus Am Hoff und Davoser Stundenbuch.* Zürich: Ex Libris, 1981.

Nelson, Timothy. "Die Bibliothek Davos—25 Jahre im 'Schweizerhaus.'" *Davoser Revue* 85 (2010): 8–11.

Powys, Llewelyn. *Swiss Essays.* London: John Lane, 1947.

Schaffer, Fritz. "Die Engländer in Davos." *Davoser Revue* 59, no. 1 (1984): 205–16.

———. "Die Engländer in Davos (2. Fortsetzung)." *Davoser Revue* 60, no. 2 (1985): 101–9.

———. "Die Engländer in Davos (3. Fortsetzung)." *Davoser Revue* 60, no. 3 (1985): 160–65.

———. "Die Engländer in Davos (4. Fortsetzung)." *Davoser Revue* 60, no. 4 (1985): 221–28.

Schmid, Christian. "Wie Davos zu einem jüdischen Friedhof kam." *Davoser Revue* 70 (1995): 11–22.

Schmid, Yvonne. "'Davos-Platz: A New Alpine Resort for Sick and Sound': Der Einfluss der Britischen Kurgäste auf die Fremdenverkehrsentwicklung in Davos während der Zeit von 1875–1914." *Lizentiatsarbeit*, Phil I Universität Zürich, 1998.

Wise, A. Tucker. *Alpine Winter in Its Medical Aspects.* London: J. & A. Churchill, 1885.

Wottreng, Willi. "Naturidyll im Todeshauch: Der Waldfriedhof bei Davos." *Turicum* 26 (1995): 60–67.

"Athens on the Limmat"

Works Cited

The Autobiography of Florence Kelley: Notes of Sixty Years. Edited by Kathryn Kish Sklar. Chicago: Charles H. Kerr, 1986.

Engel, Barbara Alpern. *Mothers and Daughters: Women of the Intelligentsia in Nineteenth-Century Russia.* Cambridge: Cambridge University Press, 1983.

Engel, Barbara Alpern, and Clifford N. Rosenthal, eds. and trans. *Five Sisters: Women against the Tsar.* New York: Routledge, 1975.

Bibliography

Hasler, Eveline. *Flying with Wings of Wax: The Story of Emily Kempin-Spyri.* Translated by Edna McCown. New York: Fromm International, 1993.

Herrmann-Rütschi, Elisabeth. *Die Staatsangehörigkeit der Kinder aus nationalgemischten Ehen.* Zürich: Juris-Verlag, 1949.

Horowitz, Helen Lefkowitz. *The Power and Passion of M. Carey Thomas.* Urbana: University of Illinois Press, 1994.

Koblitz, Ann Hibner. *A Convergence of Lives: Sofia Kovalevskaia: Scientist, Writer, Revolutionary.* New Brunswick, NJ: Rutgers University Press, 1993.

Meijer, J. M. *Knowledge and Revolution: The Russian Colony in Zuerich (1870–1873).* Assen, Netherlands: Van Gorcum & Co., 1965.

Schirmacher, Käthe. *Zürcher Studentinnen.* Leipzig-Zürich: Th. Schröter, 1896.

Shaw, George Bernard. *"In Good King Charles's Golden Days": A True History That Never Happened.* 1939. In *Selected Plays, with Prefaces.* New York: Dodd, Mead, 1948.

Siebel, Johanna. *Das Leben von Frau D. Marie Heim-Vögtlin, der erseten Schweizer Ärztin 1845–1916.* Zürich: Rascher, 1920.

Sklar, Kathryn Kish. *Florence Kelley and the Nation's Work: The Rise of Women's Political Culture, 1830–1900.* New Haven, CT: Yale University Press, 1995.

Works Consulted

Belser, Katharina, et al., eds. *Ebenso neu als Kühn: 120 Jahre Frauenstudium an der Universität Zürich.* Zürich: efeF-Verlag, 1988.

Chernyshevsky, Nikolai. *What Is to Be Done?* Translated by Michael R. Katz. 1863. Reprint, Ithaca, NY: Cornell University Press, 1989.

Churchill, Caryl. *Top Girls.* London: Methuen, 1982.

Johanson, Christine. *Women's Struggle for Higher Education in Russia, 1855–1900.* Kingston-Montreal: McGill-Queen's University Press, 1987.

Kovaleveskaya, Sofya. *Nihilist Girl.* Translated by Natasha Kolchevska with Mary Zirin. New York: Modern Language Association, 2001.

———. *A Russian Childhood.* Edited and translated by Beatrice Stillman. New York: Springer, 1978.

Neumann, Daniela. *Studentinnen aus dem Russischen Reich in der Schweiz, 1867–1914.* Zürich: Rohr, 1987.

Schiebinger, Londa L. *The Mind Has No Sex? Women in the Origins of Modern Science.* Cambridge, MA: Harvard University Press, 1989.

Schweizerischen Verband der Akademikerinnen, ed. *Das Frauenstudium an den Schweizer Hochschulen.* Zürich: Rascher, 1928.

Stadler-Labhart, Verena, ed. *"Das Parnass liegt nicht in den Schweizer Alpen . . .":*

Bibliography

Aspekte der Zürcher Universitätsgeschichte; Beiträge aus dem "Zürcher Taschenbuch" 1939–1988. Zürich: Rohr, 1991.

Dada in Zürich, Continued

Works Cited

Arp, Jean. *Arp on Arp: Poems, Essays, Memories.* Edited by Marcel Jean and translated by Joachim Neugroschel. New York: Viking, 1969.

Ball, Hugo. *Flight Out of Time: A Dada Diary.* Edited by John Elderfield and translated by Ann Raimes. New York: Viking, 1974.

Codrescu, Andrei. *The Posthuman Dada Guide: Tzara and Lenin Play Chess.* Princeton, NJ: Princeton University Press, 2009.

Foster, Hal. "Dada Mime." *October* 105 (2003): 166–76.

Huelsenbeck, Richard. *Memoirs of a Dada Drummer.* Edited by Hans J. Kleinschmidt and translated by Joachim Neugroschel. Berkeley: University of California Press, 1969.

Melzer, Annabelle. *Dada and Surrealist Performance.* Baltimore: Johns Hopkins University Press, 1994.

Motherwell, Robert, ed. *The Dada Painters and Poets: An Anthology.* New York: Wittenborn, 1951.

Pichon, Brigitte, and Karl Riha, eds. *Dada Zurich: A Clown's Game from Nothing.* New York: G. K. Hall, 1996.

Richter, Hans. *Dada: Art and Anti-Art.* Translated by Davis Britt. London: Thames & Hudson, 1964.

Zweig, Stefan. *The World of Yesterday: An Autobiography.* 1943. Reprint, Lincoln: University of Nebraska Press, 1964.

Works Consulted

Ball-Hennings, Emmy. *Betrunken taumeln alle Litfasssäulen: Frühe Texte und autobiographische Schriften 1913–1922.* Edited by Bernhard Merkelbach. Hannover: Postskriptum, 1990.

———. *Ruf und Echo: Mein Leben mit Hugo Ball.* Einsiedeln: Benziger, 1953.

Bollinger, Hans, Guido Magnaguagno, and Raimund Meyer. *Dada in Zürich.* Zürich: Arche, 1985.

Cabaret Voltaire Dada Zürich: Ein Eingriff von Rossetti + Wyss. Zürich: Institut für Geschichte und Theorie der Architecktur, Eidgenössische Technische Hochschule, 2004.

Bibliography

Dickerman, Leah, ed. *Dada: Zurich, Berlin, Hannover, Cologne, New York, Paris.* Washington, DC: National Gallery of Art, 2005.

Dickerman, Leah, ed., with Matthew S. Witkovsky. *The Dada Seminars.* Washington, DC: National Gallery of Art, 2005.

Green, Martin. *Mountain of Truth: The Counterculture Begins; Ascona, 1900–1920.* Medford, MA: Tufts University Press, 1986.

Hasler, Eveline. *Und werde immer Ihr Freund sein: Hermann Hesse, Emmy Hennings, und Hugo Ball.* München: Nagel und Kimche, 2010.

Henderson-Affolter, Leni. "Die Dame auf der neuen Fünfzigernote." *Davoser Revue* 71 (1996): 31–34.

Lanchner, Carolyn. *Sophie Taeuber-Arp.* New York: Museum of Modern Art, 1981.

Meyer, Raimund, et al. *Dada Global.* Zürich: Limmat Verlag, 1994.

Sandquist, Tom. *Dada East: The Romanians of the Cabaret Voltaire.* Cambridge, MA: MIT Press, 2006.

Schifferli, Peter, ed. *Als Dada Begann: Bildchronik und Erinnerungen der Gründer.* Zürich: Arche, 1957.

Tzara, Tristan. *Seven Dada Manifestoes and Lampestries.* Translated by Barbara Wright. London: Calder Publications, 1992.

Freiestrasse 103, Zürich

Works Cited

Botton, Alain de. "The Discreet Charm of the Zurich Bourgeoisie." In *The Best American Travel Writing 2006*, edited by Tim Cahill. New York: Mariner, 2006.

Brändli, Sebastian. *Hottingen: Von der ländlichen Streusiedlung zum urbanen Stadtquartier.* Zürich: Quartierverein, 2004.

Keller, Gottfried. *Die Leute von Seldwyla.* 1874. Reprint, Münich: Goldman, 1986.

White, Edmund. *The Flâneur: A Stroll through the Paradoxes of Paris.* New York: Bloomsbury, 2001.

Works Consulted

Craig, Gordon. *The Triumph of Liberalism: Zurich in the Golden Age, 1830–1869.* New York: Scribners, 1989.

Orelli, Susanne. *Die Alkoholfreien Wirtschaften des Zürcher Frauenvereins.* Zürich: Berichthaus, 1909.

Ulrich, Conrad. *Der Lesezirkel Hottingen.* Zürich: Berichthaus, 1981.

Bibliography

Witzig, Heidi. *Polenta und Paradeplatz: Regionaler Alltagsleben auf dem Weg zur modernen Schweiz*. Zürich: Chronos, 2000.

Basel

Works Consulted

Bouvier, Nicolas, Gordon Craig, and Lionel Gossman. *Geneva Zurich Basel: History, Culture, and National Identity*. Princeton, NJ: Princeton University Press, 1994.
Gossman, Lionel. *Basel in the Age of Burckhardt*. Chicago: University of Chicago Press, 2000.

Nueva Helvetia, California (1839)

Works Cited

Allende, Isabel. *Daughter of Fortune*. Translated by Margaret Sayers Peden. New York: HarperCollins, 1999.
Bryant, Edwin. *What I Saw in California*. 1848. Reprint, Lincoln: University of Nebraska Press, 1985.
Cendrars, Blaise. *Gold: Being the Marvelous History of General John Augustus Sutter*. Translated by Nina Rootes. 1925. Reprint, New York: Marlow, 1982.
Duden, Gottfried. *Bericht über die Reise nach den westlichen Staaten Nordamerika's und einen merhjährigen Aufenthalt am Missouri (in den Jahren 1824, 25, 26 und 1827), in Bezug auf Auswanderung und Übervölkerung, oder, Das Leben im Innern der vereinigten Staaten und dessen Bedeutung für die häusliche und politische Lage der Europäer*. Elberfeld, Germany: S. Lucas, 1829.
Hurtado, Albert L. *John Sutter: A Life on the North American Frontier*. Norman: Oklahoma University Press, 2006.
Zollinger, James Peter. *Sutter: The Man and His Empire*. New York: Oxford University Press, 1939.

Works Consulted

Abbott, John C. Abbott, ed. *New Worlds to Seek: Pioneer Heinrich Lienhard in Switzerland and America, 1824–1846*. Translated by Raymond J. Spahn. Carbondale: Southern Illinois University Press, 2000.

Bibliography

Anderson, Bill, and Penny Anderson, eds. *Dogtown Territorial Quarterly*: Special Sutter's Fort Issue 19 (1994).

Arx, Caesar von. *Die Geschichte vom General Johann August Suter: Schauspiel.* Zürich: Oprecht, 1947.

Bachmann, Bernard R. *General J. A. Sutter: Ein Leben auf der Flucht nach vorn.* Zürich: Neue Zürcher Zeitung, 2005.

Grueningen, John Paul von, ed. *The Swiss in the United States.* Madison, WI: Swiss-American Historical Society, 1940.

Lienhard, Heinrich. *From St. Louis to Sutter's Fort, 1846.* Translated by Erwin G. and Elisabeth K. Gudde. Norman: University of Oklahoma Press, 1961.

Owens, Kenneth N., ed. *John Sutter and a Wider West.* Lincoln: University of Nebraska Press, 1994.

Sutter, John A., Jr. *The Sutter Family and the Origins of Gold-Rush Sacramento.* Edited by Allan R. Ottley. 1947. Reprint, Norman: University of Oklahoma Press, 2002.

Tucker, Michael S. *Audio Tour Transcript*: Sacramento, CA: Sutter's Fort State Historic Park, 1992.

Van Sicklen, Helen Putnam, ed. *New Helvetia Diary: A record of events kept by John A. Sutter and his clerks at New Helvetia, California, from September 9, 1845, to May 25, 1848.* San Francisco: Grabhorn Press, 1939.

Wilbur, Marguerite Eyer Wilbur, ed. and trans. *A Pioneer at Sutter's Fort, 1846–1850: The Adventures of Heinrich Lienhard.* Los Angeles: Calafía Society, 1941.

Zweig, Stefan. *Decisive Moments in History: Twelve Historical Miniatures.* Translated by Lowell A. Bangerter. Riverside, CA: Ariadne Press, 1999.

New Glarus, Wisconsin (1845)

Works Cited

Comité des glarnerischen Auswanderungsvereins. *Der glarnerische Auswanderungs-Verein und die Colonie Neu-Glarus: Hauptbericht des Auswanderungscomité.* Glarus: J. Vogel, 1847.

Hoelscher, Steven D. *Heritage on Stage: The Invention of Ethnic Place in America's Little Switzerland.* Madison: University of Wisconsin Press, 1998.

Kubly, Herbert. *An American in Italy.* New York: Simon & Schuster, 1955.

———. *At Large.* Forward by Kay Boyle. London: Victor Collancz, 1963.

———. *Native's Return: An American of Swiss Descent Unmasks an Enigmatic Land and People.* New York: Stein and Day, 1981.

Bibliography

————. *Varieties of Love*. 1958. Reprint, New York: Belmont 1960.

Luchsinger, John. "The Planting of the Swiss Colony at New Glarus, Wis." In *Collections of the State Historical Society of Wisconsin*, vol. 12, 335–82. Madison, WI: Democrat Printing Company, State Printer, 1892.

Schelbert, Leo, ed. *New Glarus 1845–1970: The Making of a Swiss American Town*. Glarus: Kommissionsverlag Tschudi, 1970.

Trillin, Calvin. "U.S. Journal: New Glarus, Wis." *New Yorker*, January 20, 1975, 48–60.

Works Consulted

Grossenbacher, Paul. "Looking Back: From Burgdorf, Canton Bern, to New Glarus, Wisconsin: Autobiographical Sketch of a Twentieth Century Swiss Immigrant." *Swiss American Historical Review* 25 (1989): 5–49.

Kubly, Herbert. "An American Finds America." *Common Ground* 3 (1943): 49–56.

————. *Switzerland*. New York: Time-Life Books, 1964.

————. *The Whistling Zone*. New York: Simon &Schuster, 1963

Luchsinger, John. "The Swiss Colony of New Glarus." In *Collections of the State Historical Society of Wisconsin*, vol. 8, 411–39. Madison, WI: David Atwood, State Printer, 1879.

Morrell, Jemima. *Miss Jemima's Swiss Journal: The First Conducted Tour of Switzerland*. 1863. Reprint, London: Putnam, 1963.

Nicholas, William. "Deep in the Heart of 'Swissconsin.'" *National Geographic* 91, no. 6. (June 1947): 781–800.

Stone, Matthew. "Back in Time Book Review." *Global Postmark Travel Magazine*, December 3, 2010. Accessed January 18, 2011. http://www.globalpostmark .com/2010/12/american_in_italy/.

Tschudy, Millard. *New Glarus, Wisconsin: Mirror of Switzerland 1845–1995*. Monroe, WI: Monroe Evening Times, 1965.

Wild, Joshua. *The Story of Myself*. Translated by Maria Kundert. 1935. Accessed September 19, 2013. http://digicoll.library.wisc.edu/cgi-bin/WI/WI-idx?type= div&did=WI.NGWildStory.i0001&isize=M.

Swiss Family Robinson (1812)

Works Cited

Blackwell, Jeanine. "An Island of Her Own: Heroines of the German Robinsonade from 1720 to 1800." *German Quarterly* 58 (1985): 5–26.

Bibliography

Coetzee, J. M. *Foe*. New York: Penguin, 1987.

Cooper, Fiona. *Not the Swiss Family Robinson*. London: Virago, 1991.

Edgeworth, Maria. *Practical Education*. London: J. Johnson, 1798.

Forster, E. M. *Aspects of the Novel*. New York: Harcourt Brace Jovanovich, 1927.

Joyce, James. *Occasional, Critical, and Political Writing*. Edited by Kevin Barry. New York: Oxford University Press, 2008.

King, Russell. "Geography, Islands, and Migration in an Era of Global Mobility." *Island Studies Journal* 4 (2009): 53–84.

Miller, J. Hillis. "Reading: *The Swiss Family Robinson* as Virtual Reality." In *Children's Literature: New Approaches*, edited by Karin Lesnik-Oberstein. New York: Palgrave, 2004.

Mir, Aleksandra. "The World From Above." 2003. Accessed May 7, 2012. http://www.aleksandramir.info/projects/the-world-from-above/.

Rousseau, Jean-Jacques. *Émile; or, On Education*. Translated by Barbara Foxley. 1762. Reprint, New York: Dutton, 1955.

Sansone, Valentina. "Interview with Aleksandra Mir." *Flashart* 260, Milan, October 2006. Accessed September 19, 2012. http://www.aleksandramir.info/texts/sansone.html.

Schmidt, Heinrich. "Interview with Aleksandra Mir." *Vernissage-TV*, Zurich, August 2006. Accessed September 19, 2012. http://www.aleksandramir.info/texts/heinrich.html.

Sgualdini, Silvia. "How to Do Something with Nothing: Interview with Aleksandra Mir." *UOVO Magazine*, Torino, December 2006. Accessed September 19, 2012. http://aleksandramir.info/texts/sgualdini.html.

Spark, Muriel. *Robinson*. 1958. Reprint, New York: New Directions, 2003.

Stein, Gertrude. *The Autobiography of Alice B. Toklas*. New York: Vintage, 1933.

Swiss Family Robinson. DVD. Directed by Ken Annakin. Burbank, CA: Buena Vista Home Entertainment, 2002.

Wyss, J. D. *The Swiss Family Robinson*. Introduction by J. Hillis Miller. New York: Signet, 2004.

Yesterland. "Swiss Family Treehouse." Last modified February 13, 2008. Accessed November 13, 2009. http://www.yesterland.com/treehouse.html.

Works Consulted

Ballantyne, R. M. *The Coral Island*. 1858. Reprint, New York: Penguin, 1994.

Bristow, Joseph. *Empire Boys: Adventures in a Man's World*. London: HarperCollins, 1991.

Bibliography

Bollen, Christopher. "Interview with Aleksandra Mir." *The Believer*, December 2003–January 2004. Accessed September 19, 2012. http://www.believermag .com/issues/200312/?read=interview_mir.

Burnett, Graham D. "Maps, Bodies, States." *Lincoln Center Theater Review* 54 (2010): 21–22.

Defoe, Daniel. *Robinson Crusoe*. 1719. Reprint, London: Penguin, 1965.

Dubois, Jacques. "Du roman au mythe: un Robinson hédoniste et helvète." *Études françaises* 35 (1999): 25–42.

Fisher, Carl. "The Robinsonade: An Intellectual History of an Idea." In *Approaches to Teaching Defoe's "Robinson Crusoe,"* edited by Maximillian E. Novak and Carl Fisher. New York: Modern Language Association, 2005.

Gore, Philip. *The Imaginary Voyage in Prose Fiction*. New York: Columbia University Press, 1941.

Green, Martin. *The Robinson Crusoe Story*. University Park: Pennsylvania State University Press, 1990.

Hollings, Ken. "An Inventory of Other Islands." In *Aleksandra Mir—Switzerland and Other Islands*. Zürich: Edition Fink, 2006.

Loxley, Diana. *Problematic Shores: The Literature of Islands*. New York: St. Martin's, 1990.

Marshall, Peter H. *William Godwin*. New Haven, CT: Yale University Press, 1984.

Marryat, Frederick. *Masterman Ready, Or the Wreck of the Pacific*. 1841. Reprint, New York: Dutton, 1970.

St. Clair, William. *The Godwins and the Shelleys: A Biography of a Family*. London: Faber & Faber, 1989.

Heidi (1880)

Works Cited

Bewes, Diccon. *Swiss Watching: Inside Europe's Landlocked Island*. London: Nicholas Brealey, 2010.

Arai, Man, and Noriko Arai. *Travels with Heidi*. 1994. Originally published in Japanese as *Haiji kiko: Futari de iku "Arupusu no shojo Haiji" no tabi*. Translated for the author by Hiroe Saruya.

Heidi. DVD. Directed by Alan Dwan. Beverley Hills: 20th Century Fox Home Entertainment, 2005.

Spyri, Johanna. *Heidi*. Translated by Joy Law. New York: Franklin Watts, 1959.

Bibliography

———. *Heidi: Heidis Lehr- und Wanderjahre; Heidi kann brauchen, was es gelernt hat.* Chur: Desertina, 2000.

Tritten, Charles. *Heidi Grows Up.* New York: Grosset & Dunlap, 1938.

———. *Heidi's Children.* New York: Grosset and &, 1939.

Zeller, Hans, and Rosemarie Zeller, eds. *Johanna Spyri/Conrad Ferdinand Meyer: Briefwechsel 1877–1897.* Kilchberg, ZH: Mirio Romano, 1977.

Works Consulted

Escher, Georg, and Marie-Louise Strauss. *Johanna Spyri: Verklärt, vergessen, neu entdeckt.* Zürich: Neue Zürcher Zeitung, 2001.

Evangelische Mittelschule Schiers. *Heidi im Leben von Johanna Spyri.* Schiers, GR: Heidi Guide AG, 2001.

Gyr, Ueli. "Heidi Überall: Heidi-Figur und Heidi Mythos als Identitätsmuster." *Ethnologia Europaea: Journal of European Ethnology* 22 (1999): 75–95.

Halter, Ernst ed. *Heidi: Karrieren einer Figur.* Zürich: Offizin, 2001.

Schindler, Regina. *Johanna Spyri: Spurensuche.* Zürich: Pendo, 1997.

Schweizerische Institut für Kinder- und Jugendmedien, eds. *Johanna Spyri und ihr Werk—Lesarten.* Zürich: Chronos, 2004.

Scott, Ramsey. "Even the Hardy Boys Need Friends: An Epistolary Essay on Boredom." *Southwest Review* 91 (2006): 550–67.

Skrine, Peter. "Johanna Spyri's *Heidi*." *Bulletin of the John Rylands University Library of Manchester* 76 (1994): 145–64.

Spyri, Johanna. *Heimatlos.* 1912. Reprint, Basel: Brunnen, 1998.

Villain, Jean. *Der erschriebene Himmel: Johanna Spyri und ihre Zeit.* Zürich: Nagel und Kimche, 1997.

"Who Owns Heidi?" *Sunday Telegraph Magazine*, December 14, 1997, 13–16.

Epilogue

Works Cited

Helvetica. DVD. Directed by Gary Wustwit. Brooklyn: Plexifilm, 2007.

Hollis, Richard. *Swiss Graphic Design: The Origins and Growth of an International Style 1920–1965.* New Haven, CT: Yale University Press, 2006.

Krugman, Paul. "The Swiss Menace." *New York Times*, August 17, 2009.

"I'm Swiss" (and Other Treasonous Statements). DVD. Written and directed by Bill Maher. Chatsworth, CA: Image Entertainment, 2005.

Bibliography

Müller, Lars. *Helvetica: Homage to a Typeface*. Baden: Lars Müller Publishers, 2002.

Work Consulted

Grounding: Die Letzten Tage der Swissair. DVD. Directed by Michael Steiner and Tobias Feuter. Zürich: C-Films, 2006.

8/16